HERE IS BUT ONE OF THE MANY CHEESE PROFILES IN THIS BOOK THAT WILL GIVE YOU GOOD REASON TO SAY CHEESE—AND SMILE!

BRIE

WHERE MADE: France; almost always factory produced. . . .

HOW MADE AND CURED: Cow's milk; soft, bloomy rind; cured about 3 weeks; 45% fat content. . . .

AROMA: Full, distinct; faintly suggestive of mushrooms. . . .

FLAVOR: Savory, tangy, and a touch earthy. . . .

APPEARANCE: Thin, downy white rind; pancake-like disk. . . .

BUYING HINTS: Buy fresh-cut portions from ripe whole Bries. . . . Beware of excessive saltiness. . . .

USABLE LIFE: When ripe, should be consumed the same day. . . .

BEVERAGE MATCH: Beaujolais, St. Emilion, Cabernet Sauvignon. . . .

SIMILAR CHEESES: Coulommiers, Camembert.

No longer do you have to worry about a Brie, doubt a Parmesan, hesitate before a Pont L'Eveque or be intimidated by a Stilton. You can buy any cheese with confidence, store it with success, and serve it to perfection. This is the book that all turophiles (cheese lovers) long have wanted to explore the wide and wonderful world of cheese with limitless enjoyment.

SIGNET Books of Special Interest

THE
SIGNET BOOK
OF CHEESE

Peter Quimme

A SIGNET BOOK
NEW AMERICAN LIBRARY
TIMES MIRROR

SIGNET TRADEMARK REG. U.S. PAT. OFF. AND FOREIGN COUNTRIES
REGISTERED TRADEMARK—MARCA REGISTRADA
HECHO EN CHICAGO, U.S.A.

SIGNET, SIGNET CLASSICS, MENTOR, PLUME AND MERIDIAN BOOKS
are published by The New American Library, Inc.,
1301 Avenue of the Americas, New York, New York 10019

FIRST SIGNET PRINTING, OCTOBER, 1976

1 2 3 4 5 6 7 8 9

PRINTED IN THE UNITED STATES OF AMERICA

to William Peter Burns

ACKNOWLEDGMENTS

For their kind help and generous assistance in supplying me with information, I wish to thank the Austrian Food Center; Kraft Foods; Food and Wines from France, Inc.; the Canadian Consulate General; the Italian Trade Commission; the Roquefort Association, Inc.; the National Cheese Institute; the Switzerland Cheese Association, Inc.; Borden, Inc.; the Holland Cheese Exporters Association; the Denmark Cheese Association; the German Information Center; Gerber International Foods, Inc.; the Atalanta Corporation; the Swedish Information Center; and the New York Public Library. In particular I would like to thank Frank Sanabria of Vermonti Enterprises, Inc.; Giorgio De Luca of The Cheese Store; and Irving Horowitz and Saul Zabar of Zabar's Gourmet Foods; all of New York City, for freely sharing their vast cheese expertise with me. I am especially grateful to the first and last named of these gentlemen for taking the time to read this book in manuscript and make valuable suggestions for its improvement. In compiling the information in this book, particularly where I was not able to obtain independent confirmation, I have learned much from the works of André Simon and Pierre Androuët. These and other writings on cheese consulted during the course of my research are discussed under Further Reading. Of course, I alone am responsible for whatever errors of fact may have escaped my attention, and for the enthusiasms and opinions contained herein.

April 1976   PETER QUIMME

Contents

THE
SIGNET BOOK
OF CHEESE

A FEW
INTRODUCTORY REMARKS

Cheese is simply the food made by the process of coagulating milk and, usually, concentrating and ripening the curds. Of course, that's putting it bluntly; cheese is also one of the most remarkable of foods, comparable only to wine in its spectrum of flavors and its individuality. Highly nutritious in all forms, it provides sustenance even when it lacks gustatory interest. But the most flavorsome examples offer the palate an extraordinary range of tastes, aromas, and textures. These sometimes dramatic, sometimes subtle, but always fascinating flavor gradations are possible because cheesemaking, like winemaking, is a simple process whose steps can be varied almost any number of ways to achieve almost any number of tastes in the final product.

Then too, cheese, like wine, reflects the character of the ingredients of which it is composed and so in turn reflects its origins. Cheese reflects the type and quality of milk used, its handling and curing, local conditions such as microorganisms, climate, the pasturage the milk-giving animals feed on, and even the time of day the cheese is made. Not all cheese, certainly, is so individual; a good deal is anonymous, consistent, and practically characterless. Just as most wine is produced for drinking, not contemplating, so too most cheese is produced for eating, not savoring. What is remarkable is that so many cheeses pleasure the palate while filling the stomach. Of the thousands of different cheeses produced in the world, scores of them rank among the most toothsome foodstuffs ever created: think of the intensity of fresh goat cheese, for example, or the voluptuous succulence of perfectly ripe Brie; the savory sharpness of fine farmhouse Cheddar; the nutty, lingering quality of Gruyère; the penetrating aroma of Münster; the unsurpassable rich tang of Stilton at its best. The list is long and varied, and over the centuries responsible for creating that subclass of gastronomes known as *turophiles*, or lovers of cheese.

Indeed, the enormous range of cheese produced worldwide is bewildering to the beginning cheese enthusiast who wants to try something beyond country-store Cheddar or plastic-wrapped Swiss-type slices but has no idea what to try next. The sheer number of choices available in today's well-stocked cheese store can be confusing even to the cheese lover of wide experience. What the amateur turophile needs is a good guide-book, a Baedeker to the high points of cheesedom.

Fortunately, the passionate appreciation given to cheese over the years has also given rise to quite a long and varied list of books on the subject. But if you exclude books on cheese-making and those that consist largely of recipes for cooking with cheese, there are only a few up-to-date guides in print to the various cheeses of the world. Although some of these guides are excellent in their own way (see the Appendix on Further Reading), none of them is organized in a fashion that's truly useful to the consumer who wants concise and complete information on any given cheese. Instead, most are organized by type category (soft, blue, hard-pressed, and so on) or flavor family, or by country. Some cover the cheeses of one area in daunting technical detail; others offer scanty information that scarcely distinguishes one cheese from another. The reader who wants to know, say, what sort of cheese Caerphilly is has a hard time locating the cheese in these texts if the country of origin or category isn't known, or has to chase down the essential points on its taste characteristics, appearance, and how to buy, store, and serve it, through a number of chapters.

To avoid these problems, I've organized this book into two parts: the first, A Primer of Cheese, is a concise and complete handbook that presents general information likely to be of interest to the cheese lover. Here the history of cheese, how it is made, its classifications, how to taste, buy, store, and serve it, as well as when to enjoy it and what to enjoy it with, are all covered in detail. The second part, A Dictionary of the World's Cheeses, consists of an alphabetical listing of all the principal cheeses of the world, cross-referenced by variant names. Many cheeses currently produced are not mentioned; after all, not all cheeses are worth tasting. Some are so unenticing they would scarcely attract a mouse. Some are simply copies, sometimes good and sometimes not-so-good, of better-known cheeses. Then, too, a great many cheeses are produced for local consumption only. The cheeses covered here are primarily fine cheeses, both famous and not-so-famous, that are usually available (or at least sometimes available) somewhere in the United States and that would interest the palate of a lover of good food. Thus, the listings cover those cheeses most often seen on retail shelves.

Each entry summarizes the information most likely to be needed by someone hunting for a particular cheese or looking up one that hasn't been sampled before; the origin, type of milk, fat content, and so forth are given in capsule form, as well as complete information on appearance, aroma, and flavor. While it's true that smells and tastes are notoriously difficult to describe, I've tried to indicate whether a cheese is particularly individual in taste or nondescript, and what other cheeses it most resembles. Each entry ends with buying hints and storage information, comments on the cheese's history, general quality, suggested servings, uses, and beverage matches. In short, I've tried to put everything the prospective buyer of a given cheese would need to know right in each entry. Naturally, this makes for a certain amount of repetition when discussing similar cheeses, but this, I feel, is preferable to endless thumbing through the book to refresh one's memory on the best way to wrap goat cheese or some such essential but easily forgotten nugget of information. I hope most readers will read Part One straight through, but I imagine many would use Part Two simply as a reference, both to look up cheeses that have been bought and to browse through for cheeses that might be tried next.

Much of my task in writing this book has consisted of gathering large amounts of information from a number of sources, taking notes on endless cheese samplings, and condensing the mass into what I hope is a useful and accurate compilation. However, production worldwide is not a static industry; changes are constantly made in cheese manufacture as new techniques, markets, and demands develop. Consequently, descriptions that might have been true of certain cheeses a few years ago may not be true today, and despite my efforts to keep my information current, a cheese described herein as having a peculiar shape, rind, and unusual taste may suddenly start showing up in rindless block form and taste quite different from its ancestor. On the other hand, a few cheeses thought to have been a thing of the past have been revived in recent years.

Then, too, new, enticing cheeses are dreamed up from time to time by cheese producers to woo jaded turophiles.

Even if the effects of change are disregarded, cheese is not a subject in which definitiveness is easily achieved. Part of the problem is that many cheese names are loosely used and are often adopted for variations on a well-known (and well-liked) cheese or stretched to cover imitations of traditional types. This naturally has the effect of blurring distinctions. The result is that many authorities disagree over how such-and-such a cheese is made, its size and shape, and so forth. And it hardly needs pointing out that opinions on quality and taste are almost as various as cheeses themselves. On factual matters I've tried to be as precise as possible without suggesting a precision in these matters that doesn't exist. Where opinions on quality differ widely, I've tried to be fair. While I have my own taste preferences, I've written this book not to confirm my own prejudices but to encourage cheese lovers and would-be cheese lovers to sample with discrimination and form their own opinions. I've intended this book as an introduction for those who are just beginning to nibble their way into the subject as well as for those who have sampled widely but spottily and would like to have an overview of all the excellent cheeses left to try.

PART ONE

A PRIMER
OF CHEESE

1: A BRIEF HISTORY OF CHEESE

Cheese, like many foods, has obscure and ancient origins. Undoubtedly some form of cheese originated almost simultaneously with the discovery that milk could be obtained from wild or domesticated animals. It is mentioned in the Old Testament; it was known to the early Greeks; and the Romans recorded the use of cheese among European tribes. Like wine, tea, coffee, and a number of other foods, cheese is sufficiently unique to give rise to legends explaining its discovery.

The most common legend is about a Persian traveler who filled a bag made of animal intestines with a ration of goat's milk and set off across the desert on horse- or camelback. That night the traveler found his goat's milk had separated into semisolid curds and watery whey. The chemical action of rennin (an enzyme with coagulant action found in the lining of animal stomachs), the hot sun, and the animal's movement, so the story goes, caused the separation of milk solids from the soluble constituents. The horrified but hungry traveler found the whey drinkable, but, more important, the fresh curds both tasty and nourishing—and so cheese was born.

Actually, any milk will eventually sour to form an acid curd that will cause the milk to separate into whey and semisolid curds. Primitive peoples in various parts of the world obtain fresh cheese in this fashion, sometimes helping the coagulation by adding the juices of certain plants or animal tissues. Cheese retains almost all the food value of milk, and in a much more convenient form, since the cheesemaking process reduces about ten volumes of milk to one volume of cheese. It also has better keeping qualities than milk, and thus offers a valid means of preserving a valuable food.

The first refinements in the cheesemaking process probably came about through efforts to extend the keeping qualities of cheese. Heating and kneading the curds, keeping it in salt brine, and even the use of particular molds, all have their use

3

as preservation techniques, although today these various methods are appreciated particularly for the various flavors they impart to the final product. (Cheesemaking is described in greater detail in section 2.) These different methods of cheesemaking have their own legends as well and revolve around accidental discoveries that fresh cheese left in certain caves picked up unusual and beneficial molds, and so forth.

The legends offered for the discovery of Roquefort have shepherd boys hiding their lunch of fresh sheep's milk cheese in local rock crannies while being pursued by bandits, or conversely, while pursuing beguiling shepherdesses. When they return a few days later and discover their cheeses shot through with blue-green mold, at least one lad is hungry enough to overcome his disgust and, tentatively sampling the cheese, discovers the delicious transformation that the local microorganisms have performed on the simple curds. After that, the effect is encouraged and finally induced on the local cheeses, and Roquefort as we know it is born.

By Roman times cheesemaking and a variety of cheese types were well-established in Europe. Not only were regional cheeses popular in Rome, but cheeses were imported from as far away as France, England, and the Dalmatian coast. Then, as now, simple cheeses were a food staple (they were included in the daily ration of Roman infantrymen), whereas finer varieties were esteemed by gastronomes (the Emperor Augustus is said by Pliny the Elder to have found the cheese from Toulouse especially toothsome). Along with their other contributions to Western culture, the Romans spread the practice of cheesemaking throughout Europe. *Formia,* the Latin word for the rush baskets used to drain cheese, gives us the French and Italian for cheese, *fromage* and *formaggio,* while the English word "cheese," the German *käse,* and the Dutch *kass* derive from the Latin term for it, *caseus.*

Cheese remained an important food in the Middle Ages; a number of cheese types still familiar today had their origins in the monasteries of the time, which accounts in part for the many cheeses named after saints. Other well-known cheeses are of equal antiquity: Chesire, the oldest English cheese, has been popular since the twelfth century; Roquefort has been known in its present form since the ninth century. Although it remained an important food, cheese was not always looked upon with favor in the Renaissance. Shakespeare's references to cheese, for example, are almost all unappetizing. Whether this general outlook was due to the low quality of the cheese of the time or to Elizabethan theories of digestion is not known. But by the eighteenth century it was regarded much as it is today: a nutritious food that ranges in gastronomic interest from merely edible to simply sublime. The bad press for cheese was confined largely to poor-quality "rattrap" varieties.

The next two hundred years saw the perfecting of classic cheese types and their production, and the conscious development of new cheeses for their taste. Stilton, Camembert, Cheddar, Port-Salut, and numerous other cheeses were invented or came to fame during that time. More important for the future of cheese, however, was the start of the shift in the manufacture of cheese away from the individual farm where it had always been made. At first, farm cooperatives became more common, and finally factories appeared, at first small, local enterprises and then huge plants.

The idea of making cheese in factories is generally credited to a New York dairy farmer, Jesse Williams, who bought milk from local dairy farmers for his Rome, New York, enterprise in 1850, and soon was shipping his Cheddar wheels throughout the state. It is estimated that by 1865 some five hundred such factories followed his example and were in operation in New York State. By the turn of the century the time was ripe for even larger enterprises: J. L. Kraft, a farmboy from Fort Erie, Ontario, began his empire with sixty-five dollars in capital, which he used in Chicago in 1903 to rent a wagon and a horse named Paddy, and buy a supply of cheeses to sell to Chicago grocers. Innovations in processing and packaging fueled the expansion of the Kraft enterprise until today, some seventy years later, it does a four-billion-dollar-a-year business world-wide, of which cheese and cheese products constitute a sizable share.

Today the cheese industry operates on a number of levels and producers can be found in all sizes. Individual farmhouse producers, small local plants and dairy cooperatives, state-owned and -operated factories, and huge corporations are found in most major cheese-producing countries. Individual producers, as might be expected, are largely a thing of the past. This shift from farm to factory, combined with the application of technology, has enabled the cheese industry worldwide to achieve an admirable level of quality and reliability, so much so that today cheese forms a significant part of the national diet in a great many countries. In fact, it is estimated that some nine billion pounds of cheese are consumed throughout the world each year. Not only that, but the per-capita consumption of cheese is on the increase; for example, in the United States in 1965, the figure stood at 9.6 pounds of cheese per head of population, but by 1974 14.5 pounds per person were being consumed annually. This national hunger for cheese put the United States slightly ahead of countries such as Canada, the United Kingdom, and West Germany, but behind Italy, France, and the Scandinavian countries. The United States easily leads in sheer output, however; fully one-fifth of total world production is American. (France, next in importance, produces about 11 percent.)

The shift from farm to factory production, virtually complete today, has not *always* been to the detriment of taste. However, it is widely recognized that fewer varieties of cheeses are produced today than a hundred years ago, and that milder-tasting, bland cheeses are much more popular than strong, characterful cheeses; consequently, many cheeses are not the assertive individuals they once were. On the other hand, there is sufficient demand for fine cheese to keep a number of older, difficult-to-make varieties and unique types in production. The age of complete blandness predicted by gloomy turophiles is fortunately not yet upon us. Although total tastelessness in cheese is well-nigh universal in some quarters, there are signs that a significant and growing segment of the populace appreciates and demands full-flavored foods. This demand, one fervently hopes, will keep a lot of fine cheeses from extinction.

2: HOW CHEESE IS MADE

Although there are cheeses that are made from whey, by far the majority of cheeses consist of the curd formed when milk coagulates. Milk coagulates spontaneously if it is allowed to stand, because it sours and forms an acid curd; fresh cheeses such as farmer or cottage cheese are derived from this simple acid curd. (In modern cheese production the separation of curds and whey for such fresh cheeses is encouraged by heating the slightly sour milk for a number of hours and adding a culture of lactic-acid-producing bacteria.) With the exception of fresh cheeses, all the major cheeses of the world are initially separated by the addition of rennet; the curds, naturally enough, are therefore called rennet curds. Cured cheeses— cheeses that undergo a process of aging, however short—are all made from rennet curds. (As mentioned previously, the active ingredient in rennet is rennin, a coagulating enzyme usually obtained from the lining of calves' stomachs; the name given to the enzyme in a brine extract is rennet. About three ounces of the extract diluted some forty times in water is sufficient to curdle about a thousand pounds of milk.)

The process of obtaining fresh cheese is simply one of pressing or draining the curd and perhaps molding it into a particular shape. Rennet-curd cheeses undergo a more elaborate, though closely related process, and are then cured, or "ripened," by various methods to bring out various aromas and flavors. Important as the curing process is, variations in the basic cheesemaking process determine the character of the cheese; curing merely adds the finishing touches. It is remarkable that virtually all the major cheeses of the world are made in the same fashion; what accounts for their great differences in character are sometimes very slight differences in time, temperature, and handling of the curds.

In the cheesemaking process the cheesemaker attempts to create environments in which desirable microorganisms will

7

flourish while undesirable ones will be inhibited. Curds exposed to gas-producng microorganisms give rise to cheese with holes, or "eyes," like Swiss types; certain molds and yeasts sprayed on the cheese may develop on the surface to transform the interior, as in Brie and Camembert; mold of a certain kind introduced into the cheese results in blue-mold internal-veined cheeses such as Roquefort and Stilton; and so on. The complex changes that milk undergoes when subjected to various bacteria under various conditions are not completely understood, so that even the most modern cheese factories using the most sophisticated tools of the biochemist's laboratory have to rely on the human skills of the experienced cheesemaker. While the day may be close at hand when milk delivered at one end of a factory will emerge as some sort of cheese at the other with only the midwifery of computer-directed machinery intervening, the production of fine cheese, like the production of fine wine, will always take a good deal of experience and craft to ensure success.

Before actually taking a look at the stages of cheese production, something needs to be said about milk. Mention has already been made of cow's, goat's, and sheep's milk cheeses, but cheese has also been made from far more exotic milks, including those of yaks, reindeer, buffalo, camels, and so on, and of course could be made from porpoises, musk oxen, tigers, whales, duckbilled platypuses, and even humans, should one be so inclined. The predominance of cow's milk cheeses over all others is to be expected, however, considering that in importance as a source of milk, cows far outweigh goats, sheep, and all other milk sources combined.

The following steps apply to natural-cheese production, not that of processed cheese. (Processed cheeses are made by mixing and heating different lots of natural cheese together with emulsifiers to produce a homogenous dairy product. Like natural cheese they vary considerably in character and interest, but they never attain anything like the character of fine natural cheese.) Depending on how one looks at cheesemaking, there are six to eight stages in the production of cheese. For clarity, I'll divide the steps into eight categories (these follow the outline given in Frank Kosikowski's treatise *Cheese and Fermented Milk Foods* but omit technical details). These steps are the same for cheesemaking on any scale, from kitchen operation to factory production.

Setting and Curdling the Milk

The quality and character of milk used has a great deal to do with the character of the cheese produced from it. Cheese can even be produced from reconstituted dry milk, although, as might be expected, the finest varieties of cheeses are produced from the highest-quality milk from certain districts in certain seasons. The quality of milk used is most often determined by market considerations, but regulations of one sort or another govern the standards of milk used for certain cheeses. For example, milk used for cheese production in Switzerland cannot, by law, come from dairy cattle fed on silage (fodder kept in silos) because of the adverse flavor effects the butyric acid present in silage milk has on cheese made from it.

Just as a winemaker is concerned with the levels of acidity and sugar in his grapes, so too the cheesemaker is concerned with the acidity and fat content of the milk he begins with. Different cheeses require different acidity and fat-content levels. The richness and acidity of the milk can be adjusted to the desired levels by blending the milk from various locales, from several days' production, or even by mixing morning and evening milk, and of course cream may be skimmed off or added. Although raw, heated, or pasteurized milk is used for rennet-coagulated cheeses, almost all fresh cheeses are made from pasteurized milk, as this ensures a more uniform product. There are other aspects of pasteurization, however, and I'll return to them after reviewing cheesemaking.

Because lactic acid will increase simply by letting the milk stand (or "set" or "ripen" as it is sometimes called), the cheesemaker will allow the warm milk to set for anywhere from fifteen minutes to fifteen hours, depending on the cheese type desired. In addition a "starter"—a lactic-acid bacterial culture—is almost invariably added, and if the cheese is to be a cured or ripened variety rather than a fresh cheese, rennet is added as well. The proportions of the coagulants added, the temperature at which the milk is held, and the length of time it is allowed to set may vary considerably. The goal with any cheese is to curdle the milk and form a smooth curd block in the vessel or vat. If formed with a lactic-acid culture only, the curd may take hours to form; if curdling is initiated by rennet, it typically forms in less than half an hour. The faster the process of coagulation by rennet, the more whey is ultimately expelled from the curd and the harder the final cheese will be.

Before the milk is set, coloring may be added to give certain cheeses their characteristic orange hue. The coloring agent in almost-universal use for this is annatto, a tasteless vegetable dye derived from the Latin-American bush of the same name. Cheeses not so treated have a much lighter color.

Cutting the Curd

The curd, once formed, is "cut" or broken up into smaller pieces to allow more complete drainage of the whey by increasing the surface area of the curd. The curd may be simply cut with a knife if the amount of cheese being made is small enough, or it may be broken up by drawing a "harp" (essentially a stringed paddle) through the vat, or the entire procedure may be highly mechanized. The rennet curd is judged ready to cut when it has attained the consistency deemed proper for the type of cheese being made.

Heating the Curds

After the curd is cut or broken, it would be possible simply to drain the cheese, press and mold it, and proceed directly to the ripening stage. Most cheeses, however, are treated further in the curd stage by heating. That is, the curd is heated to some extent to contract the curds and effectively remove the whey, and to establish the desired moisture level of the cheese. Significant differences between cheeses depend on the temperature reached (90°F for Camembert, 128° for Swiss, 176° for Ricotta, and so forth). Cheeses whose curd is heated in order to harden it are usually called "cooked" cheeses. These days a good many cheeses are heated to some degree, so that the distinction between cooked and uncooked cheeses is not as clear as one might think. Cheddar, for example, is heated to about 100°F, but is commonly classed as uncooked. Heating is usually accomplished by means of elaborate jacketed vats using steam or hot water, at least in large-scale production, and when the curd has developed properly for the desired cheese type, it is ready to be drained.

Draining the Curd

Draining the curd finally separates the curd from the whey by physically removing the former from the latter. Some methods consist of draining the whey out through a sieve in the bottom of the vat (a typical method in Cheddar production), lowering a cloth on a hoop down and around the cheese mass in the vat and then lifting it out (as is done in Swiss production), or simply scooping the curds out of the vat to drain in perforated molds (as is typical in Blue-cheese manufacture). Regardless of the method, the aim is the same, although how and when it is done depends on the cheese being made.

Knitting the Curds

After drainage, the ripening process may begin at once (as in Tilsiter) or the curds may be molded first (as in Tomme de Savoie). Many cheeses, however, are taken through another step, that of "knitting" the curds so they will mat together and form a solid mass. This may include breaking up the curd further (a process called milling, or "cheddaring," after the cheese most associated with this step), and perhaps even cooking it again (as is done with Parmesan). For a cheese such as Provolone or Mozzarella this step consists of pulling and molding the cheese curd. Regardless of procedure, knitting gives the cheese its texture, and also allows the still-accumulating lactic acid to affect the curd's flavor.

Salting and Pressing

Salting enhances the texture and flavor of cheese, if not overdone, and also reduces moisture and inhibits undesirable bacterial growth. It is a relatively simple step: coarse salt may be rubbed by hand on the curd surfaces, or the curds may be immersed in a brine solution.

The purpose of pressing is to mold and form the body of the cheese to give it its characteristic shape. Fresh cheeses as well as cured cheeses may be pressed. Cheeses are pressed in bags, weighted down with a brick or subjected to considerable mechanical pressure in wooden or metal forms, or simply heaped in piles to rest lightly on itself, as is done with Roquefort.

Curing and Ripening

Of course, long before the cheese has reached the curing and ripening stage, it has received the kind of processing necessary to produce its type, but it is at this point that particular cheeses may undergo particular treatments intended to give them their final character. Blue cheese is inoculated with blue-mold spores, cottage cheese is creamed, Brie and Camembert are sprayed with white-mold spores, monastery cheeses are washed, and so forth. Many cheeses, such as Cheddars, are simply exposed to warm temperatures of up to 73°F at the proper humidity (or conversely, cold temperatures as low as 36° for longer periods) to permit further beneficial bacterial growth and internal enzymatic activity. During the ripening process (also called "curing," "aging," "maturing," and more rarely, "fermenting") the microorganisms continue to break down the constituents of the cheese: for example, only trace amounts of lactose sugar (milk sugar) remain after two weeks of aging. Carbon dioxide is given off as a common by-product of ripening and in certain cheeses is not able to escape. Consequently holes, or eyes, are formed, as in Swiss and Swiss-type cheeses. In Camembert, Brie, Limburger, and a few other surface-ripened cheeses a certain amount of ammonia is released due to the enzymatic breakdown of certain amino acids. In short, given time, a great many flavor constituents are created during the ripening process by desirable microorganisms, and these give the cheese its characteristic flavor. The converse is true as well; aging never makes up for the defects of a poorly made cheese—it magnifies them.

The period of ripening may last from two weeks to two years, and the cheese may be left unwrapped or coated with paraffin or plastic. Depending on the cheese, the surfaces may be cleaned, brushed, salted, and the cheese may be periodically turned. During aging, rinds form and thicken, and may continue to be washed, or oiled, or brushed, or scrubbed, or wrapped, or just left alone. Rinds, whether very thin and delicate or thick and tough, serve two purposes: they not only protect the cheese, but create an interior environment where proper ripening can take place.

A final thought on cheesemaking procedures: what happens to all the whey left over from large-scale cheese production? Disposal can be something of a problem, though fortunately whey can be sold for use in commercial baking, animal feeds, and even as an ingredient in candy. There are actually cheeses that are made in whole or part from whey, notably Gjetost from Norway and some types of Italian Ricotta. Of these, only Gjetost is made entirely from whey (wholly or partly goat's milk), which is stirred and cooked until it has condensed to about one-fourth its original volume. The others have various amounts of whole or skim milk or cream or buttermilk added during the process. Whey cheeses contain a good deal of lactose (milk sugar) and are consequently excellent energy foods.

A Note on Pasteurization

During 1941–44 some four hundred cases of typhoid fever in the United States and Canada were traced to Cheddar cheese produced from raw, unpasteurized milk. Although it seems clear enough that the principal cause was improper and unsanitary manufacturing, these outbreaks spurred the passage of U.S. government regulations requiring the pasteurization of milk for many cheese products. Briefly, federal regulations (and many state laws as well) require that all unripened cheeses be made from pasteurized milk, and that if ripened cheese is not made from pasteurized milk, it must be aged for at least sixty days. There are several reasons why the regulations read this way. First, pasteurization (defined as heating milk to 143°F for thirty minutes or the equivalent), although no absolute guarantee of safety, destroys significant amounts of harmful and possibly pathogenic microorganisms. Second, before the discovery of pasteurization, aged cheese had long been considered a safer dairy product than raw milk, although the reason why was incompletely understood. It is now clear that the lactic-acid fermentation that takes place in cheese-making inhibits pathogenic bacteria. Even if such bacteria are introduced to ripening cheese, they fail to survive the environment for very long, and certainly not for sixty days. The low moisture and high salt content of many ripened cheeses also adds to their relative safety among food products. Of course, it must be recognized that it is not the presence of bacteria per se in cheese that is cause for concern; it is the type of bacteria present. Most of what is regarded as the desirable flavor of fine cheese is due to the presence of beneficent and harmless microorganisms.

Requiring the pasteurization of milk for use in cheeses that will not undergo a lengthy ripening process also has another useful effect: it permits cheese factories to bring milk from great distances without spoilage, and to use milk from a variety of locations. Milk that varies in character and quality can be used without difficulty, because pasteurization kills off most of the accompanying bacteria, the composition of which often differs considerably from milk source to milk source. Were the milk used not rendered uniform by such partial sterilization, and then reinoculated with selected bacterial strains for curdling, the cheeses made from these various milks or combinations of milks would not behave or ripen in a uniform fashion, and far more defective cheeses would occur in the manufacturing process. Then, too, cheeses made from pasteurized milk have more stability and a longer shelf life. All these advantages, in addition to regulations for reasons of health, have brought about the near-universal use of pasteurization for fresh cheeses, both in the United States and abroad. (This is particularly true for cow's milk cheeses, since raw goat or sheep's milk has less bacteria than cow's milk.)

There is only one great drawback to the use of pasteurized milk for making cheese: flavor is adversely affected. Cheeses that are made from raw milk are invariably superior in flavor, texture, and aroma to those that are produced from pasteurized milk. Why? The reason lies in the fact that pasteurization kills off many of the bacteria that add a desirable complexity to the finished cheese. This has long been recognized, even in the most mechanized sectors of the U.S. cheese industry, which is why a great deal of U.S. Cheddar and Cheddar types continue to be made from raw or only partially heat-treated milk. The taste of raw-milk cheese not only is deeper, more intense, and more complex, but does not have the bitter after-taste found in many cheeses made from pasteurized milk. Cheese lovers find it ironic that the very cheese that gave rise to the concern for regulations—Cheddar—is in fact the cheese that is exempted from the necessity for pasteurization, provided it is aged for a sufficient period of time. Instead, it is the soft, fresh, and quick-ripening cheeses that suffer the most in flavor from these requirements. Given the fact that raw-milk cheeses are consumed by Europeans (and Americans abroad) without ill effects, it seems clear to gourmets, at least, that it is not raw-milk cheeses that are rightly suspect, but improperly made cheeses of any kind. Turophiles are inclined to think the U.S. cheese industry is unduly attracted to the convenience of using pasteurized milk and consequently is happy to have its products suffer no comparison from more flavorful imports. (U.S. laws require that imported cheeses meet the same regulations as U.S. cheeses, which is why none of the unpasteurized or quick-ripened raw-milk cheeses of Europe reach these shores—only their pallid, pasteurized brethren.) Actually, the growing dominance of blander cheeses everywhere has not so much to do with health regulations, whether ill-conceived or not, as it does with the growing predominance of the cheese factory worldwide and its insistence on convenience and uniformity in its products. Fresh cheeses from raw milk are becoming harder to find even in those countries that allow their production. Fortunately for the true cheese lover, a good many Cheddar and Swiss-type cheeses are still made from high-quality raw milk and consequently taste much like they did in times past. Today's fresh, soft cheeses, created with perishability and marketability in mind, find a large, appreciative audience among those who don't insist on flavor in their food. For this state of affairs, Uncle Sam's health regulations are not entirely to blame.

Cheese as Food

Cheese is an exceptionally nutritious food. It is particularly high in protein, containing significant amounts of the essential amino acids, and is also a good source of calcium and phosphorus. It contains vitamin A and some of the B vitamins too. Cheddar-cheese types, for example, have much more protein per ounce than most meats and seafoods. A half-pound of most cheeses (including processed cheeses) has as much protein, calcium, and phosphorus as one and a half quarts of milk.

The diet-conscious tend to shy away from cheese on the mistaken assumption that it is excessively caloric and fat-ridden. Many cheeses *are* high in calories: hard cheeses may have some four hundred calories per four ounces and many soft cheeses (excluding the double- and triple-crèmes) have about three hundred calories per four ounces. Fresh cheeses run only about a hundred calories for the same amount of cheese. Few concentrated high-protein foods are noted for being low in calories, however, and considering the food value of cheese, these are by no means "empty calories."

In general, the caloric content of cheese varies with the butterfat content, and certainly some cheeses do contain very high amounts of butterfat: a triple-crème, for example, may have a butterfat content of 75 percent. But those concerned about fats as well as calories in their diets should realize that a great many cheeses—including some of the tastiest—are quite low in butterfat. Ricotta and fresh cheeses such as cottage or pot cheese have 4- to 15-percent fat. Gammelost has a mere 4 percent. Cheeses with a relatively low fat content include Handkäse and Sapsago (both under 10 percent). Note that whether or not a cheese is made from skimmed milk has little to do with its actual fat content.

Don't make the mistake of thinking dry, hard cheeses are low in butterfat—many of them are in fact quite high. Almost all figures given for fat content on cheese labels (and in most cheese books, this one included) refer to the content in a dry extract of the cheese. In cheeses with little moisture content (such as Parmesan), the percentage given is quite close to the percentage by weight in serving. But as Androuët is anxious to point out, in cheeses with a high moisture content—for example, Brie, which may contain 50-percent water—a depressing figure of 45-percent butterfat can be happily halved, since Brie is consumed, one hopes, in its succulently moist condition.

Another dietary consideration should be mentioned briefly. Although much cheese is highly salted, there are a number of unsalted cheeses purposely prepared for those on a low-salt diet, including a tasty low-salt version of Dutch Gouda and several Swiss cheeses, which are not only low-salt, but low-fat as well. (Swiss St. Otho, in fact, is 95-percent fat-free.)

3: THE FAMILIES OF CHEESE

There is no single convenient system of categorizing cheeses. Instead, there are several competing systems in widespread use; all are rough guides at best to the world's cheeses. By taking a brief look at these systems cheese lovers will readily see why cheeses are so difficult to pigeonhole and can reassure themselves that even though a simple acquaintance with the taste families of cheese may not offer the sort of precision a dairy scientist needs, it is all that a turophile could want as a guide for beginning taste explorations.

The most common ways of classifying cheeses are by age, ripening agent, appearance, hardness, method and rind type, flavor, or country of origin. This last-mentioned means of distinguishing cheeses is only useful if the country produces cheeses that are all similar to one another in some way. But although it is meaningful to talk of Swiss-type cheeses, it is pointless to talk of French cheeses as if they had anything in common with one another—France produces virtually every kind of cheese there is. In brief, to know the country of origin often tells you little in itself about a cheese. The age of a cheese tells one even less, since even cheeses that are normally cured for a year or longer are often edible much younger. The age of a cheese tells one something about it only in the context of additional information.

Classifying cheeses by ripening agent seems both logical and informative, but it turns out that only a few cheeses have particularly distinctive ripening agents—notably Brie and Camembert, Blue types, Brick and its cousins, and Swiss types. A number of other factors are just as important as the ripening agent in giving a cheese its distinctive character. This method lumps together vast numbers of very different cheeses merely because they fall into the same bacterial category. Since some special ripening agents, such as those used in producing Blue cheese, do impart an individual and recognizable flavor to those cheeses, however, this method of classification is not without its uses in distinguishing some groups of cheeses.

Appearance as a means of distinguishing cheeses has another difficulty: although some cheeses are instantly recognizable by sight—Sapsago or Morbier, for example—other cheeses look very much like one another but taste very different. It is sometimes possible to anticipate a cheese's character and quality by sight, but appearance provides useful criteria more for judging cheese than for classifying it.

Hardness is one of the most common methods of organizing the variety of cheeses produced in the world, with most such systems employing four or five degrees of hardness, from the exceptionally hard grating cheeses like Parmesan to soft types like the crèmes. Kosikowski, among other authorities, points out one big problem: there is no objective measurement used in this sort of classification, so that Port-Salut, typically classed as a semisoft cheese, is actually softer than some cheeses traditionally classed as soft. Kosikowski gives examples of how the relative hardness of cheeses could be organized by moisture content. Cottage, Ricotta, and Neufchâtel have 55–80-percent moisture; Mozzarella, Brie, and Blue have 45–55-percent; Edam, Cheddar, and Provolone have 34–45-percent; Parmesan and Gjetost have 13–34-percent. He admits this system tells little about the character of the cheese, even if it does provide useful groupings.

The method and rind type of a cheese seems to offer an attractive means of classifying cheeses by the method of their manufacturing process. It doesn't seem farfetched to assume that cheeses produced in a similar way will taste similar. Androuët follows this scheme and offers a half-dozen categories based on differences in production of various cheese types: bloomy rinds, washed rinds, natural rinds, uncooked pressed, and so forth. To the confusion of the nonexpert, however, it turns out that, for all too many cheeses, several of these categories overlap. Nonetheless, these are useful descriptions, and I have adopted several of them here.

But because most cheese amateurs are quite fuzzy on manufacturing, some writers on the subject of cheese have abandoned all these somewhat technical classifications and simply grouped cheeses into families, principally on the basis of similar tastes. Aroma and flavor, texture, and taste are, after all, what interest the cheese lover, not obscure differences in cheese manufacture. For this reason it is probably the best and most reasonable single method for organizing the world's cheeses for the average turophile. There are any number of such lists of the families of cheese, but the shorter ones tend to have too many exceptions and too many very different cheeses grouped together. I've devised a list for use here that divides the world of cheese into fifteen categories.

Readers should not jump to the conclusion, however, that to know a cheese's flavor is to know all about it. It is both helpful and interesting to know how a cheese is categorized by hardness or by method of manufacture and rind, as it is to know its aroma and taste characteristics. Some of the other groups and technical categories to which a given cheese may also belong, although—as I've just argued—not always informative in themselves, taken together provide the more-experienced turophile with complete information that can be used for advanced tasting comparisons and detailed exploration of the world of cheese.

Thus, each cheese entry in this book includes a variety of information: where the cheese is made, its milk type, method and rind type, hardness, time cured, fat content, and flavor family as well as other available details. Some of the terms used for hardness and method and rind type need a bit of explanation, as do the flavor families into which I've divided the world's cheeses.

For hardness, cheeses are grouped in this book into the following categories:

Very hard: These are cheeses that are so hard they can be easily and finely grated. Typical of such hardness are the cheeses of the Grana family, such as Parmesan, and Sapsago, a spiced cheese from Switzerland.

Hard: Some examples of hard cheeses are Cheddar, Gruyère, and Asiago. These are typically cooked, pressed cheeses (like most Swiss types) or else Cheddar types. They all hold their shape well when cut. This group covers a wide range of firmness, and there are a few types—particularly from Denmark—that are not as hard as most hard cheeses but not soft enough to fall into the next category, semisoft; these are classed as semihard.

Semisoft: This group includes softer, uncooked, pressed types like Saint-Paulin, Münster, Reblochon, and most Blue cheeses. Semisoft cheeses are plastic, yielding, or resilient

to the touch, and sometimes crumbly. Some hold their shape better than others when cut, but none become runny.
Soft: Brie, Neufchâtel, crèmes, and Ricotta are all soft types, quite moist, and are more or less spreadable.

Under the method-and-rind-type classification, cheeses may be described as cooked or uncooked, pressed or unpressed, cured or uncured. (Since almost all cheese types are cured, readers can assume that any cheese has undergone some ripening unless it is described as "fresh, uncured cheese.") Cooked cheeses include those hard cheeses with tough rinds (such as Emmentaler), whereas pressed cheeses include a great many hard and semisoft types (semisoft pressed types often show some sort of imprint on the rind from the cloth or mold used in pressing). Where informative, I've described some cheeses by their ripening agent, either internal mold or surface-ripened. Internal-mold types are those of the Blue-cheese family, which have been inoculated in their interiors with *Penicillium roqueforti* or *Penicillium glaucum* and ripen and develop their characteristic flavor from the inside to the edge.

Cheeses that are surface-ripened show either a "bloomy" rind or a "washed" rind and are ripened from the outside due to the presence of molds or bacteria on their surfaces. Bloomy-rind cheeses such as Brie and certain goat cheeses have a mold growth (*Penicillium camemberti*) encouraged on their surfaces that has a downy, fluffy, or fuzzy appearance when fully developed and varies from snow-white to mottled brown and white. Washed-rind cheeses have rather thin rinds with a varnished appearance that varies from faint yellow-ocher to deep glossy red to rough orange-brown due to frequent dippings in various solutions during curing, such as brine, whey, beer, cider, or wine. The color of these rinds is due to the presence of *Bacterium linens,* among other microorganisms. These bacteria are usually present in the location where the cheeses are cured; their spontaneous growth on the surfaces of the cheese is spread evenly by frequent washings and handling. Some cheeses of this group are Münster, Pont-L'Évêque, and Livarot. Many of these surface-ripened cheeses, both bloomy- and washed-rind types, are semisoft to soft in hardness, uncooked, and either pressed or unpressed.

Of course, a cheese may not have a special ripening agent at all. Cheddar and Swiss types, as mentioned before, are simply ripened by microorganic activity in the milk and consequently show neither special internal molds nor particular surface molds or bacteria. Such cheeses have natural rinds that begin to form when the cheese is salted and are often colorless and thin (as in Cheddar) or tough, yellow-brown, and thick (as in Swiss types). Cheeses with natural rinds are unwashed but frequently brushed, oiled, scrubbed, rubbed, or wrapped, and perhaps waxed to retain moisture while the cheese ripens. This category includes cooked pressed types as well as some uncooked pressed types.

Under the dictionary entries for cheeses readers will find each cheese described as falling into one (sometimes more than one) of the following groups or flavor families:

1. Fresh Uncured Cheese

Such cheeses are the only unripened types in the world of cheese; all the rest are ripened. Stracchino, cream cheese, Ricotta, pot and cottage cheese, and Petit-Suisse are representative examples. All share the mild sweet qualities of cheese that is not far in character from the milk from which it's made.

2. Bland and Mild Cheeses

These types are grouped together not because of any similarity of method of manufacture or rind type, but because they are all simple and unaggressive in flavor. Some of these are quite delicious eating, excellent as breakfast or luncheon cheeses; some here are so lacking in character that they're better off in a sandwich than on their own. Gouda, Edam, Monterey Jack, and Muenster types are typical of this category, though it should be noted that aged examples of some bland and mild cheeses can be as sharp as Cheddars and some (Brick cheese, for example) are more properly classed as strong cheese when they are fully aged and developed.

3. Crèmes

Included in this category are the buttery, unctuous double-
and triple-crème cheeses, all of which are distinguished by
the addition of cream during cheesemaking to raise their butterfat content to 60 percent (for double-crèmes) or 75 percent (for triple-crèmes). Soft, creamy, and surpassingly rich,
they are all rather mild and milk-sweet. Boursault, Crema
Dania, Caprice des Dieux, and other brands of crèmes may
have soft, bloomy rinds like those of Brie types but are best
classed here because of their high fat content.

4. Brie and Camembert Types

These famous cheeses are distinguished by the soft, satiny-
moist, and delicious texture their interiors have when properly
ripened. Their soft, downy, mold-covered rinds are responsible for the unique and popular character of these cheeses.
Brie and Camembert are the classic cheeses of this category,
but Carré de l'Est and others are similar enough to be grouped
with them.

5. Swiss and Swiss Types

Swiss types are, naturally enough, best represented by the
nutty, hard, and mostly mild cheeses of Switzerland, of which
Emmentaler and Gruyère are the most famous. Related cheeses
of the country include Tête-de-Moine and Appenzeller. This
type of cheese has been frequently copied in the United States,
Scandinavia, and elsewhere, sometimes but not always with
great success.

6. Cheddar and Cheddar Types

English Cheddar is the most frequently copied cheese in
the world, and while the best of this sharp, rich cheese is dif-

ficult to surpass, most English Cheddar is easily matched by the very fine Cheddars in the United States, Canada, and occasionally elsewhere. French Cantal belongs in this group, as several other European cheeses by virtue of taste and manufacture. Most English cheeses are Cheddar types.

7. Grana Types

This category is limited to the exceptionally piquant, sharp, and extremely hard grating cheeses typified by Parmesan. Most of the cheeses in this category are Italian.

8. Monastery-Type Cheeses

Since many members of this family have monastic origins, it seems appropriate to call them monastery types. Port-Salut, Saint-Paulin, Pont L'Évêque, Oka, and the various Trappist cheeses produced in Europe, the United States, Canada, and elsewhere are typical of this group. Other semisoft, washed-rind cheeses, such as Reblochon and other mountain cheeses, belong here, even though not of monastic origin, because they show the same pungent, earthy scent and flavors the classic monastery types do.

9. Goat Cheeses

With the exception of this category and the one set aside for sheep's milk cheeses, all the cheeses in other categories are cow's milk cheeses. Typical of this group are the tangy to very spicy, sometimes redolent chèvres from France. All share the unique taste and texture of goat's milk cheeses.

10. Sheep's Milk Cheeses

Sometimes called ewe's milk cheeses, those in this family

are usually either very mild or rather tangy and close to goat cheese in character, and sometimes sharp and salty because they are matured in brine. Brinza, Pecorino, Kasseri, Kashkaval, and other Mediterranean and Eastern European cheeses are representative of this family.

11. Blue Cheeses

If Roquefort weren't often regarded as the king of the Blue (or internal-mold) cheeses, it would be classed as a sheep's milk cheese. But it belongs here with the other Blues, which are almost all made from cow's milk: Stilton, Gorgonzola, Bleu de Bresse, Danablu, and the other semihard to semisoft, sometimes crumbly, veined cheeses with their sharp, spicy flavors and creamy textures.

12. Processed Cheeses

Cheeses in this family are distinguished by manufacturing method and share a somewhat gummy, plastic texture, remarkable keeping qualities, and a wholly uniform and often boring flavor. The simple-flavored blocks, slices, spreads, and other forms of U.S. processed cheeses are all Cheddar-based; the ubiquitous foil-wrapped cubes, wedges, and squares of white, chewy cheeses produced in Europe are even milder; of these, some are Gruyère-based. Cheeses in this category are not themselves natural cheeses but are created from various natural cheeses to make a cheeselike product.

13. Spiced Cheeses

Leyden, Nokkelost, smoked cheeses, crèmes aux fines herbes, cheeses covered with nuts—the list of cheeses to which spices or some other flavorings have been added is lengthy and in general not very inspiring, though many of the caraway-seed cheeses of Scandinavia can be appealing.

14. Whey Cheeses

Whey cheeses are simply those that, unlike all the others in the list, are made wholly or in part from whey rather than curds. Otherwise, some of these types have little in common: Gjetost, and certain Ricottas, for example. (Ricotta, however, even when made from whey, is primarily thought of as a fresh cheese.)

15. Strong Cheeses

Very ripe, intensely flavored, and extremely redolent monastery, goat, and certain long-aged bland and mild cheeses belong to this group, distinguished by their penetrating smells and sometimes taste as well. Representative of these are fully ripe Alsatian Münster, Limburger, Livarot, and Liederkranz.

Readers should realize that cheeses within a given family do not *necessarily* taste very similar, although two cheeses from within the same group would in almost all cases taste more alike than any two cheeses from different groups. The flavor family to which any given cheese has been assigned in this book gives a rough approximation of the sort of cheese it is, and hopefully the accompanying specific description of its aroma and flavor gives a much clearer idea.

4: CHEESE EXPERTISE

Knowing Your Cheeses

Among those interested in cheeses, most are far more interested in eating them than in reading about them. But beginning cheese enthusiasts recognize that without some basic information about the kinds and types of cheese, even the most indefatigable sampler finds it difficult to keep them straight. Knowing something about the flavor families into which cheeses can be grouped, for example, enables one to select an untried cheese with a certain degree of confidence; it may not turn out to be an instant favorite, but its flavor and aroma will not be a complete surprise to the nose and mouth. By forming the habit of thinking of cheeses in terms of flavor families, a cheese enthusiast finds it much easier to remember tastes; it is much easier to remember not only the name of a new cheese but also one's sensory impressions if they can be pigeonholed in the memory under a suitable tag such as goat, crème, and so on.

Knowing something about how cheeses are made makes one much more keenly aware of how the variations in manufacture have affected a cheese. When one recognizes something about a cheese—its washed rind, perhaps, or the soft, downy bloom of a Camembert type, or the interior veining of Blue cheeses—one soon associates the taste characteristics of cheeses with the treatment they have received. Consequently one not only remembers them, but finds it easier to compare them with past samplings of similar cheeses. This is the beginning of being able to evaluate cheeses with some objectivity. In short, knowing something about cheeses enables one's sampling experiences to be organized, an approach that enhances one's appreciation and enjoyment of cheese considerably, and enables the cheese enthusiast to select and serve cheeses with confidence.

Well, then, how does the eager cheese enthusiast become more knowledgeable about cheese? Readers who have read thus far have already absorbed fairly detailed information, and if they continue to the end of this primer and use the dictionary as a guide to sampling, should be well on the way to becoming knowledgeable turophiles. To sample systematically, first become acquainted with representative cheeses from each flavor family and manufacturing method. Probably the most ideal method of exploring cheeses is to taste them where they are produced, though admittedly most people must be content to confine their turophilic travels to a visit to the cheese store. Regardless of whether one is undertaking a serious examination of cheese or merely nibbling here and there, the best and most enjoyable way to try them is by having a cheese-tasting.

How to Set Up a Cheese-tasting

Like wine-tastings, cheese-tastings can be simple or elaborate, formal or informal, serious or merely a pretext for a party. Here's how to conduct a fairly serious sampling of about a dozen cheeses with a few equally interested friends.

1. *Don't make it a meal.* A serious wine-tasting never includes cheese, because cheese makes poor wine taste better; at the least, it obscures the taste of the wine. So, too, wine does not belong at a serious cheese-tasting; it makes the cheese taste better. Of course, wine is an ideal accompaniment to cheeses on informal occasions. But when sampling carefully, confine the beverages to unsugared tea or coffee. Plain tea is best. Always provide plain white French or Italian bread or plain unsalted water biscuits to munch between cheeses and after sipping the beverage. Quarter-pound slices of cheese are more than sufficient for a serious tasting with four participants. Don't try to sample more than a dozen cheeses. Start with a half-dozen the first time; it's surprising how exhausted the palate can get.

Don't smoke, drink, or eat for at least a half-hour before sampling, and don't smoke while tasting. Even if you are used to it, nonsmokers cannot properly taste at all in the presence of tobacco smoke. It's best to taste when slightly hungry, but don't fill up while tasting. Sit comfortably at an uncluttered, well-lighted table and provide everyone with a plate or cutting board and a knife. Use tags or flags, or have stickers on the wrapping to identify the cheese and prevent mixups. Provide pencils and paper, and take your time.

2. *Taste the cheese at room temperature.* Just as wine does not show its true character when ice-cold, neither does cheese. Always remove cheeses from the refrigerator several hours before serious sampling. (If you must try a cheese cold, be sure to masticate it thoroughly in the mouth to warm it, although this trick is no substitute for letting the cheese warm to room temperature.) It is better to taste a cheese too warm than too cold. To see what a difference temperature can make, cut a cheese in half, leaving one piece in the refrigerator and the other sitting out for three hours. Then taste the two halves and compare.

3. *Always compare.* Cheeses tasted against one another quickly reveal their differences and similarities. A cheese tasted alone cannot be compared with anything except one's memory; even an expert's well-stocked memory is not as objective a means of comparison as another cheese tasted at the same time. For a first tasting, choose dissimilar cheeses to gain an idea of the differences between major flavor groups. Then gradually reduce the scope of your tastings to seemingly similar cheeses. It is surprising how sensitive even an untrained palate can be to very small sensory subtleties between, say, two Cheddars tasted side by side. Other samplings might include comparisons between similar cheeses of different ages, or different brands of the same cheese type, or a cheese type and its copies and imitations from all over the world. While a group of turophiles might find it more instructive to compare a half-dozen Bries, informal party tastings call for a wide selection of cheeses to suit a variety of tastes.

4. *Look, feel, sniff, taste.* First, look at the cheese. What sort of rind does it have? Fuzzy, mottled, thick, or thin? What color is the interior? White, yellow, orange? Does it have holes? What sort? Is the texture close-grained, waxy, oily, marbled, flaky, or crumbly? Feel the cheese through the rind, then poke gently at the interior. Is it firm, hard, supple, resilient, bouncy, rubbery, soft, mushy? Play with a small crumb between the fingers if the cheese is firm-textured. What does it feel like? Oily? Elastic?

Sniff the rind, then sniff a piece of the cheese free from all rind. Is there a difference? Does the cheese smell like earth? Mushrooms? Mold? Leaves? Ammonia? Grass? Butter? Nuts? Is it pleasant or unpleasant, faint or overwhelming, savory, mouth-watering, spicy, herby? Or is it gassy, chemical, musty, rank? Now taste it; taste a small piece, free of all rind, chewing it slowly and pressing it with all parts of the tongue from tip to back, including the sides, and spreading it against the hard palate. Concentrate on the impressions as you do. Swallow, and wait for any aftertaste. Does it linger? Disappear? Have a strange backbite? Take in a breath through the mouth and exhale through the nose so that the scent can rise in the nasal passages. Does the impression, from tongue tip to aftertaste, complement the aroma? Is it different—better or worse? Stronger or milder than the aroma led you to expect?

If tasting with others, taste first, and then discuss. Compare impressions, but everyone should first form their own. A serious tasting would include note-taking, even assigning scores for virtues and defects to each, just as is done in a serious wine-tasting. In any event, it is not a bad idea to jot down one's impressions so that later one doesn't have to rely on memory to recall which cheeses were outstanding and which disappointing. After tasting each cheese, try to fix it in your mind and take any notes before moving on to the next cheese. Add additional notes on comparisons later. Clear your palate between cheeses with a cracker or piece of bread—after drinking unsugared tea or coffee.

Cheese tasters, just like wine, coffee, or tea tasters, have their own special vocabulary to describe tastes, textures, aromas, and overall impressions of cheese. Although much of the cheese taster's vocabulary is self-explanatory, some terms have special meanings. The following glossary not only helps clarify the descriptions given in the dictionary entries but should give the cheese amateur a good idea of what to pay attention to when tasting a cheese critically. In compiling this vocabulary, I've included descriptions most commonly used by cheese authorities and those in the trade. In particular I've drawn on the list of terms in Van Slyke's treatise *Cheese*. In each case, however, I've attempted to give these nontechnical definitions.

A Turophile's Glossary

Note: An italicized term used in a definition is defined elsewhere in this list.

Acid Used to indicate a pleasant sourish tang; not to be confused with a completely *sour* character, which is a *defect*. See *tangy*.

Aged Hard cheeses are said to be at their peak of development when aged. See *ripe*.

Ammoniated, ammoniacal Ammonialike odor given off by overripe soft cheeses with bloomy *rinds* and a few other types.

Appearance Appearance includes all visual assessments of cheese: *wrapping, rind, color, texture,* what it looks like when handled or broken or cut, and so forth.

Aroma The smell or odor of a cheese. Cheese may lack aroma, have *faint* aromas, *mild* or light aromas, *pronounced* aromas (be aromatic), or even stink. Aromas are closely allied with flavors, but smelly cheeses can have mild flavors, while cheeses lacking aroma may have strong flavors. The *rind* of a cheese may have a different odor than the *interior*. Aromas may also be specific, such as *oily, barnyardy, earthy,* and so on.

Aromatic Said of cheeses with distinct, *pronounced aromas*.

Barny, barnyardy Also "cowy"; an odor suggestive of the barnyard. In all but a few cases, considered a *defect*.

Bitter An unpleasant biting flavor; a bitter aftertaste is sometimes associated with the use of pasteurized milk. See *cooked*.

Body The physical characteristics of the cheese when felt, handled, cut, chewed. A cheese may be felt or palpitated to determine its condition or ripeness. Its body may feel *supple, rubbery, firm,* elastic, soft, resilient, yielding, and so on. When rolled between the fingers or cut it may feel *oily, waxy, crumbly,* and so forth. When chewed, a cheese may feel *grainy*, gritty, mealy, *creamy*, plastic, *gummy*.

Buttery Said of a cheese with a high fat content, particularly the crèmes. Also said of cheese with a *flavor* and *texture* reminiscent of butter.

Chemical An *aroma* or *flavor* taint indicating improper manufacture or contamination with foreign materials.

Clean A cheese free of objectionable *off*-flavors and *defects*.

Close Said of the texture of cheeses with a body free of holes, fissures, or other breaks; uniform.

Color The color of the *rind* and the *interior* of any cheese is an indication of its condition and quality. In all cases the color should be characteristic of the cheese type. Cheeses naturally range from snow-white to deep yellow; orange-colored cheeses are dyed with annatto, a vegetable dye, during manufacture.

Cooked As a tasting term, cooked refers to an aroma associated with the use of pasteurized milk. (Not to be confused with cooked as a manufacturing description, which refers to the heating of the curd.)

Creamy Broad term used to describe the *appearance* of certain soft cheeses, and the taste *texture* of certain cheeses (from hard to soft types) when chewed.

Crumbly Said of the body of cheeses that break and fall apart when cut, usually due to interior veining and sometimes to excessive dryness.

Defect A spoilage factor found in the cheese due to improper manufacture or contamination.

Dirty Cheeses with this *flavor* taste as if they have been buried underground. Always unpleasant, a *defect* indicating some kind of spoilage. Not to be confused with *earthy*.

Earthy *Aroma* and *flavor* description most often applied to monastery-type cheeses. May be *faint* or intensely *strong;* not appealing to everyone, but not a defect. Not to be confused with *dirty*.

Faint Said of a fleeting very light *aroma* or *flavor*.

Feed taste A feed taste is the odor or taste found in a cheese due to the particular feed given the cow or other animal before milking. It may be unpleasant if the feed is silage or turnips, or intriguing if the feed is, say, apples.

Fermented An aroma reminiscent of alcoholic fermentation. See *fruity* and *gassy*.

Firm Said of the body of cheeses that are relatively inelastic and unyielding to the touch; typical of hard cheeses.

Fishy An unpleasant *flavor* nuance said to appear in some overcured cheeses.

Flaky Said of the *body* of a cheese that flakes when cut.

Flat A cheese is lacking in *flavor,* when marked flavor is normally characteristic; especially said of cheeses lacking in salt.

Flavor The taste of the cheese in the mouth. Flavor is partly detected by the nose when one is chewing. Flavors in order of ascending aggressiveness are termed *faint* (fleeting), *mild* (light or bland), *pronounced* (distinct), *strong (intense)*. Flavors may also be specific, as in goaty, *salty, moldy, nutty,* acidy, and so forth.

Fruity A sweet, pleasant fragrant *aroma* or *flavor* found in certain cheeses, notably semisoft monastery types and a few hard mountain cheeses. A defective note in others.

Gamy *Strong* cheeses with penetrating odors are sometimes described as gamy.

Gassy Cheeses suffering from one or more manufacturing *defects* may exhibit various gassy or sometimes synthetic scents or tastes.

Grainy Said of the appearance of certain cheeses and the texture of others, which, when tasted, do not melt and form a creamy mass but retain a coarse or mealy texture. Desirable in some cheeses, but not in others.

Grassy A weedy taste said to be imparted by cows feeding on bitterweed, leeks, onions, and so on. See *feed taste.*

Gummy Descriptive of the plastic, spreadable, but somewhat sticky consistency of some soft cheeses, particularly processed types.

High Confusing term used in two ways; (1) to describe a delicate, attractive, but fleeting, faintly volatile odor; (2) an unpleasant, *rancid,* spoiled *aroma.*

Intense Said of very strong, concentrated, and powerful odors and tastes.

Interior The cheese itself, excluding its *rind.*

Lactic A distinct milklike *aroma* or *flavor.*

Mild Said of light *aromas* and *flavors.* Stronger than faint, but not distinct or *pronounced.* Also used to describe less than fully aged Cheddar types.

Moldy Said of the scent and taste of certain cheeses, particularly bloomy-rind and interior-mold types. Should be clean and pleasant rather than musty or *ammoniacal.*

Mottled Irregular, splotchy *color* of cheese that should be regular in appearance. Not a good sign.

Mushrooms *Aroma* and *flavor* description; always *clean* and attractive. Characteristic of certain soft and semisoft types.

Nutty Many cheeses are said to resemble sweet nutmeats in flavor. Cheddars are often described as reminiscent of walnuts, fresh goat cheese and Gruyère are said to remind one of hazelnuts, and so on.

Off Off-flavors or off-odors are undesirable *flavor* or odor taints too faint to be more precisely characterized.

Oily Said of the appearance of cheeses with a rich, fatty look when cut, and the *aroma* and *flavor* of certain cheeses.

Open Said of the body of a cheese whose *texture* has numerous small openings and holes.

Paste The *interior* flesh of a cheese; more specifically, the *texture* of the *interior* of Brie and Camembert types when *ripe.*

Peppery Aged Cheddar is sometimes described as having a peppery *flavor* nuance as are aged goat cheeses.

Pronounced A distinct *aroma* or *flavor.* Stronger than *mild,* but not powerful enough to be described as strong or *intense.*

Pungent Said of a particularly redolent *aroma* or *sharp,* penetrating *flavor.*

Putrid Said of a completely spoiled cheese in a state of putrefaction.

Rancid A distinct *aroma* and *flavor* indicating a defective, spoiled, often *gassy* cheese.

Rind The outer surface of a cheese. Cheeses may have soft, bloomy rinds, washed rinds, thick or thin natural rinds, and so forth. (See sections 2 and 3 in the Primer for descriptions.)

Ripe Soft cheeses are said to be at their peak of development when ripe. See *aged.*

Robust Said of coarse, *strong aromas* and *flavors.*

Rubbery The resilient, bouncy feel or *texture* of certain cheeses. In certain cheeses an undesirable characteristic.

Salty A *flavor* impression found in almost all cheeses; especially pronounced in cheeses soaked in brine. A lack of salt makes cheese taste *flat;* oversaltiness hides flavor.

Satiny Said of the *texture* (especially when tasted) of soft, spreadable cheeses, particularly Brie types, when perfectly *ripe.*

Sharp Said of the fully developed character of well-aged Cheddar. Not to be confused with *bitter.*

Soapy An unpleasant taste like that of soap; usually associated with overage cheeses.

Sour An excessively *acid* cheese; a *defect.* See *rancid, putrid.*

Spicy Said of cheeses with a *peppery,* herby tang. Not to be confused with *grassy* or applied to cheeses that are actually spiced with caraway seeds, chives, and so forth.

Strong See *intense.*

Supple Used to describe the body of certain cheeses when felt.

Not as resilient as *rubbery* or as soft as spreadable; somewhat elastic, consistent, and yielding.

Tangy Broad term used to indicate a distinct, lingering, usually acidy flavor element. Also used to indicate specific characteristic flavors, as in a Cheddar tang, a goat tang, and so on.

Taste See *flavor*.

Texture Texture is judged visually, by feel, and also in the mouth. Textures may be *close, open, waxy, grainy,* uniform, *crumbly, creamy,* and so forth. Expected texture depends on cheese type. See *body*.

Waxy A cheese *body* or *texture* with the *appearance* (and sometimes the taste texture) of wax.

Wrapping The exterior material in which a cheese may be enclosed: leaves, plastic, cloth, paraffin, foil, and so on. The condition of the wrapping is one indication of the condition of the cheese.

5: HOW TO BUY
AND STORE CHEESE

The first thing one notices about the range of cheeses available in cheese departments and stores in major cities is that most of them are European imports. There are several reasons for this. Europe produces not only 40 percent of the world's cheese, but an enormous variety of them. France alone offers about seventy distinct types (several hundred if you include obscure cheeses and local variants). Any selection of the world's best cheeses would thus include a disproportionate number of European cheeses. This isn't to say there aren't superb American cheeses—there are—but the sorts of U.S. cheeses likely to intrigue a gourmet are far outnumbered by their bland brethren. Although the United States produces more cheese than any other single country, the vast majority of its products are the ubiquitous sliced and prepackaged cheeses and processed cheese foods and spreads, and such humble items as cottage cheese. Consequently a significant share of the growing U.S. taste for fine cheeses is supplied by foreign imports. Once only 4 or 5 percent of cheese consumption in the United States, imports now account for around 10 percent of the cheese consumed by Americans. Of course, imports to this country consist, by and large (though not exclusively), of the better cheeses of the exporting country. There is, too, an undeniable element of exoticism that attaches itself to imported cheese—a false exoticism compounded partly out of snobbism both for imported products and against domestic efforts. But despite the romantic antiquity of European cheeses, the truth is that these days the vast majority of them are produced in factories no less mechanized than American ones. The turophile who is willing to be guided by taste rather than prejudice will find a number of very fine to outstanding U.S. cheeses available.

Cheese and the Law

Despite the excellence of American cheeses, the United States has for many years placed import quotas on foreign cheeses, particularly inexpensive ones, presumably to protect the domestic cheese industry. Current quotas limit imports to about ninety million pounds per year. The result has been that imported cheeses have risen sharply in cost due to demand and to the fact that the imports must reach certain price levels to be brought in at all. Good, inexpensive foreign cheeses are excluded and thus offer no competition to inexpensive American-produced varieties.

The United States does not regulate use of most foreign names of cheeses. Roquefort is one exception to this general state of affairs, but Swiss, Provolone, Camembert, Mozzarella, Edam, and so on have all been adopted as names for cheeses made here, some of which bear little resemblance to the original. This is complicated by the fact that few other countries respect one another's nomenclature either, so that a cheese labeled "Imported Swiss" is no guarantee that the cheese in fact came from Switzerland.

One might think cheeses should not be allowed to be labeled with the names of cheeses of other countries and districts, but the problem becomes quite complicated in the case of a cheese like Cheddar. The original Cheddar is English, but if this name were not allowed to be used as a generic name, what would one call the billions of pounds of that style of cheese (some of which is quite excellent) that are produced in the United States, Canada, New Zealand, and elsewhere? Most countries have imitated one another's cheeses, often very well: the "genuine" or original versions of every cheese type are not *always* the best of their kind, though sometimes, of course, they are. In short, cheeses have to be judged on their own; after all, it's not the labels that are eaten.

An additional aspect of cheese labeling to be aware of: importers and distributors market cheeses under a bewildering variety of brand names concocted to fulfill various marketing strategies. Since the same cheese may be sold under a variety of fancy names, the cheese lover does well to pinpoint the origin of the cheese before concerning himself with the label.

Where to Buy Cheese

A variety of cheeses are now offered in the dairy section of many supermarkets across the country, but most of these cheeses are prepackaged and of ordinary quality. In certain sections of the country, stores do offer local cheeses cut to order; these are usually quite superior to the prepackaged types. Unfortunately, however, for a broad selection of the world's better efforts at cheesemaking, one has to go to a major metropolis. In large urban centers, a cheese lover has three sources of cheese: cheese departments (sometimes this is part of the gourmet department) of department or fancy food stores; delicatessens and food shops catering to an ethnic group; and cheese specialty stores.

The ethnic food shop can be an excellent source of supply, although its cheeses are understandably limited to those enjoyed by the particular ethnic neighborhood; some of these shops make their own fresh cheeses, like farmer or Ricotta, and they are among the best, if not *the* best sources of these cheeses. But the specialty cheese store or cheese department is the obvious general source for cheese and often the only source of certain hard-to-find cheeses—chèvres, for example, or properly ripened Bries. By specializing in cheese, such outlets can usually offer well-chosen cheeses in bulk and can steer customers to the types they want or to new ones they might like to sample.

Regardless of type of outlet, however, knowledge about and concern for the careful handling and proper storage of the cheeses vary considerably. Unfortunately, whenever a food item, whether it be wine, coffee beans, or fine cheese, becomes increasingly popular, merchants spring up ready to fill the role of a specialty-food-shop owner in all respects but those that really matter to the customer: expertise, reliability, and honesty. Frankly, many specialty cheese shops, more interested in making money than purveying quality cheese, make a practice of carrying the cheapest available cheese of any given type, often those that are available from importers at a reduced price because of damage in transit or simple overaging. Sales methods employed are designed to push cheese, not guide customers. Although it is possible to get a bad cheese even from the most reliable merchants, one is lucky to get a decent cheese at the worst outlets. Fortunately, it isn't difficult to spot the dubious cheesemonger.

First, be wary of specialty stores or cheese departments claiming to carry upwards of a thousand different cheeses. Although there are three thousand varieties of cheese in the world, most of these are only local variations of one or another main cheese and are not produced in sufficient quantity to be exported. Even well-known cheeses are not always available; despite mechanization, some cheeses are obtainable only on a seasonal basis. Sadly enough, some merchants do not hesitate to offer mislabeled cheeses—thus some three hundred distinct cheeses may be "multiplied" by being given one thousand different names. Even if all were actually different cheeses, it would be extremely difficult, if not impossible, for a cheese merchant to offer that many in perfect condition. It is far preferable to pick from a small, carefully chosen selection (even if it is only dozens) than from a vast selection of which the majority are poor or dubious examples. Besides, a reputable cheese store will not carry a cheese that does not live up to its quality standards, and rightly so; few cheeses are so unique that a flattering imitation could not substitute for it. Do not assume that the best cheese stores are the ones that offer the largest number and the most exotic varieties. A good, correctly labeled Vermont Cheddar is preferable to a poor Italian Caciocavallo masquerading as a Bulgarian Kashkaval.

Second, consider the shop's storage and handling of the cheese. Does the store smell fresh or foul? If it smells like a spoiled, moldy cheese, that is a sure sign of uncleanliness. Cheeses stored under such conditions are likely to pick up such unpleasant odors themselves. Cheeses will also pick up one another's odors if stored right on top of each other. Piling cheeses of the same type on top of one another is fine, so long as they are carefully wrapped and sold quickly. Otherwise, cheeses should all be given breathing space from their neighbors so that air can freely circulate between them. The sharing of scents is one of the reasons why better cheese outlets wrap almost all their cheeses in plastic wrap, except for prepackaged cheeses and odd items that need special handling, such as storage in brine.

Storing cheeses at the proper temperature and humidity is another essential. To retain character and moisture and to prevent too rapid ripening and spoilage, cheeses must be kept cool—about 45° to 50°, at high humidity—about 85 to 90 percent, and wrapped. This means refrigerated storage is necessary. Most stores do have a few cheeses out at room temperature for display (usually carefully wrapped), particularly ones to be sold the same day, but cheeses displayed on shelves (and even in windows) at room temperature for weeks on end are suffering improper storage, regardless of their enticing appearance from a distance. Close examination of such cheeses usually reveals a warning sign: unappetizing appearance. All cheeses, no matter how unfamiliar, should look appetizing: Blues should look moist, not dried out; a fresh-cut hard or semisoft cheese should not be sagging under its rind; soft bloomy-rind cheeses should not be covered with grayish-pinkish mange and have a sunken, shriveled look. In the worst shops, the Swiss types often look covered with sweat from heat, even the Edams may show distress signals like sticky, oily cellophane wrapping, and lifting the lid on a triple-crème or Bleu de Bresse subjects you to a smell as powerful as a blow on the nose.

Overripened cheeses are a commonplace in such stores; rapidity of turnover, particularly with fresh and soft cheeses, is thus of considerable importance. In fact, virtually all cheese stores in the United States sometimes sell both underripe and overripe soft cheeses. This emphasizes not only that such cheeses are difficult to bring to the peak of development, but that few stores are willing to subscribe to the idea that a cheese-monger should sell only cheeses ready to eat in forty-eight hours. It is no secret that even reputable stores put slightly overripe soft cheeses on sale so that they can be sold before they get too ripe to sell at any price. Perhaps one of the reasons why many of the less-reputable cheese suppliers seem to make such a specialty of cheese spreads is so that their overripe cheeses can be given a second chance with customers, this time liberally laced with something spiritous to hide their senility and enlivened with pimento and nuts.

Although it would be possible for large shops to age some of their cheeses further, few have the space, proper facilities, or the capital to tie up large amounts of cheese for years at a time. Most exported cheeses are shipped ready to consume; few would benefit rather than suffer from extended keeping. Consequently most stores in the United States do not attempt to age their hard cheeses further or carefully ripen their soft and semisoft cheeses, with the possible exception of Brie types, which better stores attempt to nurture properly. In short, it is essential to know something about cheese, not only so that one can make a reasonably good assessment of the quality of a source of cheese, but so that one can insist on quality.

The third and in some ways the most important means of judging the quality of a cheese store or department is how the store treats its customers; the following sections suggest what the wise customer should expect from a reputable cheese store and some hints for buying various types of cheeses.

Choosing and Buying Cheese

SAMPLING All cheese authorities exhort a prospective cheese buyer to sample cheeses before buying any. Although sampling a cheese in a store cannot be as critical as careful, unrushed, concentrated sampling at home—particularly because the cheese is almost always too cold—this is excellent advice. Unfortunately, many cheese stores actively discourage giving samples because it presents difficulties for the staff even in the best-run outlets. There are always people who will abuse such a privilege and insist on tasting a half-dozen expensive cheeses all of which have to be unwrapped and then wrapped again, merely to select a quarter-pound of Wisconsin Swiss for lunch. Nevertheless, there are shops where samples are not given grudgingly and clerks do not attempt to browbeat customers into buying a given cheese. A store that will let you sample only after cutting your piece (and cutting the sample from your purchase) obviously intends to make a fuss over a decision not to purchase it. It is perfectly reasonable to ask to sample several cheeses that interest you without being rushed before making a decision, though common sense tells you not to do this when the store is jammed and you have a long line behind you.

Soft cheeses and small packaged cheeses present special problems, because no store is willing to cut into one (although some stores occasionally sacrifice a small one and set it out to encourage customers to buy a whole one). Once a soft cheese has been cut into, it will not keep very long. If such cheeses are within reach, it should be perfectly all right to open the lid, examine the wrapping for signs of mold growth, stickiness, runniness, or other warnings of excessive age or spoilage, to sniff for off-odors, and even to press the wrapped surface gently to check on its ripeness. If you must ask for the cheese, ask to look inside, and whether the cheese is sitting out or not, be sure to ask before unwrapping. Ask before poking at the Bries too, since there is only so much poking a soft cheese can take before it looks shopworn. It is also reasonable to ask to look at the rind or label of a cheese; a store that has nothing to hide should not be reluctant to show you all the signs of authenticity that may accompany the cheese on its label or rind.

WEIGHING AND CUTTING Weighing and cutting in cheese stores make for a certain amount of irritation on both sides of the counter. Most cheese consumers have long noticed that ninety-eight times out of a hundred when you ask for a half a pound or pound of a particular cheese, the clerk invariably cuts it a little large and then says in a surprised tone, "Gee, it's a little over . . . is that all right?" Usually the customer makes no fuss, even though he feels that more than he wants is being pushed on him. Merchants rightly point out, on the other hand, that it is difficult to guess weight with many cheeses and that customers are annoyed when additional scraps of cheese must be added to a chunk to reach the desired weight. Besides, merchants will say, most people don't want a precise amount; they want a nice-looking piece of cheese. Thus some merchants simply ignore requests for a certain poundage and indicate a certain size wedge with their knives. "Is that about right?" they ask and, given the nod, hack away. Since this sort of thing can lend itself to abuse, a customer does well to be precise: "I want a little under a half-pound, please," or "No more than a pound." Reassure the merchant that you don't mind if the weight is a little under. If you asked for a pound and the clerk cuts one and a half pounds, you should insist on a pound. But any customer who insisted that a one-pound one-ounce piece of cheese be trimmed to exactly one pound would be persona non grata in that cheese store, since the scrap will not be able to be sold.

A note on scraps: merchants do not want to create wastage and thus will attempt to sell off the last bits of a wheel of cheese. If recently cut, there will be nothing wrong with it, but if old and tired-looking, don't feel forced to accept it, particularly if you want a larger amount. Simply state that you want a fresh-cut piece or you don't want it at all.

Each dictionary entry in Part Two suggests what the cheese should look and taste like, but there are some basic buying hints and general cautions for each flavor family that every cheese lover should try to remember.

BUYING FRESH, UNCURED CHEESES The cheese should be truly fresh and, of course, look fresh, moist, and appetizing.

BUYING BLAND AND MILD CHEESES Most cheeses of this type, particularly mild American cheeses like Muenster and the mild Scandinavian types, are quite reliable. Since they rarely are aged for long periods, endeavor to buy young ones that have not dried out, become tired, or been mishandled—in which case they look as if they've seen better days. Watch out for sticky wrappings, sagging middles, cracked rinds of wax, even moldy blotches.

BUYING CRÈMES Double- and triple-crèmes and other small high-butterfat cheeses are relatively expensive and often have soft, bloomy rinds. Always take off the lid and see that the cheese is not sticking to the wrapping or shrunk down inside its own rim; it should be plump and fill its box (though it should not look as if it is about to burst it either) and be soft and somewhat yielding to the touch (but not mushy). Any such cheese with signs of mold on the outside of the wrapping or a noticeable ammonia scent should be avoided; a pleasant trace of a mold scent is not objectionable. If possible, look beneath the wrapping: the rind should not be dead white and thick or entirely mottled gray-brown, but typically should show some slight degree of mottling, which may vary from ivory to rosy to slightly brownish on the edges of the cheese. Mottling increases with age. Nothing can be done about an overaged crème, but one bought a little young can be given a few extra days at home in the refrigerator.

BUYING BRIE AND CAMEMBERT TYPES Since, like the crèmes, these cheeses also have a soft, bloomy rind, much the same advice should be followed, particularly with the smaller cheeses, such as Coulommiers or small packaged U.S. Bries and Camemberts that aren't sold by the piece. French Bries and Camemberts, however, are often sold by the wedge, and it is usually possible to see the rind, sniff, and—if the wedges are plastic-wrapped on display—examine the interior. Make sure the cheese has softened throughout and has no unripened, hard, chalky line running through the center. Since the cheese will not ripen properly if wedges are cut out of it, a piece of cut Brie or Camembert should be ready to eat. The interior should look satiny, and moist, and bulge (if wrapped) or be on the verge of oozing out. Examine a whole, uncut Brie or Camembert with the same method that a cheese merchant uses to determine if the cheese is ready to cut: gently palpitate the cheese from the rim to the center to feel for hard spots. The precise response of a properly ripe cheese is difficult to describe, but quite easy to feel. Admittedly few merchants will let you handle whole Bries, but they should at least let you look at an uncovered portion of the rind. The mottling or pigmentation should be evenly and lightly flecked on the surface of the cheese and the cheese should have only a pleasant moldy scent, not an ammoniated smell. A large Brie with a faint trace of ammonia mingled with a predominant smell of mold may have a perfectly sound interior. But if the interior, stripped of all surface mold, has an ammoniated flavor or scent that lingers in the aftertaste, it is too old or has not ripened properly. Unfortunately, only experience can teach you how much of an ammoniated trace is too much, and people differ in their sensitivity to it. On the whole, it is best to avoid Bries, Camemberts, and other soft, bloomy-rind cheeses with the slightest hint of ammonia.

Canned Camemberts and Bries should be avoided entirely, and French Bries and Camemberts should be bought warily, if at all, during the summer months, not only because the best season runs from about October to April for these cheeses, but also because spoilage is more likely in summer heat.

BUYING SWISS AND SWISS TYPES These cheeses are among the most reliable types to purchase, not only because they can almost always be sampled, but also because they keep so well. Nonetheless, be sure they are neither dried out nor rubbery, and always determine, either by examination of the rind or other identifying marks or by asking, whether the cheese is genuine Swiss or a European or American Swiss type. Genuine Swiss cheeses are almost always superior to imitations, but some Swiss types made elsewhere are of very high quality. A few are as good as the originals. Many Swiss types are quite inferior, however, so be sure and pay accordingly.

The holes in Emmentaler should be about the size of a quarter and be spherical rather than irregular or oval. Gruyère holes are dime-sized or smaller; Appenzeller has even smaller holes. Huge, odd-shaped holes are a sign of poor manufacture. If the rinds of Emmentaler and Gruyère are overly thick and grayish toward the edge or split with cracks, the cheeses may be old and oversharp. Emmentaler and Gruyère should be sweetish and clean-tasting, and Gruyère should not be too gritty and grainy in texture. Other Swiss cheeses such as Appenzeller and Tête-de-Moine are stronger-tasting. Non-Swiss types should come close to Swiss character.

BUYING CHEDDAR AND CHEDDAR TYPES There are many non-English Cheddars that equal all but the rare farmhouse English Cheddar, so do not pay inflated prices for the English product without first sampling. Again, beware of dry-looking cracks and crumbling, indicating excessive moisture loss, or cheeses with white mold specks, splotchy, streaky, or mottled colors, or bulgy, wet-looking rinds: all are signs of faulty manufacture and/or storage. Don't buy Cheddars with traces of bitterness in the aftertaste or dried-out Caerphillies and white Wensleydales.

BUYING GRANA TYPES Be sure that the Parmesan or other Grana-type cheese you purchase is Italian. Check the rind and its identifying marks; if they are not visible, ask. If the cheese isn't Italian, pay accordingly. Since most grana types produced outside Italy have none of the sweet-salty graininess of the genuine article, always sample. Despite their keeping qualities, Granas can dry out.

BUYING MONASTERY TYPES These are fairly reliable cheeses to buy. Try to obtain these by the piece instead of buying a whole small one, so you can sample it before purchasing. Be aware of the range of quality (and price) in Port-Salut; there are Danish, American, and other types, as well as a variety of French Saint-Paulins, some of which are far superior to others. The cheese should not be dried out, have excessive holes, have cracked or moldy rinds if paraffined, or, in the case of Reblochon and the various Tommes, have abnormal mold formations on the rind. Wrapped, boxed types, such as Pont-L'Évêque, should look clean and unsticky in the box, and have a resilient texture and a pleasant hint of redolence. With monastery or mountain cheeses, do not make the mistake of thinking that pronounced scent indicates pronounced taste.

BUYING GOAT CHEESES Goat cheeses are quite individual.

They should conform to their particular character and should not show mold growth abnormal for their type, and so on. Fresh goat cheese should be fresh; indeed, if it is not, the smell and taste will give it away. Old, dry ones are not to everyone's taste.

BUYING SHEEP'S MILK CHEESES These range from mild to sharp in flavor depending on age; their principal defect is excessive saltiness. Examine the cheese to see that it is moist and fresh, and taste it for flavor and saltiness.

BUYING BLUE CHEESES With the exception of small wrapped Blue cheeses, which, like other prepackaged cheeses, can only be examined by sight, most Blues can be purchased by wedge or slice. Blue cheeses should always look attractive, show even distribution of veins, and be moist and not excessively crumbly when cut, although thin slices may break into large chunks. The color of the cheese, apart from veining, should be whitish rather than gray or brownish, uniform, and not dark toward the outer edge. Roquefort is a protected name; look for the identifying mark on the foil wrapping. If you can, taste Blues for excessive saltiness and age before buying.

BUYING PROCESSED CHEESES A processed cheese would have to be frightfully mishandled before it would show signs of spoilage; consequently it is more reliable to buy than any natural cheese, and is usually inexpensive. Unfortunately, these cheeses are not particularly interesting. Gourmandise is one of the few that is sold in bulk and thus can be sampled first for flavor.

BUYING SPICED CHEESES Spiced cheeses cover the range of cheese types from hard to soft, bland to strong, so that one should note whatever cautions would apply to the cheese if it were not spiced with caraway seeds, herbs, and so on.

BUYING WHEY CHEESES With the exception of Ricottas produced from whey, which must be fresh to be at their best, most of the other whey cheeses are hard, durable, and reliable, and come prepackaged.

BUYING STRONG CHEESES Cautions that would govern the cheese if it were milder and thus belonged in other categories also apply here. Remember that even if the cheese is supposed to exhibit a strong heavy smell, there is a difference between a rustic redolence and a truly rank, spoiled stench. Experience with strong cheeses that have not reached full ripeness and those that have long passed it quickly teaches one the difference. If possible, taste; smells with these cheeses can be deceptive.

RETURNING CHEESES If you have had the misfortune to purchase a spoiled, damaged, bitter, or otherwise unsatisfactory cheese, return it. Many people are highly reluctant to do this. The biggest hesitation seems to come from the fact that few people are confident about their assessment of a cheese and are apprehensive they'll simply be told, "Well, that's the way it's supposed to look, smell, and so on." All too often that's the answer the hapless customer gets, even if the cheese is in an advanced state of putrefaction. It does not take long, however, to gain a working familiarity with good examples of standard cheeses sufficient to know an overripe cheese when you smell it. Few customers are allowed to purchase a mature Livarot, Handkäse, or other smelly cheese without being warned what to expect. There will always be a few customers who'll simply return something perfectly sound simply because they didn't like it, but the fact is that a good cheese store does not argue with customers who are unhappy over a purchase any more than a good wine store argues with those who return a bottle. Even the best cheese store cannot prevent the occasional poor piece of cheese from being sold any more than the best wine merchant can assure the quality of every wine he sells without uncorking it.

A NOTE ON BUYING CHEESE IN SEASON As Androuët points out, the best cheeses are made from the best milk of the season and should be purchased at the proper time of the year. Unfortunately, it is extremely difficult to act on this sound piece of advice, because it really applies only to farm cheese produced from local milk. Only a handful of cheeses are farm-produced today; most are manufactured in large commercial plants from milk brought in from various districts and sometimes considerable distances. The efforts of a cheese factory are all bent toward year-round consistency of production both in quantity and in quality, and whatever seasonal differences might be found in the quality of the local milk are lost when it is mixed with milk from other districts, frozen curds, and so on.

The only generalizations one can make are that the fall and winter are good seasons to buy many cheeses because they benefit from being made from the rich summer milk, while spring and summer cheeses (other than the fresh ones and long-curing cheeses) must be made from the thinner milk of winter; it is also true that French Brie, Camembert, and cheeses such as Pont-L'Évêque are not at their best during the summer. Other than this, as Androuët admits, there is really no "best season" for factory-produced cheeses. With farm cheeses, seasons do make a difference, but it is extremely difficult to determine modes, methods, and times of production with any assurance. Chances are farm cheeses will be sold at their best season because that is the only season they are available. One can only ask a reliable cheese merchant, and let your taste be your guide.

ON BUYING CHEESE BY MAIL In recent years it has been possible to order cheese from large cheese shops or mail-order houses and have it shipped directly to any part of the country. But since this procedure has several drawbacks, look around first and make sure a cheese department or shop hasn't opened within a convenient distance. If not, look closely at various mail-order plans. Remember you won't get a chance to examine the cheese, much less taste it, and are therefore not in a position to be fussy. Many mail-order plans require you to purchase processed cheeses and other uninteresting fare each month and freely substitute inferior cheeses for the mouth-watering types described in their catalogs. It is best to do your own selecting and order large blocks of hard, excellent-keeping cheeses rather than risky, perishable types that do not ship well, such as Brie and Camembert types and soft cheeses. It is not merely a question of not ordering cheeses during the summer; cheeses can spoil just as easily by sitting in an over-heated or unheated warehouse during the winter.

How to Store Cheese

The first rule of storing cheese: don't buy more cheese than is needed at a time. Storage of cheese at home is difficult for certain varieties and requires rather frequent attention for all but a few types. It is possible to have an actual cheese cellar in one's house, but few homes have the necessary cool, moist conditions. Furthermore, although a number of cheeses benefit by additional aging, a collection of aging cheeses is not like a collection of aging wines. Wines are best left to age undisturbed, but cheeses need to be turned, brushed, washed, or at least watched carefully as they develop. Few turophiles' interest in cheese is great enough to warrant setting up a true cheese cellar. Most cheese lovers are better off learning to select good cheeses as they appear on retail shelves and purchasing them fairly frequently. That way, storing cheeses becomes a simple problem of keeping them reasonably fresh and moist.

In buying cheeses that will not be consumed within a day or two, be guided by the usable life span that is typical for the particular cheese. There is no way to keep a perfectly ripe Brie from becoming overripe once it has reached its peak of development, so always buy cheeses with such short life spans for immediate use only. Cheddars and other long-lived types, on the other hand, will keep for months if properly stored, and can therefore be bought in larger quantities.

Unless you have a cool cellar or pantry (about 50° F) with very high humidity, keep cheeses in the refrigerator—a very suitable place if it is not kept too cool. (One exception: frost-free refrigerators have very low humidity and consequently tend to dry out cheese much faster than the conventional kind.) Somewhere around 45° F is just about right for most cheeses, particularly if they are kept in the vegetable drawer. (If your lettuce usually freezes, cut back on the temperature dial and spare your cheese.) Remember that all cheeses, with the exception of processed types, will continue to age and develop to some extent even in the refrigerator, and thus will become sharper with age. This is particularly true of Blues, so if you like your Blues on the mild side, buy them in small quantities.

Of the so-called improvements that modern technology has brought to the world of cheese, none is probably more useful than polyethylene or plastic wrap. This material satisfies the two principal requirements for cheese storage other than temperature: it keeps moisture in and air out. (In particular, I prefer Saran brand wrap, since it is the least permeable and doesn't have any odor, something that certain other brands appear to have.) When in doubt or in a hurry, wrap any cheese in plastic wrap to protect it. Only a few cheeses are better wrapped in something else. When wrapping hard cheeses and semisoft types, trim uneven cut surfaces or smooth them with the flat of a knife so that they have flat faces; wrap tightly, taking care to press the plastic flat against the cut surfaces, removing air pockets. That way, little drying out will take place, and the cheese will keep for weeks to months, depending on type.

Goat cheeses can be allowed to dry out, but many people find their flavor overbearing when so treated. Since an unwrapped cheese, especially a strong one, will lend its odor freely to the cheese stored next to it, wrap goat cheeses in plastic film as well. Leave Camembert and Brie types and all small prewrapped and packaged types in their original wrappings until used. Unused portions of crèmes and many soft cheeses can be wrapped in plastic and returned to the refrigerator.

Blues can also be wrapped in plastic wrap, but some authorities recommend wrapping them in damp cloth and then placing them in a plastic box or under a cheese bell. While plain water is quite adequate, some perfectionists insist on preparing a brine solution for the damp cloth, consisting of a pinch of salt and a spoonful of vinegar to a half-cup of water.

Foil is excellent for wrapping cheese, although it must be tightly closed to retain moisture as well as plastic. Nonetheless, it is preferable for fresh or soft cheeses, which easily lose their shape, and is handier to use when wrapping very small scraps of Blue.

Don't subject any cheese to an endless round of temperature changes. If you've purchased a large wheel of cheese, don't let it sit out to warm every time a portion will be eaten, no matter how impressive it looks. The cheese will only sweat or sag and then toughen up again when returned to the refrigerator. Repeating the process over and over again will rapidly tire and dry out the cheese and reduce its quality. Cut off the portion intended to be consumed at one time and leave the rest of the cheese to hibernate in the refrigerator. Although uneaten portions of fresh cheeses, crèmes, semisoft, and hard cheeses can all be returned to the refrigerator sucessfully, Brie and Camembert types should simply be wrapped and left out for consumption at the next meal, unless the room temperature is very warm. Very dry cheeses such as Parmesan and a few others need not be refrigerated at all if the house is cool.

If abnormal spots of mold develop on the cheese, cut them off to keep them from growing bigger. When the cheese is reduced to scraps, use them up in cooking, canapés, and spreads. Old bits of Blue cheese, if not too old, can be made into long-keeping spreads by mixing with butter or with cream cheese and spirits.

Cheese can even be frozen, but this is never an ideal method of storage. Cheddar, Swiss, and many mild types can be frozen if the cheese is cut into half-pound or smaller chunks (but not small cubes), tightly wrapped, and put into a subzero freezer. While storage life can be extended for months, texture may become mealy and crumbly, which, of course, is perfectly all right for cooking purposes. Thaw frozen cheese slowly in the refrigerator.

6: HOW TO SERVE
AND ENJOY CHEESE

When to Serve Cheese

When to serve cheese may seem an odd question, considering how basic a foodstuff it is. Certainly cheese can be enjoyed at any time and can be a meal in itself. Cheese lovers looking for new ways to enjoy their favorite food should consider adding some of the mild, bland cheeses to their breakfast table, like the Dutch do. The English have long held a lunch of English cheese, hearty bread, and good English ale in high esteem, and those who haven't enjoyed the many delightful combinations of fresh fruit with various cheeses as the ideal snack simply haven't been exercising their gustatory imaginations.

But serving cheese with main meals can be a bit of a problem. Although many people consider cheese the ideal appetizer, it is a mistake to serve it in any quantity before a meal, particularly if there will be a long wait before sitting down to the main course. Cheese is certainly appetizing, but it is also very filling, and the generous host and hostess are liable to find that their guests have had their appetites not only whetted but half-satiated as well. Of course, there are cheeses that could perform as hors d'oeuvres—small amounts of light, spicy chèvres or a bit of Blue cheese are especially good if you are serving one wine with a not overly elaborate meal and wish to serve the wine as an aperitif as well.

At the end of a meal, however, cheese really comes into its own on the menu. Cheese and fruit make a delightful dessert, particularly after a heavy entrée, when a rich sweet dessert would be too much. The English often serve cheese *after* the dessert, but this seems a peculiar practice to all but the English. It seems more logical to serve it beween the main dish and a sweet dessert; nothing will complement the dinner wine better than the cheese, so it makes sense to serve it to accompany the last of the wine served with the main dish. If salad is served after the entrée, serve the cheese after the salad to counteract the acidic sharpness of the dressing. Since the dressings of almost any salad will make wine taste terrible, one has to serve the cheese either at the same time as the salad or shortly thereafter. Androuët recommends the latter procedure.

What cheeses should be served after a meal? Since few people will want to open a different wine to accompany the cheese, the cheeses should be chosen to complement the wine served and to continue and complement the tastes of the entrée. Just as it makes sense to serve heavier, more powerful wines after younger, lighter wines, so too it pleases the palate more to encounter progressively richer and more intense tastes. A mild, buttery-rich triple-crème might be perfect after a trout dinner and Rhine wines, but would seem anticlimactic after roast beef and Burgundy. A slice of Parmesan would not be out of place following a spicy northern Italian meal and full-bodied Piedmontese wines such as Barolo; nothing could be better than a rich fine Blue cheese such as Stilton following game. A ripe Brie marries beautifully with the last of a fine Burgundy, so long as the previous courses haven't been excessively rich or creamy. Small tastes of intriguing, aromatic, spicy, or luxurious soft or semisoft cheeses are called for at the end of a meal, not cheeses that can be meals in themselves, like Cheddar or Swiss types.

If one wants to serve something less than a formal meal to guests, but more elaborate than potluck snacks from the refrigerator, a selection of cheeses on a board, some breads, crackers, and a bottle of wine are ideal. Cheese and wine are also an excellent alternative to the usual canapés and hard liquor served at cocktail parties. Whether you're having four guests or forty, cheese is served the same way.

How to Serve Cheese

There are no hard-and-fast rules about serving cheese, but the most appropriate way is to present them on a cheese board. Unwrap the cheeses, place them on a large tray, and let guests serve themselves the cheeses of their choice. Cheese is a farm product, at least in origin, not a creation of the kitchen, and should be served in a manner that reflects its rustic sources. Most cheese enthusiasts feel a wooden cutting board not only shows off cheeses well, but also allows for ease in cutting and slicing. Another good choice is a marble slab, which shows off cheese beautifully. The last traces of redolent cheese smells can be cleaned off marble easily, something difficult to do with porous wooden boards. Cheeses deserve to sit on something more thoughtful than a dinner plate. There is one school of thought that feels cheeses look naked and forlorn unless placed on napkins, doilies, reed mats, or leaves; I always omit these on grounds that cheeses are much easier to cut when they don't slide around the tray. Decorations, it should be said, do not belong on a cheese board, no matter how artistic. Cheeses are attractive themselves and do not need gimmicks or disguises.

How many cheeses should be served? Androuët stipulates four choices as a minimum, although he admits it is better to serve one perfect cheese than a host of indifferent ones. A small selection allows for preferences among your guests, however, and permits arrangement from mild to strong, fresh to aged, buttery to tangy. It is wise to include at least one well-known and well-liked cheese for guests who are not inclined to experiment with the farther reaches of cheesedom. Emmentaler or Gruyère, a ball of Edam, or a wedge of Cheddar are instantly recognizable and readily welcomed by the unadventurous. Select others from the various flavor families of cheese that offer something different—a goat's or sheep's milk cheese, a Coulommiers, Livarot, Mondseer, Petit-Suisse, Blue Castello, and so forth. Just be sure to offer a variety of tastes; trays of just Blues or just chèvres are for turophiles who can appreciate the often subtle differences among cheeses that fall within the same flavor family.

Take the cheeses out of the refrigerator in advance, so that each can come to room temperature. If you're serving hard, semisoft, and soft cheeses together, you may have to take them out at different times. Cover them with a damp cloth or leave wrapped. Always pretaste the cheeses, since some perfectly sound-looking cheeses can have a bitter flavor or manifest some other taste defect. Leave plenty of space around each cheese; arrange them so that they can be cut easily. A very strong, odiferous cheese should not be placed right next to a mild cheese, lest it lend its aroma to its neighbor. One use of the cheese bell is to isolate such an aggressive cheese from the others.

Cheeses should be served without wrappings. Scrape off any extraneous mold that may have cropped up on the cheeses and trim them up so that they look inviting. Never serve tiny scraps of cheese to guests; they look unappetizing. Don't serve much more of each cheese than you expect will be consumed. It looks impressive to bring out big wheels, but the cheese will suffer by undergoing frequent and unnecessary temperature changes. If you think your guests would like it—and this may be a good idea for a large cheese party—place small cards next to the cheeses to identify them.

Don't preslice cheeses or cut them into numerous wedges before serving, since small cut portions dry out quickly. Do, however, cut into the cheese to encourage guests to do the same. Make the appropriate cut before bringing out the tray so that guests will know how the cheese is to be cut or sliced. Pie-shaped flat cheeses should be cut into wedges; Edams and small Goudas are cut like an apple; blocks and logs are cut into slices; pyramids are cut into wedges from the top. Proper cutting is particularly important with Stilton; people still have the mistaken notion that it should be scooped from the top and then enlivened with port wine. Stilton goes well with port, but the two should not be thrown together to create a sort of pulpy dip, which is a waste of the cheese and the wine. Slice through the top parallel to the surface and about one and a half inches below, and then start cutting small wedges. When that layer is finished, slice through again, and start cutting the next layer into wedges. (This method works well for other Blue cheeses in large cylinders.)

Guests should be given plates, knives, and napkins. Each cheese on the board should, ideally, have its own knife, although two will do for four cheeses if the cheeses are not so soft that they stick to the knife. Supply individual knives for Bries and Blues. Roquefort requires a wire cutter to keep it from crumbling when cut. A small cheese server—something that looks like a miniature pie server—is another useful tool to add to the tray. A cheese slicer—the kind that looks like a pie server with a planelike slit in the middle to slice very thin slivers when drawn across the cheese surface—is good for most hard cheeses and essential for Gjetost.

Don't expect your guests to cope with complicated, difficult-to-cut, or excessively crumbly cheeses. Cut these into portions as requested. Most cheeses require little fussing, but it is helpful to remove the hard inedible rinds from certain cheeses, such as the waxed coatings of Cheddar types. Don't remove the rind of cheeses guests can remove easily themselves, even if it's not edible. It's possible to scoop out the interior of a wedge of Brie with little fuss, for example, and certain cheeses would look rather odd on the cheese board without their characteristic rind—Edam or Reblochon, for instance.

There are a very few cheeses that have edible rinds. Among these are the extremely thin-skinned natural rinds of some washed-rind cheeses such as American Muenster and some bloomy-rind types like Boursault, and certain Blues. There are those cheese fanciers who find the rinds of Brie and even goat cheeses edible and even go so far as to claim they are the "best part of the cheese." I disagree. In fact, I remove the rind from virtually every cheese I eat. Androuët asserts one should never eat the rind of a cheese, and cautions the cheese lover to turn a deaf ear to those who advise otherwise. Cheese enthusiasts who doubt the wisdom of this procedure should try the following experiment. Remove the rind of a cheese that you would normally eat with the rind, and eat the cheese *sans* rind. Note the taste. Now eat the pieces of rind you just cut off. Compare the flavor. Do you honestly think the rind's flavor improves the taste of the cheese? Brie lovers who are always complaining about bitter cheeses should try the simple expedient of just eating the interior.

Those who claim moldy rinds are *good* for you, incidentally, are also completely misguided. According to Kosikowski, penicillin is not derived from the penicillium molds used in cheesemaking, and in fact the molds found in cheese actually inactivate penicillin. As discussed previously, the rind in many cheeses is the source of bacterial activity that transforms the flavor of the interior of the cheese. The proper focus of gustatory attention on cheese is the *result* of this bacterial activity— the interior—not the bacteria themselves. Those who think cutting the rind off cheese is wasteful are like those who insist on draining old wines to the dregs instead of leaving the sediment undisturbed in the bottom of the bottle: in both cases the best part is ruined by mixing it with what should have been discarded.

What to Serve with Cheese

Wine is a delightful companion to cheese, but bread is an essential accompaniment. While small bits of hard cheese can be picked up and eaten with the fingers, soft cheeses would be difficult to eat in that fashion without adopting some rather rustic manners. This is one reason why cheeses are always served with a selection of breads and crackers: they serve as a handy means to convey cheese to the mouth. Bread is also the perfect foil to the tastes of cheeses: its dry texture can accent a cheese's moist creaminess without competing with its flavors. Intense, spicy, and rustic cheeses should be served on strong, flavorful, and rustic breads, while the mildest cheeses call for milder breads such as plain French or Italian, which lightly enhance the flavor of a mild cheese without distorting it. But no matter how mild the cheese, don't serve it on a slice of flavorless factory bread, whose texture and taste are more like that of a foam mattress than nature's grains. No soft cheese can be spread on the spongy, insubstantial slices, and cheeses eaten on such bread taste like they've been wrapped in cotton.

Serve two or three fresh-baked breads, including at least one white and one or two darker breads such as rye and pumpernickel, with your cheese board (but don't put them on the board itself). Just before serving, slice each into thin slices, cutting large slices into halves to make smaller, more manageable pieces. For an informal group, let guests slice their own.

Crackers are less essential than breads, but simple plain water-biscuit types are excellent with crèmes and the thin, crisp Scandinavian rye crackers and flatbreads are superior with hard cheeses. Don't serve salted crackers; most cheeses are salty enough. (If you're serving Gjetost, include some of the sweeter English digestive biscuits; they go surprisingly well together.)

Butter goes well with most types of cheese and especially well with oversalty Blue cheeses. Make sure that it is *sweet* (unsalted) butter, and always serve it in a side dish. Whether to serve additional garnishes or not depends on the cheeses and the occasion. A bowl of walnuts makes an interesting addition to the enjoyment of those two inseparables, Stilton and port. But slathering a fine Gruyère with mustard is not my idea of

how to savor such a cheese, and it is pointless to encourage
such gastronomic barbarisms by offering the mustard pot unless the cheese is processed or about to disappear between
the layers of a sandwich. Pickles, scallions, chives, shallots,
parsley, and so on go very well with many fresh cheeses and
add considerable interest to otherwise dull cream and cottage
cheeses. Other fresh types may well be overwhelmed, however.

Fruit stands out as one of the most successful foods to serve
with cheese, especially for a light meal. Apples with sharp
Cheddars, wild strawberries and Petit-Suisse, fresh figs and
Parmesan, are only a few of the fruit-and-cheese affinities for
the turophile to explore.

Choosing beverages to serve with cheeses is second only in
importance to choosing bread. Only a half-dozen beverages
really complement cheese; of these the most important is wine.
But the best wine to serve with cheese is not always *fine* wine.
Serve fine wines and fine cheeses together, but not if either
is so rare and precious that it is best appreciated in the com-
pany of foods and beverages that will stay in the background
and not influence the taste. To marry a fine wine and a fine
cheese is to create a sublime taste experience, but it is achieved
only by submerging, to some extent, their individual character.
If the opportunity to mate a rare wine with a unique cheese is
irresistible, decide which one is to be the "star" of the meal
or tasting, and taste that one first, all alone, with a clear
palate.

In picking wines to accompany cheeses, don't be daunted by
the lists of wine-and-cheese combinations that are sometimes
given in cheese books (and wine books). For the most part
these are highly arbitrary and reflect biases that have little
basis in actual tastings. The injunction that cheeses ought to
be accompanied by wines from the local region, for example,
sounds reasonable at first—after all, shouldn't the local drink,
which springs from the same soil as the cheese, go especially
well with it? But the fact is that great cheeses and great wines
are rarely made in the same districts. Port and Stilton could
hardly be produced in more different climatic regions, and
yet their affinity is widely acknowledged. In many instances
the local drink is taken with the local cheese simply because
it is the local drink, and the combination is familiar and ac-
cepted as complementary to palates accustomed to it. Game
dishes are thought to call for substantial red wines, but in
Germany the natural wine choice is German white wines, a

choice elsewhere thought suitable only for delicate dishes like trout. In short, try traditional local combinations, but don't feel constrained by them. Merely because Fontina d'Aosta is well matched by Barbera d'Asti is no reason why another combination—an Australian wine, perhaps?—might not be just as interesting. Wine choice may depend on the season, too: one turophile claims a chilled rosé may be perfect with Caerphilly in the summer, while medium-dry sherry is a better choice in the winter. Many cheeses are better accompanied by beer than wine; spicy, flavorful Munich-type beers, ales, and stouts with plenty of tangy hop character stand up well to very strong cheeses with penetrating aromas, and are excellent with Cheddar types. With certain cheeses, fruit wines, cider, and even spirits (providing none of these are overly sweet) may be a better match. Both tea and coffee (so long as they are drunk without sugar) go well with cheese. I find a properly pot-brewed fine Keemun (the classic English breakfast type) one of the best choices, whereas almost any rich, aromatic variety of coffee is superb. Other beverages, though not particularly complementary to cheese, can be consumed with it without misgivings.

In spite of these remarks, cheese-and-beverage listmaking is not pointless. There *are* wine-and-cheese affinities, just as there are wine-and-food affinities. It is merely that such lists can provide only general guidelines, not infallible combinations. The success of such combinations depends to a great extent on the quality and character of the cheese and wine (or other beverage), which, as anyone knows who has tasted much of either, may not be true to type or live up to their reputations. The following list, then, should be taken only as a starting point; try these suggestions first, then work out your own favorite matches at your own table. Above all, keep an open mind and don't assume there is one right wine or even one right beverage for every cheese.

FRESH UNCURED CHEESES While cottage cheese rarely calls for anything more than coffee, the better cream cheeses are very enjoyable with soft, light white wines and lively rosés; try Vouvray, Tavel rosés, California Grenache rosés, Chenin Blanc, and Emerald Riesling. Cheeses in this category are also excellent with light pilsner-type beers (most American beers and light European ones are this type).

BLAND AND MILD CHEESES In general, cheeses in this group are unassertive and mate well with a variety of beverages. The mild cheeses of Scandinavia are particularly good with Scandinavian beers; cheeses such as young Edam and Gouda can be enjoyed with fruity inexpensive red wine or black coffee. Monterey Jack is excellent with California Chardonnay, Bel Paese with Italian Soave or Orvieto, young Provolone with Bardolino or Valpolicella, Muenster with pale ale, and so on.

CRÈMES Rich, luxurious, but on the whole mild, these dessert cheeses are superb with fine German Rhines and Moselles, particularly Spätleses and Ausleses, although many light not-quite-dry white wines and rosés harmonize with them equally well. Rich aromatic coffee is an excellent nonwine choice to accompany crèmes.

BRIE AND CAMEMBERT TYPES The best examples of these cheeses are incomparable when accompanied by fine red wines with generous bouquets; fine Beaujolais—say, Morgon or Moulin-à-vent—are among the better choices, although fine red Burgundies and red Bordeaux and first-rate California Cabernet Sauvignon are not out of place, provided the cheese is also outstanding. A tasty but not sublime Coulommiers would call for a good California Zinfandel or Beaujolais-Villages.

SWISS AND SWISS TYPES Aromatic reds are sometimes recommended as companions to these cheeses, but I would serve them only with the stronger-tasting types such as Appenzeller, and pick light, dry, sprightly white wines to accompany fine Emmentaler or Gruyère. Alsatian Rieslings, dry Graves, Sancerre, and California Rieslings and Sauvignon Blancs would be good choices.

CHEDDAR AND CHEDDAR TYPES While these cheeses can go quite nicely with red wines, I find them more successful with characterful ales and stout. Hard cider and even dry country fruit wines such as elderberry are possible and unusual alternatives, and in winter one can successfully match these with medium-dry sherries. Coffee and tea are good choices here too, and Caerphilly and white Wensleydale are among the first choices of cheeses suitable to accompany but not intrude upon a tasting of first-growth claret or top-flight California Cabernet Sauvignon.

GRANA TYPES Parmesan and related types call for substantial red wines, and the first choice here is northern Italian wines, notably Barbera, Barbaresco, Gattinara, and Barolo, or full-bodied California Barbera. The more intense and concentrated the flavor of the cheese, the more intense and concentrated the accompanying wine should be.

MONASTERY CHEESES The range of this family of cheeses is wide enough to call for red, white, or rosé wines, depending on the age and character of the cheese. Port-Salut and Saint-Paulins in particular seem to compliment any soft fruity wine and even coffee, while Pont-L'Évêque calls for progressively sturdier, more full-bodied wines as it matures. Try it with young Burgundies or California Pinot Noirs. Many Tommes and Reblochon go very well with dry white wines.

GOAT CHEESES Goat cheeses range from very mild to potent and peppery. Consequently they can be enjoyed with very dry, crisp whites—Alsatian Gewürztraminer, Muscadet, Chablis, Meursault. California Pinot Blanc, for example—and when older and more powerful, tackled with tannic, rough country reds—Rhône wines, and California Petite Sirah and Ruby Cabernet. In general, goat cheeses do not call for fine wines; the more rustic the cheese, the more rustic the wine.

SHEEP'S MILK CHEESES Very salty, briny types call for light spicy beers or rough red country wines; match the less salty ones to Spanish Riojas, Portuguese Dãos, Italian Chianti, and inexpensive Zinfandel.

BLUE CHEESES The outstanding cheeses of this group have long been considered fit companions to the finest red wines. Roquefort is frequently paired with fine Burgundies and red Bordeaux, and even Brut Champagne or Cognac. The frequently oversalty specimens that are exported (as well as other French Blues) are best matched with something less exalted, but full-bodied and flavorful: Hermitage, fine California Zinfandel, even medium-dry sherries and tawny ports. Although Stilton is thought to have no better accompaniment than fine port, it is certainly at home with fine, sturdy red wines. The same is true of Gorgonzola, which is fittingly matched with fine northern Italian reds or Chianti Riserva. Danablu calls for something solid and red, but not necessarily a fine wine. The adventurous pair Blues with well-chilled Sauternes or Barsac.

PROCESSED CHEESES One needn't fuss with this category of cheese. The best of them are perfectly at home with red, white, or pink *vin ordinaire* or jug wine, and equally happy with coffee or tea.

SPICED CHEESES The best spiced cheeses—for example, Leyden—are excellent with stout or dark, spicy, and characterful European beers, particularly the Scandinavian and Munich types. Soft, herb-flavored types such as Boursin are delightful with inexpensive sparkling wine. Many flavor variants in this family require experimentation with a variety of beverages.

WHEY CHEESES Again this category varies considerably. Gjetost, to my taste, calls for rich, black coffee.

STRONG CHEESES These may go well with full-bodied red wines with generous aromas (such as California Petite Sirah, Barbera, Zinfandel, and even Ruby Cabernet) as well as with Côtes du Rhône, Saint-Emilion, Cahors, or spicy whites like Gewürztraminer, or spicy beers (especially Munich types) and strong, characterful ales.

In general, Italian cheeses go best with Italian reds, English cheeses with beer and ale, and Scandinavian cheeses with Scandinavian beers, but it is difficult to generalize about American and French cheeses. Usually, the stronger the cheese, the stronger and sturdier the wine or beverage should be. If I had to pick a single wine to accompany a wide range of cheeses, in most instances, it would probably be a *good* Beaujolais or California Gamay.

PART TWO

A DICTIONARY OF THE WORLD'S CHEESES

Note: Cheese entries are listed here by cheese name or type. (Example: Cheddar is discussed under **Cheddar;** Canadian Cheddar will be found under **Cheddar, Canadian.)**

Appenzeller

Switzerland, in the cantons of Appenzell, Saint-Gall, and others; made in mountain chalets.

HOW MADE AND CURED

Type of milk: Unpasteurized whole or skimmed cow's milk. Skimmed-milk version called Appenzeller Rass Cheese.

Method and rind type: Hard, pressed, cooked; natural rind, whole-milk version steeped in cider or white wine and spices before aging.

Time cured: Three to six months.

Fat content: 45 percent; skimmed-milk version, 20 percent.

AROMA

High, pungent aroma.

FLAVOR

Flavor family: Swiss.

Taste: The whole-milk version has a delicate, rounded taste when young; it becomes stronger, more pungent, and zingier with age. It is a more robust and tangy cheese than Gruyère, which it resembles. The skimmed-milk version has a stronger flavor than the whole-milk one.

Texture: Very firm, but moister and creamier than Gruyère.

APPEARANCE

Exterior: A fairly thick, lightly wrinkled brown rind with a pebbly look to it.

Interior: Whole-milk version is pale-golden-yellow with some small eyes distributed throughout the cheese. In the skimmed-milk version the eyes are smaller—about the size of a pinhead.

Size and shape: Wheel-shaped, with convex sides; 14 inches in diameter, 3 inches thick, weight 13 to 18 pounds.

BUYING HINTS

Swiss cheeses are quite reliable; federal inspectors grade the cheeses according to strict standards. Swiss law prohibits the use of artificial additives, artificial coloring, and milk from cows fed on silage. Appenzeller should have very small round holes; it should not have cracks in the rind or a hard, crumbly texture. The shades of its color may vary with the seasons. Best seasons for the cheese are summer, autumn, and winter.

USABLE LIFE

Can age more than six months and still be good, though it will be stronger. From three to eight months old is best. For those who like blander cheeses, the younger the cheese the better. Once cut, will keep about one to two months if stored properly.

STORAGE AFTER PURCHASE

Wrap airtight in plastic wrap; refrigerate.

SERVING AND EATING

A good eating cheese. Serve with whole-wheat bread and butter or French bread and butter, and Golden Delicious apples. Makes a nice end to a meal of veal or chicken.

BEVERAGE MATCH

Fruity white or red Swiss wines are excellent; light beer and German white wines are also good.

COMMENTS

Named for canton where it is made and where it originated. It is believed to be a very ancient cheese, made since the reign of Charlemagne.

SIMILAR CHEESES

Gruyère, Emmentaler.

Asiago

WHERE MADE

Italy, most in area of Vicenza, some near Padua, Verona, Trento, Venice, and in Lombardy; principally made on farms. Imitated in U.S.

HOW MADE AND CURED

Type of milk: Unpasteurized, partly skimmed cow's milk; sometimes whole milk.

Method and rind type: Hard, pressed, semicooked, with a natural, brushed rind.

Time cured: Four to ten months for table cheeses; twelve to twenty months for grating cheese.

Fat content: 30–45 percent.

AROMA

Faint, pleasant.

FLAVOR

Flavor family: Cheddar type/Grana type.

Taste: Taste strengthens and sharpens with age. When young has sharp, tangy flavor reminiscent of Cheddar; savory, rich, salty; sometimes described as smoky, but few contemporary examples show this. When aged, similar to Parmesan, but not as subtle or complex.

Texture: When young, firm, slightly granular texture in mouth, flaky. When aged, very hard, granular.

APPEARANCE

Exterior: Glossy, smooth rind; sometimes covered in gray-black wax.

Interior: Cream-colored, almost whitish to slightly straw-yellow; becomes yellow-brown with age. Paste when young has small holes and cracks; when aged surface gets granular look, as though covered with sand, and looks brittle.

Size and shape: Small wheel shape, 13 to 18 inches in diameter, 3½ to 4½ inches thick, and weighing from 17 to 27 pounds.

BUYING HINTS

Whether you want a young Asiago for table use or an aged one for grating, the rind should not be cracked, there should be no flecks of white mold on the paste, and the color of the paste should be uniform with no off-color spots. A young Asiago should not be crumbly, but firm with a slightly granular texture. An aged one should look more like Parmesan. U.S. versions of Asiago are undistinguished.

USABLE LIFE

Uncut, continues to mature and can be used eventually as a grating cheese. However, proper conditions for aging one yourself are difficult to achieve. If cut, young Asiago will keep in a large piece for several months. Correctly wrapped, a piece of aged Asiago will keep indefinitely.

STORAGE AFTER PURCHASE

Wrap airtight in plastic wrap or in a damp cloth. Rub the flat of the knife across the cut surface to seal pores and prevent moisture escaping from a young cheese. Refrigerate.

SERVING AND EATING

Good eating cheese when young; makes an excellent and interesting substitute for English Cheddar. Good with rustic breads, butter, celery, and in sandwiches. Melts well, especially when aged. Aged used especially for grating in place of Parmesan. Asiago is excellent with dates.

BEVERAGE MATCH

Best with full-bodied red wines such as California Barbera and Italian Barolo and Barbaresco.

COMMENTS

Named for Asiago plateau where the cheese was first made about 1870. It was originally made from sheep's milk and called Pecorino di Asiago.

SIMILAR CHEESES

English and Canadian Cheddar closest to young; Pecorino Romano and Parmesan closest to aged.

Bagnes, see *Raclette.*

Banon (also called Banon de Provence or Le Banon)

WHERE MADE

Throughout the area of Provence, France; in dairies (cow's milk), on farms (sheep's and goat's milk).

HOW MADE AND CURED

Type of milk: Pasteurized goat's, sheep's, or cow's milk; the latter two sometimes mixed with goat's milk.

Method and rind type: Soft, natural rind; cured in leaves; sometimes dipped in marc and stacked in earthenware jars.

Time cured: Two weeks to two months.

Fat content: 45 percent.

AROMA

Fresh and lactic to very strong, depending on age and type.

FLAVOR

Flavor family: Goat, sheep, or mild.

Taste: Mild and milky to sweet-nutty and deliciously savory, depending on age and type.

Texture: Light, creamy, yielding.

APPEARANCE

Exterior: Under leaves, slightly sticky rind.

Interior: White, creamy, slightly dry texture.

Size and shape: Small disk about 4 ounces in weight, 3 inches across, 1 inch high, wrapped in chestnut leaves and tied with raffia. Also shipped in 1½ pounds bulk form.

BUYING HINTS

Purchase fresh; wrapping should look new and attractive,

not overly dry or mold-spotted. Should be firm but yielding to the touch. If cannot be purchased in bulk and therefore sampled, try one first to make sure the entire lot is not dried out before buying several.

USABLE LIFE

Will keep for several weeks, but grows stronger with age; eat when fresh and moist.

STORAGE AFTER PURCHASE

Refrigerate; need not be wrapped further unless cut; if cut, wrap tightly in plastic wrap or foil.

SERVING AND EATING

End of simple meals, luncheons, particularly in summer; exquisite when served with raspberries.

BEVERAGE MATCH

Fruity, inexpensive red and white wines.

COMMENTS

There is a spiced Banon covered with sprigs of savory (*sariette*) variously called Banon au Pèbre d'Aï or Poivre-d'Âne, and even a pepper-covered version. These lack the leaf wrappings and are of course spicier.

SIMILAR CHEESES

All fresh and young French chèvres.

Beaufort

WHERE MADE

Jura and Savoy Mountains, France; in mountain chalets and dairies.

HOW MADE AND CURED

Type of milk: Unpasteurized cow's milk.

Method and rind type: Hard, cooked, and pressed with thick natural brushed rind.

Time cured: Three to six months.

Fat content: 50 percent.

AROMA

Mild, faintly gamy scent.

FLAVOR

Flavor family: Swiss type.

Taste: Rather like a rich, strong Gruyère.

Texture: Buttery, somewhat elastic.

APPEARANCE

Exterior: Rough, even, thick rind.

Interior: Very few small eyes, if any, in very smooth yellow-ivory interior of soft waxy appearance.

Size and shape: Large wheels 2 feet by 5 inches thick with straight sides, weighing 90 to 130 pounds.

BUYING HINTS

Watch out for cracked rind, numerous holes, dark subcrust under rind—a sign of overage—a gritty texture, and oversaltiness. The best and most sumptuous Beaufort is labeled "Beaufort haute-montagne" and is aged at least six months.

USABLE LIFE

Keeps for months in large well-wrapped pieces when refrigerated.

STORAGE AFTER PURCHASE

Wrap in plastic wrap and refrigerate.

SERVING AND EATING

For lunch or snacks with green grapes or peaches.

BEVERAGE MATCH

Fruity white wines; white Graves, Alsatian wines, Sancerre, California Pinot Blanc.

COMMENTS

A very old cheese that may have been known in Roman times.

SIMILAR CHEESES

French and Swiss Gruyères.

Beaumont

WHERE MADE

In the Departments of Savoie and Haut-Savoie in France; produced in factories.

HOW MADE AND CURED

Type of milk: Pasteurized cow's milk.

Method and rind type: Semisoft, pressed, uncooked.

Time cured: Five to six weeks.

Fat content: 50 percent.

AROMA

Faint milky, vegetative scent.

FLAVOR

Flavor family: Monastery.

Taste: Earthy, rustic; mild, but resembles other monastery and Trappist types. An attractive cheese.

Texture: Creamy, with a consistency like Reblochon.

APPEARANCE

Exterior: Light-beige crust over light-yellow rind.

Interior: Creamy ivory color, darkens with age; supple feel to rind, soft interior.

Size and shape: 3-pound 6-ounce disks, about 8 inches in diameter and about 2 inches thick.

BUYING HINTS

Should not be dried out, bitter in taste, or display a barnyardy scent.

USABLE LIFE

Will keep for weeks if well-wrapped in refrigerator; continues to develop and ripen slowly. Small cuts should be eaten within a few days.

STORAGE AFTER PURCHASE

Refrigerate tightly wrapped in plastic wrap.

SERVING AND EATING

End of meals, with French/Italian bread and blackberries.

BEVERAGE MATCH

Calls for sturdy red wines: Côtes du Rhône, California Zinfandel.

COMMENTS

First made in 1881 in Beaumont, for which it is named; contemporary Beaumont is a successful factory-produced version of a local traditional Alpine cheese.

SIMILAR CHEESES

Reblochon, Oka, Tomme de Savoie.

Beau Pasteur

Brand name of a processed cheese produced in France; comes both plain and flavored (or spiced). See *Fromage Fondu.*

Beer Cheese, see *Weisslackerkäse.*

Belalp, see *Raclette.*

Bellétoile

Brand name of French triple-crème. See *Triple-crème.*

Bel Paese

WHERE MADE

Italy, near Melzo in Lombardy; in factories; imitations also made in the United States, Canada, and other European countries, in factories.

HOW MADE AND CURED

Type of milk: Pasteurized whole cow's milk.

Method and rind type: Soft, ripened by bacteria, pressed, uncooked, with washed rind.

Time cured: Five to nine weeks.

Fat content: 45–50 percent.

AROMA

Mild, pleasant, lactic.

FLAVOR

Flavor family: Bland and mild cheeses.

Taste: Sweet, mild, creamy, delicate, round.

Texture: Soft, smooth, moist, yielding.

APPEARANCE

Exterior: Surface rind slightly gray and thin; sometimes paraffined; wrapped in foil with name on it.

Interior: Creamy ivory to cream-colored; smooth, close, creamy texture.

Size and shape: Small wheel shape with slightly convex sides; diameter of 6 to 8 inches, thickness of 2 inches, weight of 4½ pounds.

BUYING HINTS

A very reliable cheese. Quality is almost always uniform and dependable. The rind should not swell or bulge or be discolored, indicating the cheese has been overheated. It should not taste sharp or bitter, especially in the aftertaste. The copies made in the United States are not as good as the original. Look for the cheese covering with a beige and green map of Italy on it; an American copy has a map of North and South America on it in the same beige and green colors. Bel Paese is a trade name of this type of cheese; American copies, such as Bel Paesino, often have a slightly bitter aftertaste.

USABLE LIFE

If cut, keeps well for two weeks at the most.

STORAGE AFTER PURCHASE

Wrap airtight in plastic wrap. Refrigerate.

SERVING AND EATING

An extremely versatile cheese; good for snacks, it also melts well. It is especially good as a dessert cheese after a meal of veal, chicken, or fish. Try it with persimmons.

BEVERAGE MATCH

Light, soft white wines such as Italian Soave and Orvieto or California Chenin Blanc. A full-bodied white such as Chardonnay is good, too, so long as it isn't steely.

COMMENTS

Invented by Galbani, head of a huge cheese business, in 1920, although this type of cheese had been made in area around Melzo for about twenty years at that time. Name is factory trademark. Bel Paese, used in Dante and Petrarch to refer to Italy, means "beautiful country." It is a very popular cheese in Japan.

SIMILAR CHEESES

Taleggio, Saint-Paulin, American copies such as Bel Paesino.

Belsano

This cheese is a buttery version of Raclette; see *Raclette*.

Bierkäse, see *Weisslackerkäse*.

Bleu

Bleu, or Fromage Bleu, refers to French cheeses with internal molds; they are also called Fromage Persillé after their marbled or mottled appearance. French Bleus are members of the Blue-cheese family. Most French Blue cheeses are simply called Blue cheese from a specific place, as in Bleu d'Auvergne. Most are made from cow's milk, although the most famous Blue cheese of France, Roquefort, is made from sheep's milk.

Bleu d'Auvergne

WHERE MADE

In the province of Auvergne, France; produced principally in dairies and a few farms.

HOW MADE AND CURED

Type of milk: Cow's milk, usually pasteurized.
Method and rind type: Soft, internal mold, scraped rind.
Time cured: Varies; two to three months.

Fat content: 45 percent.

AROMA

Heavy, pungent; moldy.

FLAVOR

Flavor family: Blue.

Taste: Sharp, intense, tangy, savory, rustic. Excellent; one of the best French Bleus.

Texture: Creamy and rich.

APPEARANCE

Exterior: Yellow-brownish checkered thin skin, usually foil-wrapped.

Interior: Veins well-distributed throughout whitish cheese.

Size and shape: Flat cylinder 8 inches across, 4 inches high, weighing about 5 pounds.

BUYING HINTS

Beware of overly strong smell and excessively sharp flavor; dried out, crumbly interior, gummy rind.

USABLE LIFE

Keeps for weeks if tightly wrapped in refrigerator.

STORAGE AFTER PURCHASE

Wrap tightly in plastic or damp cloth and refrigerate.

SERVING AND EATING

After meals on thin, plain or flavored crackers, with or without sweet butter; or use in salads. Excellent with pears.

BEVERAGE MATCH

Hearty red wines: Cahors, California Petite Sirah, and Châteauneuf-du-Pape.

COMMENTS

Originated in mid-nineteenth century as an attempt to produce a Roquefort-like cheese from cow's milk. Bleu de Laqueuille is Bleu d'Auvergne made in the Laqueuille district. It is said to be somewhat milder than Bleu d'Auvergne in general.

SIMILAR CHEESES

Other French cow's milk Bleus: Bleu de Bresse, Pipo Crem', Bleu des Causses, Bleu du Haut Jura.

Bleu de Bresse

WHERE MADE

Eastern France; produced in factories.

HOW MADE AND CURED

Type of milk: Pasteurized cow's milk.

Method and rind type: Soft, internal mold; thin, natural rind.
Time cured: Varies with size of cheese; two to three months.
Fat content: 50 percent.

AROMA
Light to heavy mold scent.

FLAVOR
Flavor family: Blue.
Taste: Savory, rich, unctuous, and milk-sweet; excellent if not too old and sharp.
Texture: Creamy, moist, and soft.

APPEARANCE
Exterior: Thin, whitish, pebbly mold tinged with pink and brown; foil-wrapped, boxed if small.
Interior: Very soft whitish interior with blue streaks.
Size and shape: Cylindrical-shaped in various sizes, from 2½ inches across and 1½ inches thick, weighing about 4½ ounces to 4 pounds.

BUYING HINTS
A small boxed one in good condition is not easy to find; most are too old. Watch out for ammoniated smell, a sign of excessive age, as is heavy mold growth. If possible, buy pieces cut from bulk sizes in order to sample first. Of the many Blue varieties called Bleu de Bresse, Androuët claims the best is Le Bresse Bleu from the Servas cooperative in Ain.

USABLE LIFE
A small boxed one should be consumed in a few days; in any event, best consumed young, although will keep for a week or two tightly wrapped in the refrigerator.

STORAGE AFTER PURCHASE
Store in original package if small; otherwise use plastic wrap or foil, and wrap cheese airtight. Refrigerate until day of consumption.

SERVING AND EATING
End of meals; elegant snacks. May call for sweet butter if overtangy; particularly nice on plain crackers.

BEVERAGE MATCH
Sturdy, rich red wines: Corbières, California Pinot Noir, Saint-Emilion, Pomerol; even Amontillado (medium-dry) sherry.

SIMILAR CHEESE
Pipo Crem.

Bleu des Causses

WHERE MADE

South central France, in the Departments of Aveyron, Gard, and Hérault; in commercial dairies.

HOW MADE AND CURED

Type of milk: Cow's milk.

Method and rind type: Soft, internal mold; thin, natural rind.

Time cured: Varies; about two to three months.

Fat content: 45 percent.

AROMA

Pronounced moldy smell.

FLAVOR

Flavor family: Blue.

Taste: Full, savory flavor; similar to Bleu d'Auvergne. A fine Blue cheese.

Texture: Creamy, rich.

APPEARANCE

Exterior: Thin, ivory mottled rind; foil-wrapped.

Interior: Blue-green streaks in ivory-white interior.

Size and shape: Flat cylinders 8 inches across by 4 inches high; weight, about 5½ pounds.

BUYING HINTS

Sample for sharpness and excessive smell before purchase; watch out for dry, crumbly character.

USABLE LIFE

Weeks, if well-wrapped and kept in refrigerator.

STORAGE AFTER PURCHASE

Wrap in plastic wrap, or airtight in foil, or else in a damp cloth, and refrigerate.

SERVING AND EATING

Use at end of meals with French/Italian bread or plain crackers; with or without sweet butter. Also salads.

BEVERAGE MATCH

Strong, firm, tannic red wines: Cahors, Hermitage, sturdy Italian reds, and California Barbera, Charbono, Ruby Cabernet.

COMMENTS

Inspired by the example of Roquefort, this cheese is also matured in caves.

SIMILAR CHEESE

Bleu d'Auvergne.

Bleu du Haut Jura
(also called Gex or Septmoncel)

WHERE MADE

Franche-Comté, France, in the Departments of Ain and Jura; produced by dairies and farms.

HOW MADE AND CURED

Type of milk: Cow's milk.

Method and rind type: Soft, internal mold, slightly pressed, thin, natural rind.

Time cured: Two to three months.

Fat content: 45 percent.

AROMA

Faint; trace moldy.

FLAVOR

Flavor family: Blue.

Taste: Tangy, savory, a trace bitter; but very high quality.

Texture: Close, fine texture.

APPEARANCE

Exterior: Dry, pebbly, gray to mottled, almost orange rind.

Interior: White cheese streaked with almost royal-blue veins; a handsome cheese.

Size and shape: Thick fat disk about 1 foot across and 3½ inches thick; weight, about 13 pounds.

BUYING HINTS

Watch out for dry crumbling interior, excessive veining, or excessive bite to taste.

USABLE LIFE

Keeps well if tightly wrapped in refrigerator.

STORAGE AFTER PURCHASE

Wrap tight in plastic wrap or damp cloth and refrigerate.

SERVING AND EATING

End of meals, with rustic breads, crackers; with or without sweet butter as an accompaniment.

BEVERAGE MATCH

Red wines; Chinon, Bourgueil, Beaujolais, California Gamay.

COMMENTS

Produced at an altitude of over 2,500 feet in the Jura Mountains, Bleu du Haut Jura is highly prized among the French Bleus.

SIMILAR CHEESE

Pipo Crem'.

Bleu de Laqueuille, see *Bleu d'Auvergne.*

Blue Castello (also called Blå Castello)

WHERE MADE
   Denmark, in factories.
HOW MADE AND CURED
   Type of milk: Pasteurized whole cow's milk with cream added.
   Method and rind type: Soft-ripening; inoculated with both blue- and white-mold cultures; bloomy rind; almost a triple-crème.
   Time cured: Ten days to three weeks.
   Fat content: 70 percent.
AROMA
   Distinctive smell of blue mold mixed with fresh creamy scent.
FLAVOR
   Flavor family: Combined blue-veined cheeses and crèmes.
   Taste: Tastes like a cross between a luscious, unctuous triple-crème and a tangy Blue. Delectable contrast between sweet, rich, piquant creaminess and rich mold taste.
   Texture: Thick creamy texture; as warms will become almost consistency of custard.
APPEARANCE
   Exterior: Reddish-brown rind covered with mold—typical of mature cheese. Comes wrapped and packaged in blue and white box.
   Interior: Snow-white to cream-colored with few large blue veins. The veins do not run right through cheese. Creamy-looking.
   Size and shape: Packed in half-decagon box, weight 4¾ oz.
BUYING HINTS
   Difficult to choose a perfect specimen as it is sold in packages. This cheese is very perishable and often is sold too old; thus, it is important to buy this cheese at a store that has a good turnover. The wrapping of the cheese inside the box should be clean and fresh, not brown, sticky, or unpleasant-looking. The cheese should not smell ammoniated or have any kind of strong smell, other than that of slight blue mold. Before cutting it, make sure that the rind has a faint reddish-brown tinge, and is covered with mold. Older versions lack

creaminess, have stronger, less creamy rich flavor, and are generally less appealing.

USABLE LIFE

Although only cured by manufacturer for ten days to three weeks, Blue Castello is at its best around five weeks. Usually it is about that old when it appears in the cheese stores. Keeps only for a few days at its peak.

STORAGE AFTER PURCHASE

Leave in wrapping and box and refrigerate. Serve as soon as possible.

SERVING AND EATING

Leave out for several hours (up to seven or eight) before serving. Rind can be eaten. Serve at end of dinner with un-salted crackers or to finish off French bread.

BEVERAGE MATCH

Good with excellent red wines.

SIMILAR CHEESES

Triple-crèmes and creamy Blues.

Blue Cheese, Norwegian

WHERE MADE

Norway, mostly in area around Trondheim; in factories.

HOW MADE AND CURED

Type of milk: Pasteurized whole cow's milk.

Method and rind type: Semisoft, internal-blue-mold rip-ened.

Time cured: About two to three months.

Fat content: About 45 percent.

AROMA

Slight moldy scent.

FLAVOR

Flavor family: Blue.

Taste: Distinctive, lean, piquant. A good Roquefort copy, with more character than Danablu. Complex in taste.

Texture: More crumbly than creamy; not as creamy as Danablu.

APPEARANCE

Exterior: Thin, pale-brown rind; packed in foil.

Interior: Very white with greenish-blue veins throughout. Veining is not so dense as in Danablu. Has a slightly dry, less creamy appearance.

Size and shape: Large cylinder, also comes in precut indi-vidually wrapped portions.

BUYING HINTS

A reliable cheese with uniform quality. The foil covering should look clean; the cheese should look moist, not dry and cakey, but will look less creamy and moist than Danablu. The veins should look clearly defined; their color should contrast with the cheese. The color of the cheese should not be grayish. Beware of excessive saltiness and harshness of flavor.

USABLE LIFE

Carefully stored, will keep up to three weeks. The cheese develops even after being cut and refrigerated, and sharpens with age. If you don't like sharp Blues, eat within a few days.

STORAGE AFTER PURCHASE

Wrap in aluminum foil or damp cloth and put in plastic box or cover with plastic cheese dome. Refrigerate.

SERVING AND EATING

Use a very thin sharp knife or fine wire cheese cutter when cutting it, drawing it through the cheese slowly to prevent crumbling. Serve with butter and French or Italian bread at the end of a meal. It is good with fruit, especially juicy Comice pears.

BEVERAGE MATCH

Excellent full-bodied red wines.

COMMENTS

One of the best values in blue-veined cheeses—excellent and reasonably priced.

SIMILAR CHEESES

French Bleus, Danablu.

Blue Vinny (also called Blue Vinney, Dorset Blue Vinny, Blue Vinid, Blue Dorset, and Double Dorset)

WHERE MADE

Dorsetshire, England, originally near the town of Sherborne.

HOW MADE AND CURED

Type of milk: Pasteurized cow's milk, almost completely skimmed.

Method and rind type: Hard, internal-mold ripened, with thick rind. At one time aged six months in cider.

Time cured: Four to six months.

Fat content: May range from 8.8 to 27.6 percent.

AROMA

Fairly strong mold smell.

FLAVOR
Flavor family: Blue type.
Taste: Strong, rich, with lingering taste. Sharp and frequently acid; sharper than other Blues. More salty than Stilton.
Texture: Open texture, crumbly, dry, hardens with age.

APPEARANCE
Exterior: Thick, hard rind.
Interior: Very moldy; chalky-white with blue veins. One thick blue vein runs through horizontally.
Size and shape: Circular and flat; 6 inches high by 8 inches in diameter; weight, 10–12 pounds.

BUYING HINTS
Rarely seen. Examples in this country liable to be not genuine. Interior should not look dried out. Mold veins should look clearly defined. Rind should not swell or bulge. Old specimens may be as hard as a rock.

USABLE LIFE
Short-lived. Must be eaten before it hardens, immediately after curing time.

STORAGE AFTER PURCHASE
Wrap in damp cloth and put in plastic box. Refrigerate.

SERVING AND EATING
Cut into wedges. Layer cut by cutting wedges 1–1½ inches in height all around top first; cover, then cut next 1–1½ -inch layer, and so on. Serve at end of meals or mix with butter and brandy and serve as spread, with plain crackers.

BEVERAGE MATCH
Full-bodied red wines such as Bordeaux and Burgundies; vintage port.

COMMENTS
First made at least two hundred years ago. The name "Vinny" comes from the old West country words *vinew* (pronounced vinny), meaning mold, and *vinewed* (pronounced vinid), meaning moldy. The cheese developed as a skim-milk cheese because Dorset was (and is) famed for butter; cream was always skimmed off to make butter, only skimmed milk was therefore available to make cheese. Only if it turned blue (which it didn't and doesn't always) was it good to eat.

When regulations required that cheese manufacture no longer take place where animals were housed, cheeses ceased to turn blue. It turned out that previously cheesemakers had been dipping harnesses in the milk each night, and a bacteria on them caused the development of the mold.

For many years an extinct cheese, it is now being revived.
Written about by many gastronomes, Blue Vinny was said to
be the favorite cheese of Dorsetshire novelist Thomas Hardy.
Its rarity more than its taste has caused the interest. One story
has it that Blue Vinny is so hard that a train once used the
cheeses for wheels.

SIMILAR CHEESE

Stilton.

Bonbel

Brand name of a French Saint-Paulin; see *Saint-Paulin*.

Bondon, see *Neufchâtel*.

Boulette d'Avesnes, see *Maroilles*.

Boursault

A brand of French triple-crème. See *Triple-crème*.

Boursin

A brand of French triple-crème flavored with herbs and
garlic or pepper-covered. See *Triple-crème*.

Bresse Bleu, see *Bleu de Bresse*.

Brick Cheese

WHERE MADE

Mostly in the state of Wisconsin, United States; factory-
produced.

HOW MADE AND CURED

Type of milk: Cow's milk, pasteurized.
Method and rind type: Semisoft, pressed, washed-rind type.
Time cured: Two months.
Fat content: 50 percent.

AROMA

Very faint to quite pungent.

FLAVOR

Flavor family: Mild to strong, depending on age and example.

Taste: Lightly tangy and mild to sweet and pungent; a very tasty cheese that gains in strength with age.

Texture: Soft and yielding.

APPEARANCE

Exterior: Reddish-brown rind, often waxed.

Interior: Cream-colored, firm elastic body, open texture with numerous small irregular holes.

Size and shape: Brick-shaped loaves 10 inches by 5 inches by 3 inches thick, weighing about 5 pounds as well as larger and smaller loaves and prepackaged portions.

BUYING HINTS

Purchase from bulk sizes in order to sample flavor first; both mild and strong forms are attractive if characterful. Watch out for bitterness.

USABLE LIFE

Will last for a week or more if well-stored, but gains strength with age.

STORAGE AFTER PURCHASE

Wrap airtight in plastic wrap and refrigerate.

SERVING AND EATING

A fine Brick cheese is excellent for lunch with dark breads and adds interest to a cheese board. Goes well with peaches.

BEVERAGE MATCH

This cheese calls for beer: light beers when mild; strong spicy beers and ales and even dark beers when strong.

COMMENTS

This is one cheese that is indisputably American, as it was invented in the United States. Its name comes not only from its shape but from the fact that at one time bricks were used to press the cheese.

SIMILAR CHEESES

Mild: Muenster; strong: Handkäse.

Brie

WHERE MADE

Île-de-France and other districts in France; Brie types produced elsewhere in Europe and the United States. Almost always factory-produced; farm Brie now rare even in France.

HOW MADE AND CURED

Type of milk: Cow's milk, usually pasteurized.

Method and rind type: Soft, bloomy rind; surface-ripened.

Time cured: About three weeks.

Fat content: 45 to 50 percent (some new "double-crème" versions have 60 percent).

AROMA

Full, distinct, complex, attractive bouquet sometimes faintly suggestive of mushrooms. The rind may have a faint, clean moldy smell.

FLAVOR

Flavor family: Brie-Camembert type.

Taste: At its appetizing best, Brie is exquisitely savory, tangy, and lingering; a touch earthy, fruity, nutty, mushroomy perhaps, but always harmonious. Many Brie types lack delicacy and fall considerably short of sublime, but are still enjoyable. The best Bries are produced in the Île-de-France area, and are known as Brie de Meaux. (The rare farm-produced Bries are known as Brie de Meaux Fermier.)

Texture: Spreadable, satiny rich paste.

APPEARANCE

Exterior: Thin, downy-white rind, tinged with pink-brown pigmentation. Brie types produced outside France often show less pigmentation.

Interior: Heavy, thick, ivory-yellow glossy, satiny paste that when ripe bulges and finally oozes out from under rind of cut wedge.

Size and shape: Brie is produced in a large flat, pancakelike disk, either 15 inches across by 1 inch thick and weighing about 4½ pounds, or 10 inches across by 1 inch thick and weighing about 2¼ pounds. It also comes in smaller disks and in portions. Brie de Melun, a creamy, heavy tasting, slightly more salty, and less common variant, is a little thicker in shape: 10 inches across by 1¼ inches thick and weighing about 3½ pounds. Other less common local variants of size and manufacture include Chervu and Ville-Saint-Jacques (or Brie de Montereau).

BUYING HINTS

Traditionally, the best season for Brie is the fall, but factory production has made individual selection more important than season, particularly for imports. Buy fresh-cut portions from whole Bries if at all possible. Inspect the whole cheese and if possible sample it; even the best Bries are notoriously uneven in quality. Beware of a stink of ammonia given off by the rind, a grayish rind color, an unyielding feel (it should be supple from rind to center), and an excessive saltiness or bitter aftertaste. When cut, Brie should not show a hard white layer in the interior, but rather a uniform soft ripeness throughout. The cheese should not, on the other hand, be completely runny. (For more detail, see Buying Brie and Camembert Types in section 5 of the Primer.) Traditionally, the best Bries come from the Île-de-France area (do not confuse with the brand name) and are known as Brie de Meaux, but French-produced Bries from outside this area are often quite good. Bries produced elsewhere in Europe, as well as U.S. Brie types, can be good.

USABLE LIFE

Brie has a short peak period of a day, at most, when it is properly ripe (mishandled or poorly manufactured Bries never ripen properly at all), and should be consumed during that time. Rerefrigeration of unused portions may cause toughening of the flesh, but there is little choice if it cannot be consumed the same day, unless you have a rather cool pantry.

STORAGE AFTER PURCHASE

Purchase Brie at its peak of ripeness and consume shortly thereafter, or else purchase—from a trustworthy merchant—a not-quite-ripe Brie and, following his advice, either refrigerate at not overly cold temperatures or let stand in a cool room for a few days to let ripen.

SERVING AND EATING

While fine Brie has few competitors among cheeses as the connoisseur's choice with which to end a meal, it can be used— sparingly, for it is rich and filling—as an appetizer.

BEVERAGE MATCH

The best call for fine wines—the best Beaujolais (Morgon or Moulin-à-Vent, for example), fine Burgundies (Corton or Chambertin, for example), fine Pomerol or Saint-Emilion, and fine California Cabernet Sauvignon. A fine ripe Brie can overwhelm the wine, so pick one you would be willing to see take a back seat to the cheese. Less sublime Bries call for fruity red wines.

COMMENTS

No cheese has received the praise that Brie has. Known and held in high esteem since the eighth century, the most famous anecdote attached to this cheese dates from 1815, at the Congress of Vienna. As relaxation from the daily business of redrawing the map of Europe after the Battle of Waterloo, the assembled diplomats of the thirty nations represented held dinners, including one where the merits of various cheeses were discussed. One of Talleyrand's minor diplomatic achievements was to offer a Brie, which won out, it is said, over sixty other cheeses presented, and was unanimously hailed as "the King of Cheeses."

SIMILAR CHEESES

Coulommiers, Camembert.

Brie de Coulommiers, see *Coulommiers*.

Brillat-Savarin

Brand name for a French triple-crème. See *Triple-crème*.

Brinza (also called Brindza)

WHERE MADE

Hungary, Czechoslovakia, Romania, and other Balkan countries; also copied in the United States. Farm- and factory-produced.

HOW MADE AND CURED

Type of milk: Sheep's milk, sometimes goat's milk.

Method and rind type: Semisoft, unpressed, rindless cheese; macerated in brine.

Time cured: About one month.

Fat content: 45 percent.

AROMA

Strong sheep's milk smell similar to Kashkaval.

FLAVOR

Flavor family: Sheep.

Taste: Rather salty; almost like oversalty ham. Moist when young. A sharp, biting, oily, appealing rustic cheese. A flavor cousin to Feta.

Texture: Creamy, softly granular to the palate.

APPEARANCE

Exterior: No rind; large cauliflowerlike chunks kept in brine.

Interior: Off-white, moist, crumbly when older.

Size and shape: Enormous variety, up to 60 pounds in weight.

BUYING HINTS

Always sample for excessive saltiness and lack of moisture.

USABLE LIFE

Will keep in brine for months, but best when young and moist.

STORAGE AFTER PURCHASE

Keep packed in original brine, or use salt water and keep it in a plastic container. A damp cloth covering or an airtight plastic bag will suffice for a few days. Refrigerate.

SERVING AND EATING

An interesting luncheon cheese with dark breads, onions, and pickles, and dark cherries.

BEVERAGE MATCH

Spicy Munich-style beers seem to go best with Brinza.

COMMENTS

In Hungary this cheese is called Liptauer, but this name is associated here with the cheese when it has been highly spiced with peppers, capers, chives, anchovies, paprika, garlic, and so on.

SIMILAR CHEESE

Feta.

Bucheron

A large log-shaped goat cheese. See *Chèvres*.

Butter Cheese (also known as Damenkäse)

An extremely mild, buttery cheese almost without scent, made in Germany and Austria. Semisoft, with a light-brown rind and an interior the color of butter, it is usually shaped into small loaves or sausage shapes.

Cabichou, see *Chabichou*.

Caciocavallo

WHERE MADE

Italy, mainly in the south, some made in north and central areas; made in factories.

HOW MADE AND CURED

Type of milk: Unpasteurized whole cow's milk.

Method and rind type: Pasta fileta, or drawn-curd cheese;

hard, uncooked, pressed or molded by hand, sometimes smoked; thin natural rind, sometimes oiled.

Time cured: Three to four months for table use; six to twelve months for grating cheese.

Fat content: 44 percent.

AROMA

Mildly smoky, pleasant, tangy scent.

FLAVOR

Flavor family: Cheddar type/Grana type.

Taste: Increases in sharpness and tang as ages. When young, mild but tangy, slightly spicy and peppery, salty, mildly smoky; great depth of flavor, attractive, As ages, begins to resemble sheep's milk cheeses, becomes tangier and spicier.

Texture: When young, soft, crumbly texture in mouth, pliable, although dense and compact. When older, granular, hard.

APPEARANCE

Exterior: Smooth golden to brownish-ivory glossy, waxy rind, with origin and cheese name stamped in red.

Interior: Ivory color turning darker near rind and becoming darker with age. Dense and hard-looking when aged.

Size and shape: Traditionally shaped like a gourd, with a pointed bottom and a head and neck at the other end. Usually about 6 to 9 pounds in weight.

BUYING HINTS

A fairly reliable cheese. But it shouldn't have surface cracks in the rind or holes in the paste and the aftertaste shouldn't be bitter or sharp.

USABLE LIFE

Keeps well. If uncut, keeps indefinitely. If cut and young, will keep about two to three months in large piece. Hard, aged, grating cheese keeps indefinitely.

STORAGE AFTER PURCHASE

Wrap airtight in plastic wrap or damp cloth. Refrigerate.

SERVING AND EATING

When young, serve with fruit—especially tiny strawberries —at end of meals or as a snack with butter and Italian bread. When aged, use grated as condiment or in cooking.

BEVERAGE MATCH

Fruity red or white wines are excellent: Chianti, Valpolicella, Bardolino, Orvieto, and California Gamay and Pinot Blanc.

COMMENTS

Name means "horse cheese." Two possible explanations for origin of name: one, the cheese might originally have been made from mare's milk; two, the name might refer to the usual method of drying these cheeses—two cheeses are tied together with braided straw and hung over a pole as though hanging astride a horse. Thus the name might come from *cacio a cavallo,* or "cheese on a horse."

The cheese has probably been known since the Middle Ages. It is suited for making in warm climates. Although the gourd shape is the usual one, the cheeses are sometimes braided, made into horses' heads, and so on. Caciocavallo from Sicily is sometimes pressed into oblong blocks.

SIMILAR CHEESES

Provolone. A similarly produced cheese, but made from sheep's milk, is produced in central Europe; see *Kashkaval.*

Caciotta (also called Formagella in north of Italy)

This name applies to many kinds of cheeses made in Italy on small farms and given local names. Depending on the location, they may be made from cow's milk, goat's milk, or sheep's milk; they may be cured from ten days to a month, are usually small and similar to Bel Paese, and are rarely exported. The numerous varieties include Bagozzo, Caciotta Toscana, Caciotta di Urbino, Chiavari, Fresa, and the most famous, Cacio Fiore Aquilano and Cacia Fiore.

Caerphilly

WHERE MADE

Originated in Caerphilly, Glamorganshire, Wales; now made mainly in the West country of England—Somersetshire, Wiltshire, Devonshire, and Dorsetshire. Most is made in factories.

HOW MADE AND CURED

Type of milk: Primarily whole, pasteurized cow's milk; some from part skim milk.

Method and rind type: Hard, uncooked, pressed, steeped in brine; thin natural rind with little or no mold, frequently coated with wax, which is usually light straw-yellow.

Time cured: Ten days to three weeks.

Fat content: About 40 percent.

AROMA

Fresh and pleasant.

FLAVOR

Flavor family: Mild Cheddar type.

Taste: Distinct buttermilk tang, slightly salty and acid; clean and fresh-tasting, very creamy-moist; mild and delicate.

Texture: Firm, but somewhat crumbly when cut; flaky and moist.

APPEARANCE

Exterior: Thin yellowish-white rind or wax; also sold in rindless blocks.

Interior: Snow-white, moist and creamy-looking, semihard and flaky.

Size and shape: Traditionally and still flat, circular; 9 inches in diameter, 2½ to 3½ inches thick; weight, 8 pounds, also in blocks of 10 pounds.

BUYING HINTS

The interior should not look dried-out or yellowish—signs of excessive age. It should be uniform in color, and the rind should not bulge or swell. A perishable cheese often sold past its prime, older specimens are slightly bitter and chewy. Buy in small amounts. Caerphilly made in the summer is the richest and best.

USABLE LIFE

Short-lived; best when two to three weeks old; eaten and sold in Britain as young as five days old.

STORAGE AFTER PURCHASE

Wrap airtight in plastic wrap or damp cloth. Refrigerate.

SERVING AND EATING

Good eating cheese on its own. Delicious for sandwiches, with bread and butter, with celery, and in salads. Particularly refreshing in the summer when it is hot. Makes an interesting, light fondue.

BEVERAGE MATCH

English ale and beer; rosé wines, especially Tavel rosé in summer; sherry or light red wine in winter.

COMMENTS

Caerphilly has been made for generations in Wales as a mainstay of miners' diets. The height (2½–3½ inches) was supposedly chosen so a slice of the cheese could be held easily between a miner's thumb and finger and he could thus avoid getting coal dust on it; sometimes miners wrapped slices of the cheese in cabbage leaves. Caerphilly also attained popularity because it is one of the most easily digested of cheeses; it is popular among makers because of its yield: seven gallons of milk yields a seven-and-a-half-pound cheese.

SIMILAR CHEESE
White Wensleydale.

Cambridge, see *York*.

Camembert

WHERE MADE
Normandy and other districts in France; widely copied in Europe and the United States. Produced in factories and a very few Normandy farms.

HOW MADE AND CURED
Type of milk: Cow's milk, usually pasteurized.
Method and rind type: Soft, bloomy, surface-ripened type.
Time cured: One to two months.
Fat content: 45–50 percent.

AROMA
Pleasant moldy scent; a trace fruity.

FLAVOR
Flavor family: Brie-Camembert type.
Taste: Milky to tangy taste, simple to complex; at best, delicious.
Texture: Spreadable, smooth, rich paste.

APPEARANCE
Exterior: Downy white surface, tinged with pink-brown pigmentation. Non-French Camemberts often much whiter and fluffier.
Interior: Soft, creamy, ivory-yellow paste that oozes out from under rind of cut wedge when ripe.
Size and shape: Small disk, 4½ inches across by 1¼ inches high, weighing about 9 ounces. Also sold in halves and wedges (demi-Camembert and Camembert en portions). There are even canned versions.

BUYING HINTS
Camembert is so widely copied a cheese that its quality ranges from awful to superb. Today, many Camemberts are identical with small Bries. The phrase "Syndicat du Veritable Camembert de Normandie" denotes a group of genuine Normandy Camemberts, but bear in mind that non-Norman French Camemberts can also be excellent, as are, for that matter, occasional non-French Camemberts. Since Camembert has a brief period when it is properly ripe (although some will

never properly ripen), it is important to select it carefully. Boxed, individually wrapped specimens should be inspected for signs of ammonia stink, shrunken, sticky wrappers, and a hard, unyielding feel. If possible, try to buy larger sizes that can be examined more carefully for suppleness from rind to center when felt gently with the fingertips, which indicates complete softness of the interior. Reject those that feel as if they have a hard center, unless you trust your merchant and will not be using it for a few days. Look for a tinge of pink-brown pigmentation flecked across the downy rind, particularly on French Camemberts, a sign of ripeness; avoid gray-looking rinds, a sign of overage. Do not buy a completely runny one; it has surely passed its peak. Avoid buying small portions if possible, unless these have been fresh-cut from larger cheeses, and avoid canned Camemberts altogether. Chances are you will not be able to sample Camembert before purchase, but if you can, watch out for saltiness or bitter aftertaste. Summer is not the best season to buy French Camembert.

USABLE LIFE

As Camembert, like Brie, is at its peak of ripeness for a very short time, it must be consumed then. As a rule, do not buy Camemberts unless you plan to consume them within a day or two. Buying unripe ones to ripen at home should only be done with caution and from a merchant you trust.

STORAGE AFTER PURCHASE

Unused portions can be stored for a day or two in the refrigerator if tightly wrapped in plastic wrap or foil, but need not be if the cheese will be finished off within a day—unless, of course, the weather is warm. The cheese will not be as good, however, as it was when first cut into.

SERVING AND EATING

End of meals is the traditional time to serve Camembert, but it is equally tasty almost any time, particularly if it is served as a light lunch with a variety of bread, crackers, and fresh fruit.

BEVERAGE MATCH

Almost any fruity red wine: Beaujolais, California Gamay and light Zinfandel, and Italian Bardolino, Valpolicella, and so on.

COMMENTS

Camembert, one of the best-known cheeses in the world, has been flattered by numberless imitations. It dates from the 1790s and its invention is sometimes credited to Marie Harel, a farm woman of Camembert in the Orme region; it is more likely that she simply perfected one of the traditional cheeses of the area. Nevertheless, she had a statue erected in her honor at nearby Vimoutiers until it was destroyed in World War II. Simon credits M. Ridel of Vimoutiers with spreading the fame of Camembert, for in 1890 he invented the wooden box that permitted the cheese to be shipped all over the world.

SIMILAR CHEESES

Brie, Carré de l'Est, Coulommiers. Simon also lists a number of other cheeses as Camembert cousins, including Chaource, Olivet, and Saint-Benoît.

Cantal

WHERE MADE

In the departments of Puy-de-Dôme, Aveyron, Corrèze, and Haut-Loire, France. Factory-produced; also made by a few farms.

HOW MADE AND CURED

Type of milk: Unpasteurized cow's milk.

Method and rind type: Hard, pressed, uncooked cheese with a natural, brushed rind, cloth-covered.

Time cured: Two and a half to six months.

Fat content: 45 percent.

AROMA

Lactic, milky when cut.

FLAVOR

Flavor family: Cheddar type.

Taste: Nutty-sweet, milky-mellow; distinct flavor all its own; very toothsome, superb eating cheese.

Texture: Springy-firm, compact. A bit crumbly when mature.

APPEARANCE

Exterior: Thin brown-gray callused rind with thin cloth covering.

Interior: Even straw-yellow color with small occasional thin line cracks; waxy-oily Cheddar-like appearance.

Size and shape: Large cylinders 12 to 20 inches across by 15 inches high, weighing about 75 to 120 pounds; also smaller sizes weighing about 16 pounds.

BUYING HINTS

Watch out for "cowy" or barnyard" scent, cracked rind, excessive dryness, bitter aftertaste.

USABLE LIFE

Lasts for months in large, well-wrapped refrigerated pieces.

STORAGE AFTER PURCHASE

Wrap airtight in plastic wrap and refrigerate.

SERVING AND EATING

Snacks; excellent on plain or flavored crackers, rustic breads. Serve with sweet dark cherries, or California strawberries.

BEVERAGE MATCH

Traditional matches are fruity red wines, even fine Bordeaux; but it goes well with beer, too, particularly European ales.

COMMENTS

Said to be one of the oldest, if not the oldest French cheese. Its prototype, made as today in the Cantal Mountains, may have been one of the cheeses referred to by Pliny the Elder as one of those known to ancient Rome.

SIMILAR CHEESES

Fine Cheddars; English cheeses in general, particularly Cheshire.

Caprice des Dieux

WHERE MADE

In the Bassigny area of the department of Haut-Marne, France; factory-produced.

HOW MADE AND CURED

Type of milk: Enriched pasteurized cow's milk.

Method and rind type: Soft, double-crème, bloomy rind.

Time cured: Several weeks.

Fat content: 60 percent.

AROMA

Fresh, buttery smell—rind should have pleasant mold smell.

FLAVOR

Flavor family: Brie-Camembert type; also crèmes.

Taste: Simple, rich, buttery; lacks complexity but is nonetheless luxurious and delicious.

Texture: Spreadable paste.

APPEARANCE

Exterior: Snow-white rind; slight tinge of pink-brown pigmentation.

Interior: Creamy ivory paste.

Size and shape: 5½-inch-long oval loaf, 1½ inches high; weight, 7 ounces.

BUYING HINTS

Prepackaged in box, so beware of ammoniated stink, moldy, sticky wrappers, shrunken, rock-hard feel (should be yielding but not mushy).

USABLE LIFE

Use when slight tinge appears on downy white rind, and feel is like heavy paste under rind; a slightly underripe one is also enjoyable. Will keep in refrigerator in its own box for a week, perhaps longer.

STORAGE AFTER PURCHASE

Keep in its own box or rewrap in plastic or foil if cut into; unused portions will keep for a few days in the refrigerator.

SERVING AND EATING

A dessert cheese, to be served with plain, delicate crackers and breads, and fresh fruit.

BEVERAGE MATCH

Fruity wines, particularly reds, although Vouvray or California Chenin Blanc is nice; so is rich black coffee.

COMMENTS

Caprice des Dieux is a brand name.

SIMILAR CHEESES

All plain double- and triple-crèmes, Carré de l'Est.

Carré de l'Est

WHERE MADE

In eastern France; produced in factories.

HOW MADE AND CURED

Type of milk: Pasteurized cow's milk.

Method and rind type: Soft, bloomy rind, surface-ripened.

Time cured: Three weeks.

Fat content: 45–50 percent.

AROMA

Light mushroom scent.

FLAVOR

Flavor family: Brie and Camembert types.

Taste: Mild, slightly mushroomy; close to Camembert in style but blander and less complex; simple, attractive.

Texture: Soft and creamy.

APPEARANCE

Exterior: Very downy white rind.

Interior: Soft ivory paste; somewhat like cream cheese.

Size and shape: Flat and squarish, about 3¼ by 4 inches and an inch thick, and 4½ to 9 ounces in weight.

BUYING HINTS

As Carré de l'Est comes boxed, look for the danger signs of bloomy prepackaged cheeses: ammoniated smell; shrunken, hard cheese; sticky, discolored, or moldy paper; gray-brown rind. The cheese should smell pleasantly moldy, be uniformly soft and yielding, and fill out its wrapper neatly.

USABLE LIFE

This cheese keeps well and remains ripe for a number of days without deterioration if well-stored.

STORAGE AFTER PURCHASE

Unused portions should be tightly enclosed in plastic wrap and stored in the refrigerator.

SERVING AND EATING

End of meals, luncheons; excellent on dark bread, rye crackers, wheat crackers if not overly salted.

BEVERAGE MATCH

Inexpensive fruity wines; coffee or tea.

COMMENTS

According to Simon, there is also a washed-rind version that is said to have the flavor of a mild Maroilles.

SIMILAR CHEESES

Coulommiers, Camembert.

Cendré de Champagne

These rustic French cow's milk cheeses from the vineyard districts of Champagne are called *cendrés* after the ashes of vine twigs used to cover them. Scarce.

Chabichou (also called Cabichou, Cabécou, or Chabi)

WHERE MADE

In the province of Poitou, France; produced by dairies and farms.

HOW MADE AND CURED

Type of milk: Goat's milk.
Method and rind type: Soft, bloomy rind.
Time cured: Cured dry for several weeks.
Fat content: 45 percent.

AROMA

Pronounced goat smell.

FLAVOR
Flavor family: Goat.
Taste: Sharp, intensely goaty, tangy, peppery.
Texture: Soft, creamy.
APPEARANCE
Exterior: Soft, thin white rind with pink-brown pigmentation.
Farm Chabis have a thin bluish rind.
Interior: Moist, soft, creamy ivory.
Size and shape: Small short cone or cylinder about 2½ inches
across by 2 inches high, and weighing about 3 ounces. Also
comes in a large rectangle.
BUYING HINTS
Watch out for overage specimens with excessively gray rinds
and rank odors. Early fall cheeses are the best.
USABLE LIFE
Will keep for weeks but sharpens with age.
STORAGE AFTER PURCHASE
Can be left unwrapped to dry out in refrigerator (an ac-
quired taste), but most will want to wrap it in foil or plastic
wrap. Unused portions will keep for several days.
SERVING AND EATING
With simple meals, particularly at the end; young speci-
mens can be used sparingly as appetizers. Serve with rustic
breads and crackers.
BEVERAGE MATCH
Simple, even rough, young spicy reds: Zinfandel, California
Ruby Cabernet, Spanish Rioja, Cahors.
COMMENTS
Thought of as one of the best of the soft Poitou cheeses.
SIMILAR CHEESES
Any French chèvres. See *Chèvres.*

Chaource

WHERE MADE
In the province of Champagne, France, and nearby regions;
produced in small dairies.
HOW MADE AND CURED
Type of milk: Cow's milk.
Method and rind type: Soft, bloomy-rind type.
Time cured: From two weeks to two months.
Fat content: 45–50 percent.

AROMA
Faint mushroom smell.

FLAVOR
Flavor family: Brie and Camembert types.
Taste: Milky, rather mild to pungent, and slightly acid, with a nutlike flavor; rustic, simple cheese.
Texture: Spreadable.

APPEARANCE
Exterior: White, downy rind tinged with pink-brown pigmentation.
Interior: Soft, ivory-colored, light.
Size and shape: Cylinders; large ones about 5 inches across by 2½ thick weighing about 1½ pounds, and smaller ones weighing about ½ pound.

BUYING HINTS
Watch out for grainy texture, saltiness, overly pigmented rind, ammoniated smell.

USABLE LIFE
Several weeks, but can get strong.

STORAGE AFTER PURCHASE
Wrap tightly in plastic wrap or foil and refrigerate.

SERVING AND EATING
End of meals, with rustic breads, breadsticks, crackers.

BEVERAGE MATCH
Both red and white wines: Chablis, Mâcon, Mercurey, California Pinot Noir, Chardonnay, Pinot Blanc.

COMMENTS
Said to have originated as a copy of Camembert.

SIMILAR CHEESES
Camembert, Coulommiers.

Chaumes, see *Münster.*

Chavignol, see *Crottin de Chavignol.*

Cheddar

WHERE MADE
Originated in Mendip Hills, near Cheddar Gorge and town of Cheddar, Somersetshire, England; now made throughout West country of England—Somersetshire, Wiltshire, Devon-

shire, Dorsetshire. Most made in factories, called Creamery Cheddar; some still made on farms, called Farmhouse Cheddar. Towns of Wells and Shepton Mallet center of Farmhouse Cheddar making. Widely copied worldwide.

HOW MADE AND CURED

Type of milk: Factory cheeses, pasteurized whole cow's milk from many different herds; farmhouse cheeses, unpasteurized whole cow's milk from only one herd.

Method and rind type: Hard, uncooked, pressed with natural rind; cured dry; rind oiled; usually covered with cotton cloth on top and bottom, bandaged around side, and then dipped in paraffin or wax.

Time cured: Three to six months, can be aged up to four years; connoisseurs vary on best age: most say minimum is nine months, preferable eighteen months to two years.

Fat content: 45 percent.

AROMA

Light when young, gaining intensity as ages. Pleasant.

FLAVOR

Flavor family: Mellow Cheddar type.

Taste: Tangy, rich, moist, with depth of flavor and lingering finish. Complex even when six to nine months; complexity increases with age. Sharp but without bitterness. Slightly salty. When fully mature has finish reminiscent of sweet nuts, and is savory and penetrating.

Texture: Firm, oily, but not rubbery; semihard but porous; close-grained, not crumbly. Younger cheeses are more close and firm, older ones more buttery but porous.

APPEARANCE

Exterior: Usually wax- or paraffin-coated with black wax or light yellow-white wax.

Interior: Light yellow-white and smooth; natural granulation; small infrequent fissures.

Size and shape: Several sizes, from 1–70 pounds; usually 12 inches to 15 inches in diameter, between 60 and 70 pounds. Always made in cylinder.

BUYING HINTS

Genuine English Cheddar is hard to find; unscrupulous merchants often sell inferior New Zealand or Canadian Cheddar as English Cheddar. Ask to see the label. Should not be excessively hard, crumbly, or grainy. Taste should not be bitter in aftertaste. Rind should be smooth and even; interior should be uniform color and texture—or the cheese may be bitter.

Can be bought throughout year; best Farmhouse Cheddars are made from April through September.

USABLE LIFE

Best at nine months to two years. If purchased whole and uncut, will continue to mature.

STORAGE AFTER PURCHASE

Wrap tightly in plastic wrap or damp cloth dipped in water mixed with small amount of vinegar. Refrigerate.

SERVING AND EATING

Excellent eating cheese; young versions particularly good with homemade bread and butter, toast, or plain crackers with sweet pickles on side. Older versions delicious alone at end of meals. Also good for Welsh rarebit.

BEVERAGE MATCH

Younger versions good with hard cider, English ale and beer, fruity red wine; older versions good with port, red Bordeaux, California Cabernet Sauvignon, or red Burgundy. Traditionally served with elderberry wine.

COMMENTS

Cheddar has been made in England since the latter part of the sixteenth century, when it was first made in the village of Cheddar (for which it is named) in Somersetshire. It is mentioned in many writings of the late 1500s and 1600s as an exceptionally delicious cheese.

English settlers are known to have brought the cheddaring process to New England in the 1600s; English Cheddar eventually became the model for American Cheddar cheese. Now, by law, to protect the American Cheddar industry, very little genuine English Cheddar is allowed imported.

Before World War II, Farmhouse Cheddars were matured in calico corsets with brass eyelets for lacing up and tightening.

The biggest Cheddar cheese ever made was one weighing 1,100 pounds given to Queen Victoria for a wedding gift. The farmers who made it borrowed it back to exhibit around the country. Afterward the queen refused to accept it back after its lengthy tour.

SIMILAR CHEESES

Cheshire, Dunlop (Scotch Cheddar), Canadian Cheddar (a good one such as Black Diamond), Vermont Cheddar.

Cheddar, American

WHERE MADE

All over United States, but principally in Wisconsin, New York, and Vermont. Almost entirely factory-produced; made on only a few farms.

HOW MADE AND CURED

Type of milk: Cow's milk, usually but not invariably pasteurized.

Method and rind type: Hard; uncooked, pressed, thin-natural-rind cheese.

Time cured: Two months or longer (much longer for best examples).

Fat content: 45 percent.

AROMA

Faint, clean and milky, to full, aromatic Cheddar scent, depending on type, age, and quality.

FLAVOR

Flavor family: Cheddar.

Taste: Ranges from extremely bland and simple to very complex, rich, nutty, and intense. The best examples (very much in the minority) are among the best Cheddars made.

Texture: Wholly uniform, soft and yielding, to exceptionally creamy on the palate.

APPEARANCE

Exterior: May come in plastic-wrapped rindless blocks or traditional cotton-bandaged, paraffin-dipped form.

Interior: Almost always orange-colored (due to the use of annatto) and uniform in appearance, from almost-processed-looking to slightly granular and flaky; firm to the touch.

Size and shape: Almost every possible size and shape, including various prepackaged wheels, wedges, bars, sticks, and so on. Various shapes and sizes are given fanciful names—Longhorns, Twin Flats, Daisies—but apart from huge or odd-shaped specimens for promotional purposes or bite-sized cocktail bits, the standard sizes are ½-, 3-, 5-, 10-, 20-, 40-, and 150-pound wheels or blocks.

BUYING HINTS

Since hundreds of millions of pounds of Cheddar cheese are produced in the United States yearly, the quality range of this cheese varies enormously. Some are merely edible, some are more than excellent. Cheddars are often labeled according to their state of origin, Wisconsin, New York State, and Vermont

Cheddars in particular. Smaller areas and districts may also be indicated. Herkimer County cheese (named for Herkimer County, New York) is well-known because U.S. production of Cheddar was first perfected there in the nineteenth century, and because it is a high-quality, yellow-ivory, slightly crumbly Cheddar. (Today one more commonly sees small orange-colored wheels of Herkimer cheese.) Tillamook is an excellent Oregon Cheddar (see *Tillamook*).

Vermont produces among the best Cheddar and Cheddar types in the United States, including a number of excellent unpasteurized farm- and dairy-produced types. Some high-quality Vermont producers of wide repute are Cabot, Coolidge, Crowley, and the Seward family. The Cabot Farmer's Cooperative makes its fine unpasteurized product in Cabot, Vermont. Coolidge—actually the Plymouth Cheese Corporation, begun by President Coolidge's father—is located in Plymouth. (Their cheese, technically speaking, is not precisely a Cheddar, but a "granular curd cheese" that is not "cheddared" during processing. It has a very pleasant sourish tang.) Crowley Cheese, produced for over a century and a half in Healdville, Vermont, is another Cheddar-type variant, called Colby, Colby Cheddar, or by those who recognize no other Colby worthy, "Crowley." See *Colby*.

In addition, there are a number of small producing farm operations throughout the United States that supply local and loyal customers, and these should not be ignored by those in search of a fine authentic Farmhouse Cheddar or Cheddar type. U.S. Cheddars are commonly if loosely described as mild (or mellow), medium (or medium-sharp), sharp, extra-sharp, super-sharp, and so on, according to the age and intensity of flavor. The actual age may be stated on the label; in all cases where possible, however, sample the cheese before purchase to avoid oversimple, oversalted, and bitter specimens. Beware, too, of dry, crumbly cheeses, and those showing peculiar mottled splotches in the interior, as these are likely to be bitter or damaged in some way.

USABLE LIFE

May vary from weeks to years, but rarely will home conditions permit proper lengthy aging. Plan to use within a month or two.

STORAGE AFTER PURCHASE

Wrap airtight in plastic wrap, and then again in foil if keeping for some time. Refrigerate.

SERVING AND EATING

A fine American Cheddar can be a meal in itself with good country breads and fresh, crisp apples. A good one will grace any cheese board and is hardly surpassed for snacking.

BEVERAGE MATCH

Cider, beer, red wine or medium-dry sherry, and even coffee are excellent companions to U.S. Cheddar.

COMMENTS

As stated before, the notion that all U.S. Cheddars are made from pasteurized milk is not true; in fact, about 25 percent are not, and a good percentage is not colored orange with annatto vegetable dye either, but is as yellow-white as the best Canadian or English Cheddars.

SIMILAR CHEESES

Canadian and English Cheddars.

Cheddar, Canadian

WHERE MADE

All over Canada; factory-produced.

HOW MADE AND CURED

Type of milk: Unpasteurized cow's milk.

Method and rind type: Hard; pressed, uncooked, thin natural rind.

Time cured: Three, six, or nine months, depending on size and flavor desired; can age for years.

Fat content: 45 percent.

AROMA

Faint lactic smell when young; attractive Cheddar scent when aged.

FLAVOR

Flavor family: Cheddar.

Taste: Tangy, rich, and complex, with depth of flavor and lingering aftertaste that varies in intensity with age. Sharp and pleasantly salty, with nutty and savory overtones. Usually excellent, sometimes great.

Texture: Firm, close-grained, buttery-oily if rolled in fingers; very creamy, yielding texture in mouth.

APPEARANCE

Exterior: Thin natural rind usually covered with cotton-cloth bandage, then dipped in paraffin, either clear or black.

Interior: Close-grained, uniform, slightly flaky when aged, handsome, pale-yellow fairly uniform color.

Size and shape: Fat cylinder sections or wheels from 2 to 10 to 40 pounds in weight; also larger sizes and small pre-packaged wedges, bars, and sticks.

BUYING HINTS

Very reliable cheese; nonetheless it is best to buy it in pieces from bulk sizes in order to be able to sample. Some examples are oversalty and lack complexity. When buying from large wheels, determine age (whether cured three, six, or nine months); older ones are less mellow, but more intense in flavor. Two brands in particular are considered especially fine: Black Diamond (comes in black paraffin) and Cherry Hill. Beware of Cheddars that are excessively hard, crumbly, or grainy, or show pinpoints of white mold in the interior. Also watch out for nonuniform rind and mottled color splotches in interior—the cheese may be bitter.

USABLE LIFE

Will keep for months, even a year, if purchased whole and uncut and properly stored; will continue to mature. Cut portions keep well, but it is difficult to keep cut cheese from drying out when attempting long storage.

STORAGE AFTER PURCHASE

Wrap tightly in plastic wrap and then again in foil if storing cut portion; no need for wrapping if entirely paraffined. Refrigerate.

SERVING AND EATING

Excellent eating on its own; serve as a lunch with various hearty breads. Try with peaches and even oranges.

BEVERAGE MATCH

Cider (if not too sweet), substantial ales and beers, and red wine; also good with tawny ports.

COMMENTS

Probably the best Cheddar type, on the whole, produced outside England. The use of unpasteurized milk doubtless contributes to the high level of quality generally attained. The best examples are the equal of factory-produced English Cheddars and are nearly as good as the scarce English Farmhouse Cheddar.

Like English Cheddar and unlike most American Cheddars, no annatto is added to the cheese to color it orange.

SIMILAR CHEESES

American Cheddar, English Cheddar.

Cheshire (called Chester in France)

WHERE MADE

Center of area is in Cheshire, England, also made in neighboring counties of Shropshire, Flintshire, and Staffordshire. Most made in factories; some on farms.

HOW MADE AND CURED

Type of milk: Pasteurized whole cow's milk; farmhouse Cheshire made with unpasteurized milk.

Method and rind type: Hard, uncooked, pressed; traditionally bandaged and with natural rind; most now waxed.

Time cured: Most made now are cured six weeks to two months. In past three types were made: early ripening, cured three weeks and sold locally; medium ripening, cured six weeks to two months; and late ripening, cured ten weeks to ten months. Blue Cheshire is cured six months.

Fat content: 45 percent.

AROMA

Distinct, pleasant smell. Blue has faint smell of mold.

FLAVOR

Flavor family: Medium-mild Cheddar type; Blue somewhat similar to other Blues.

Taste: Not overly sharp. Mellow and pungent; a very solid, satisfying flavor. Slightly moist and intensely salty, though does not seem so at first. Aged, late-ripening version has a richer, more penetrating flavor—most of these are farmhouse cheeses. Blue Cheshire is rich, creamy, and mellow, but without the distinctiveness of Stilton; it does have a pronounced Blue tang.

Texture: Firm, but more loose and crumbly than Cheddar and not so compact. Blue is more compact and close, creamy-smooth.

APPEARANCE

Exterior: Most cheeses are waxed. Blue has some mold on rind.

Interior: Red Cheshire is colored orange with annatto—it is a sort of apricot color; white Cheshire is pale, pale yellow. Both look loose and flaky. Blue Cheshire is light yellow-orange with occasional blue veining and fissures—the veining is close to the rind and not extensive throughout the cheese.

Size and shape: Usually 11-inch by 11-inch cylinders, weighing 20–40 pounds. Blues are usually the same size, or slightly higher and wider in diameter.

BUYING HINTS

Interior should not have grainy texture or shows flecks of white mold, color should be uniform; rind should not bulge or swell. Not a troublesome cheese, almost always excellent. Medium-ripening usually made in May and June; late in July and August during best grazing late-ripening are made.

USABLE LIFE

Medium-ripening good for three to four months; late-ripening best at twelve to eighteen months. If uncut, late-ripening cheese can be aged to two years. Well-wrapped cut cheeses can last one or two months.

STORAGE AFTER PURCHASE

Wrap airtight in plastic wrap or in a damp cloth. Refrigerate. Seal pores of cheese by running flat of knife over exposed surface before wrapping.

SERVING AND EATING

Good eating cheese. Fine on its own, with bread and butter, or with raw vegetables such as celery and watercress. Also excellent toasted on bread or in Welsh rarebit. Not a dessert cheese. Blue best for snacks and appetizers, also good mixed with butter for a spread.

BEVERAGE MATCH

English ale, beer, fruity or dry red wines; traditionally with elderberry wine.

COMMENTS

The oldest cheese in England, Cheshire is believed to have been made even before the Romans conquered Britain. Legends of the origins of the town of Chester (the county seat of Cheshire) suggest that the Romans built it so they could control the district where the cheese was made. A cheese called Cheshire is mentioned in the Domesday Book, which dates from the eleventh century. It was made as we know it at least several hundred years ago. Declared the finest cheese in Europe by a historian during the Elizabethan period, it was also popular in the eighteenth century with Dr. Johnson, who ate it at Ye Olde Cheshire Cheese.

It was originally made in cat-shaped molds, from which the Cheshire cat in *Alice in Wonderland* took its name.

The area in which Cheshire is made is near a town noted for salt-mining; it is believed that the saltiness of the meadows in which the cows feed is responsible for the cheese's character. Even the French consider it a classic cheese.

SIMILAR CHEESES
   Cheddar, Double Gloucester.

Cheshire-Stilton

An English cheese made and developed like a Cheshire cheese, but inoculated bit by bit with the blue mold peculiar to Stilton. Sometimes called Blue Cheshire, see *Cheshire*.

Chèvre Long, see *Sainte-Maure*.

Chèvres

Chèvres is the name given to all French goat's milk cheeses. Usually small—three to eight ounces—they are made as small as one ounce and as large as several pounds. Sometimes mixed with sheep's or cow's milk, only cheeses made entirely from goat's milk may be labeled *pur chèvre*. A considerable amount is still made on farms, although a growing number are factory-produced. Chèvres are made in a bewildering variety of shapes: pyramids, cones (usually truncated), logs, balls, flattened balls, disks, buttons, and so on. Farm chèvres show thin bluish-gray natural rinds, while factory-produced ones are usually covered with a downy, soft, bloomy white rind showing brown pigmentation to some degree. Fresh chèvres are best bought during spring and summer. Factory chèvres are fairly reliable year round. Some factory-produced chèvres are ash-covered. The texture is close, white to ivory in color, and mildly and deliciously tangy when young to incredibly powerful, dramatic, and intensively spicy when aged. All goat cheeses have a basic similarity. Robert Courtine, the French gastronome, points out that many goat cheeses made in France are simply local variants that use some variation of the word "chèvre" in their names as well as a more specific place-name identification. Some examples are Chevreton d'Ambert, Chevrette des Bauges, Chevrine de Lenta, Chevrotin des Aravis, and Chevroton de Beaujolais. *Chevrotin* is a generic term referring to a wide group of goat cheeses, and it is thus listed separately here. Others which can be distinguished, but also share many characteristics, are also listed. These include *Banon* (and the variants *Poivre-d'Âne* and *Sariette*), *Sainte-Maure, Valençay,*

Selles-sur-Cher, Crottin de Chavignol, Saint-Saviol, Montra-chet, and *Chabichou.*

Chevrotin

WHERE MADE

In the province of Bourbonnais, France; produced by factories and farms.

HOW MADE AND CURED

Type of milk: Goat's, sometimes mixed with cow's milk.
Method and rind type: Soft, bloomy rind, surface-ripened.
Time cured: Two weeks to two months.
Fat content: 45 percent.

AROMA

Rind can smell moldy and goaty; interior smells rather buttery.

FLAVOR

Flavor family: Goat.
Taste: Not overly goaty; rich, oily, tangy, strong. Strength varies with age.
Texture: Soft, resilient texture.

APPEARANCE

Exterior: White, thin, downy rind tinged and flecked with brown. There is also a gray-rind version.
Interior: Small irregular holes, darker near rind, ivory color.
Size and shape: Various shapes; small wheel (6 inches in diameter by 2 inches thick) or short cone (about 2 inches high). These weigh from 4 ounces to 1½ pounds.

BUYING HINTS

Sample if possible for age desired; avoid shrunken, abnormally moldy examples and ones with rank smells.

USABLE LIFE

Can last for weeks if properly stored, but gains considerably in strength (an acquired taste).

STORAGE AFTER PURCHASE

Wrap tightly in plastic wrap or foil and refrigerate.

SERVING AND EATING

End of meals; sparingly as appetizer. Particularly good with rustic breads, very crusty breads, and rye crackers.

BEVERAGE MATCH

Almost any fruity wine, but stronger cheeses call for reds such as Barbera, sturdy Rhône, California Ruby Cabernet.

COMMENTS

Chevrotin (or Chevrotin du Bourbonnais) is the name given to the various chèvres of the Bourbonnais province.

SIMILAR CHEESES

Any French chèvres. See *Chèvres.*

Chiberta

WHERE MADE

Throughout the Pyrénées, in France. Produced by both farms and factories.

HOW MADE AND CURED

Type of milk: Cow's milk.

Method and rind type: Pressed, semisoft cheese. Thin, natural rind.

Time cured: About two months.

Fat content: 45 percent.

AROMA

Earthy, redolent, monastery-type smell.

FLAVOR

Flavor family: Mild monastery.

Taste: Simple, direct, clean-flavored, with an attractive milky tang; the taste is different from what the aroma leads one to expect.

Texture: Soft, supple.

APPEARANCE

Exterior: Thin rind with orange-red pigmentation on pitted surface.

Interior: Light yellow with small irregular holes; firm but springy.

Size and shape: Flat wheel about 2¼ inches high, weighing 8 ounces.

BUYING HINTS

Watch out for rank odor; cracked, moldy rind; unclean taste.

USABLE LIFE

Keeps for many weeks if well-wrapped and stored.

STORAGE AFTER PURCHASE

Wrap tightly in plastic wrap and store in the refrigerator.

SERVING AND EATING

After simple meals; luncheon snacks; also contrasts well with strong cheeses on a cheese board. Serve with crusty bread.

BEVERAGE MATCH

Young, inexpensive red wines.

COMMENTS

A Basque country cheese, it is both interesting and popular with experienced and inexperienced cheese palates.

SIMILAR CHEESE

Tomme de Savoie.

Coeur de Bray

A heart-shaped Neufchâtel. See *Neufchâtel*.

Colby

Colby is a U.S. cheese produced by a process similar to that used for Cheddar, except that the curd is not matted and milled. Colby has a more open texture than Cheddar, and is softer and more moist. It does not keep as long as Cheddar. Invented in Wisconsin and named after one of its towns, some of the best examples today are made in Vermont.

Comté (also called Gruyère de Comté or French Gruyèı

WHERE MADE

In the province of Franche-Comté, France; dairy-produced.

HOW MADE AND CURED

Type of milk: Unpasteurized cow's milk.

Method and rind type: Hard, cooked and pressed; thick natural brushed rind.

Time cured: Three to six months.

Fat content: 45 percent.

AROMA

Faint, clean, and pleasant.

FLAVOR

Flavor family: Swiss type.

Taste: Flavorful, sweet-nutty, lingering; perhaps a little more intense than Swiss Gruyère but not as sweet.

Texture: Grainy but creamy texture.

APPEARANCE

Exterior: Relatively smooth thick rind.

Interior: Yellow-beige with scattered small cherry-sized holes in smooth, waxy interior.

Size and shape: Firm, solid, large flat wheels 26 inches across by 4 inches high with very slightly bulging sides, weighing about 80 pounds.

BUYING HINTS

Beware of disturbed, broken, cracked, or bulging rind; frequent large holes, thick gray subcrust, rubbery texture, excessive sharpness or dryness in taste.

USABLE LIFE

Keeps for months in large pieces if well-wrapped and well-stored.

STORAGE AFTER PURCHASE

Wrap in plastic wrap (wrap again in foil for long storage) and store in the refrigerator.

SERVING AND EATING

An eating cheese—that is, one can make a meal of a few ounces of Comté and a variety of breads, particularly crusty ones. A good choice for the cheese board both as a contrast to unusual cheeses and for those guests with unadventurous palates.

BEVERAGE MATCH

Light, fruity or dry white wines: Sancerre, Alsatian whites, dry Graves, Vouvray, and California Sauvignon Blanc and Chenin Blanc.

COMMENTS

Known since the thirteenth century; thus it is not an imitation of Swiss Gruyère, but an equal cousin of considerable antiquity and achieves equal quality.

SIMILAR CHEESES

Gruyère (Swiss), Beaufort.

Coon

Coon is an American Cheddar type cured at high temperature and humidity, which encourages mold growth. It is then waxed. The result is a dark, crumbly, and very sharp-flavored cheese.

Cotherstone (also called Yorkshire-Stilton)

Made in the valley of the Tees, Yorkshire, England, on farms, this is a double-crème, blue-veined cheese made from cow's milk. It is said to be very similar to blue Wensleydale and Stilton. Rarely seen even in England, it is sometimes available in specialty cheese shops there.

Coulommiers   (also called Brie de Coulommiers)

WHERE MADE

Île-de-France and elsewhere in France; produced in factories and a few farms.

HOW MADE AND CURED

Type of milk: Cow's milk, usually pasteurized.

Method and rind type: Soft, bloomy rind, surface-ripened.

Time cured: One month.

Fat content: 40–50 percent.

AROMA

Very Brie-like scent; somewhat mushroomy.

FLAVOR

Flavor family: Brie and Camembert types.

Taste: Not as complex as larger Brie de Meaux; often less subtle, but can be very attractive, savory, and appetizing; rather nutty—with a taste of sweet almonds—and mushroomy.

Texture: Soft, creamy paste.

APPEARANCE

Exterior: Very downy white rind, as if covered in white felt. Slightly tinged with traces of brownish-pink pigmentation.

Interior: Soft, beige paste that oozes out from rind of cut wedge when cheese is ripe.

Size and shape: Small disks about 5 inches across by 1 inch thick weighing a little over 1 pound. Somewhat larger sizes are traditionally called Brie de Coulommiers.

BUYING HINTS

As with Brie and Camembert, the cheese should be supple and yielding to the touch when felt gently with the fingertips from rind to center. Coulommiers, like all Brie types, has a hard unripe layer in the center of the cheese that softens through when ripe so that the interior has the uniform consistency of soft, spreadable paste. Since it comes in small sizes it may not be possible to buy it in wedges and thus sample for oversaltiness and bitterness, but one should examine at the least the box and wrapping in which it is usually sold for an ammoniated smell (a sign of overripeness), a shrunken, hard-rind cheese feel (a sign of overage), or a sticky or moldy wrapper (sign of damage). If you can peek under the wrapper, beware of a fluffy-white cheese devoid of any sign of pigmentation; such cheeses may not just be underripe but "dead"—that is, will never ripen. Best bought from a reliable merchant.

USABLE LIFE

While perhaps a little less tempermental than large Bries, they should still be bought when ripe, or a few days before their peak of ripeness, from a reliable merchant. The period of peak ripeness is short, and Coulommiers should be eaten then.

STORAGE AFTER PURCHASE

Keep in original packaging until use; since it is small, it should be consumed entirely when at peak, but unused portions can be plastic-wrapped and refrigerated if necessary. This is liable to toughen the cheese, so if possible keep it wrapped in a cool room for the next meal.

SERVING AND EATING

End of meals; sparingly as an appetizer. Since Coulommiers is small and attractive, it is an excellent choice when a whole Brie would be too much but a whole cheese is wanted. Plain French/Italian bread or plain unsalted crackers are all that is necessary.

BEVERAGE MATCH

Fine Beaujolais—Fleurie, Morgon, Moulin-à-Vent—or fine California Gamay or Gamay Beaujolais is perfect, but any fine red wine can be used.

COMMENTS

According to some authorities, Coulommiers is identical with the smallest size of Brie. In any event it is very close to Brie in taste, and any differences may be accounted for by slight variations in manufacture and the fact that it is usually intended to be eaten younger.

SIMILAR CHEESES

Brie, Camembert.

Cream Cheese, American

WHERE MADE

All over the United States; factory-produced.

HOW MADE AND CURED

Type of milk: Cow's milk, pasteurized.

Method and rind type: Fresh, uncured, rindless, soft cheese.

Time cured: None.

Fat content: Usually 35–40 percent.

AROMA
Fresh.

FLAVOR
Flavor family: Fresh.
Taste: Fresh, delicately tangy-sour, simple, and attractive.
Texture: Very soft.

APPEARANCE
Exterior: Rindless; exterior looks like interior.
Interior: Snow-white, extremely uniform, soft, spreadable.
Size and shape: Variety of sizes and shapes, usually foil-wrapped or packed in containers; from 3 ounces on up.

BUYING HINTS
Freshness is the only criterion; otherwise extremely reliable.

USABLE LIFE
Three weeks, perhaps longer.

STORAGE AFTER PURCHASE
Simply store in original packaging until use; foil wrapping can be refolded if not entirely used or else cheese can be wrapped in plastic; always refrigerate.

SERVING AND EATING
Excellent on rolls, bagels, muffins for breakfast; as a snack on breads, crackers, rolls, and so on. Also nice with preserves. Although there are flavored and spiced versions available, your own mixes will be tastier.

BEVERAGE MATCH
Coffee or tea.

COMMENTS
The most famous U.S. brand, Kraft's Philadelphia Brand Cream Cheese, was never made in Philadelphia; it was simply named after that city in the late 1880s.

SIMILAR CHEESES
Fresh American Neufchâtels.

Crema Dania

WHERE MADE
Denmark, in factories.

HOW MADE AND CURED
Type of milk: Pasteurized whole cow's milk to which cream is added.

Method and rind type: Soft-ripening; bloomy rind; almost a triple-crème.

Time cured: Three weeks.
Fat content: 72 percent.

AROMA

Fresh and sweet.

FLAVOR

Flavor family: Crèmes.

Taste: Delicate; very creamy taste with earthy undertones; rich and luscious, but not complex.

Texture: Brie-like at its best; spreadable like butter; very smooth and creamy; unctuous.

APPEARANCE

Exterior: Pure white thin bloomy rind, with chalky texture.

Interior: Pale yellow-white with a few tiny holes; creamy, smooth-looking; glossy when ripe.

Size and shape: A rectangular "stick," weighing 6 ounces, wrapped in foil, and packaged in a cardboard box.

BUYING HINTS

Extremely reliable cheese; ripens with great evenness and ripe ones are almost always ripe throughout interior. Rind should be pure white and show no discoloration. When pressed, cheese should feel firm but resilient equally throughout, not lumpy. Cheese should be pale yellow-white. Scent should not be strong or ammoniated. Similar Danish bloomy-rind cheeses include Crème Royal.

USABLE LIFE

Life span is three to four weeks.

STORAGE AFTER PURCHASE

Keeps much better than French Brie. Wrap airtight in plastic wrap or aluminum foil. Refrigerate.

SERVING AND EATING

Leave out at room temperature an hour before serving. A dessert cheese, excellent with delicate fruit such as sweet cherries. Serve after a dinner of delicate food, such as fish, oysters, and so on.

BEVERAGE MATCH

Good with dry white wine or light rosé.

COMMENTS

Invented in 1957 by Henrik Tholstrup of Copenhagen, whose ancestors were cheesemakers for three generations. Many think it the only new cheese of real importance and distinction invented in the past fifty years. Invented as a low-cost luxury cheese.

SIMILAR CHEESES
Other Danish bloomy-rind cheeses such as Creme Royal, Brie, Camembert.

Crème de Gruyère, see *Fromage Fondu.*

Crème de Savoie, see *Fromage Fondu.*

Creme Royal, see *Crema Dania.*

Crescenza, see *Stracchino.*

Crottin de Chavignol (also called Chavignol)

WHERE MADE
In the town of Chavignol and neighboring villages in the province of Berry, France. Principally farm-produced.

HOW MADE AND CURED
Type of milk: Goat's milk.
Method and rind type: Soft, bloomy natural rind.
Time cured: Traditionally two to three months, but sometimes as little as two weeks.
Fat content: 45 percent.

AROMA
Faintly goaty to rank, depending on age.

FLAVOR
Flavor family: Goat.
Taste: Tangy to extraordinarily pungent and sharp, depending on age. When aged, a cheese principally for chèvres enthusiasts.
Texture: Soft and smooth when young.

APPEARANCE
Exterior: White and pink-brown rind when young; dark gray when old.
Interior: White and smooth when young; darkens with age.
Size and shape: Small flattened balls about 2 ounces in weight. Originally the old, dry, blackened cheeses of Chavignol were called *crottin* (horse dung) because of shape and

appearance, but now most of the young as well as old cheeses of Chavignol are called Crottin.

BUYING HINTS

Beware of overmoldiness or rank smell, unless this is what you're looking for. Examples should not be too salty.

USABLE LIFE

Will keep for weeks in the refrigerator, but gains in strength.

STORAGE AFTER PURCHASE

Unwrap and let dry out in the refrigerator if intensity of flavor is desired (an acquired taste); otherwise, wrap tightly in plastic wrap or foil and refrigerate.

SERVING AND EATING

After meals with rustic breads; sparingly as appetizer (when young) with breadsticks and crackers. Adds drama to cheese boards, not to mention use as conversational gambit.

BEVERAGE MATCH

White wines of Sancerre, California Sauvignon Blanc, Grey Riesling.

SIMILAR CHEESES

French chèvres.

Curé Nantais

WHERE MADE

In the province of Brittany, France; produced in factories.

HOW MADE AND CURED

Type of milk: Cow's.

Method and rind type: Pressed, uncooked, washed rind.

Time cured: One month.

Fat content: 40 percent.

AROMA

Distinct "monastery" nose; redolent.

FLAVOR

Flavor family: Monastery.

Taste: Pronounced full earthy taste, rather like Pont-L'Évêque, but not as complex.

Texture: Soft and nearly spreadable.

APPEARANCE

Exterior: Orange-brown washed rind.

Interior: Soft yellow and moist-looking.

Size and shape: A 3½-by-3½-inch rounded square about 1½ inches thick, weighing about 7 ounces.

BUYING HINTS

Bitterness of flavor should be avoided; also watch out for dry, shrunken rind and lack of suppleness.

USABLE LIFE

Will keep for weeks in refrigerator if properly wrapped.

STORAGE AFTER PURCHASE

Keep in original wrapping if boxed; otherwise wrap in plastic wrap and refrigerate.

SERVING AND EATING

At the end of meals with rustic breads, also good choice to add to cheese board.

BEVERAGE MATCH

Muscadet, California Grey Riesling, French Colombard, Folle Blanche; but sturdy young reds can be used as well.

COMMENTS

Also called Fromage du Curé, or "priest's cheese," for it was invented by a parish priest of the seaport town of Nantes in the 1890s.

SIMILAR CHEESES

Livarot, Maroilles.

Danablu (also called Danish Blue Cheese)

WHERE MADE

Denmark, in factories.

HOW MADE AND CURED

Type of milk: Pasteurized, homogenized, rich whole cow's milk.

Method and rind type: Semisoft, internal-mold-ripened; scraped rind, packaged in foil.

Time cured: Several weeks, ripens rapidly.

Fat content: 50 percent minimum, can be more.

AROMA

Slight moldy scent.

FLAVOR

Flavor family: Blue cheeses.

Taste: Distinctive, strong, rich, sharp, piquant. Very salty, but saltiness is offset by milk-sweet creaminess in the best examples. Appetizing and thirst-provoking, but not as complex as Blues such as Stilton, Roquefort, or Gorgonzola.

Texture: Crumbly, with soft consistency; spreadable.

APPEARANCE

Exterior: Yellowish-white (sometimes very white) surface that feels slightly greasy; cheese is usually wrapped in foil.

Interior: Milk-white color with dense networks of blue veins. Texture appears creamy but crumbly.

Size and shape: Comes in a variety of sizes—most common is 6-pound cylinder with diameter of 8 inches and height of 4 inches. Also comes in large rectangular and square blocks. Small consumer sizes are also sold individually in foil-wrapped packets—1 ounce, ¼ pound, and ½ pound—and ¼–½ pound plastic cups.

BUYING HINTS

A fairly reliable cheese, though it is sometimes sold too old. The covering on the cheese should look even and clean; the cheese should look moist, not dry, cakey, or granular; the veins should be clearly defined and their color should contrast pleasantly with the cheese; the color of the cheese should be milky, creamy white, not grayish or yellowish. The taste should not be bitter. The outer wrapping should be marked with the percentage of fat.

USABLE LIFE

Carefully stored, will keep up to two weeks after purchase.

STORAGE AFTER PURCHASE

Wrap airtight in foil and put in plastic bag. Refrigerate or keep in cool cellar with temperature not higher than 46°F.

SERVING AND EATING

Cut with any very sharp knife. Serve as a snack, in salads, or after dinner. The Danes think it is particularly good with blue grapes. It makes a good ending to a heavy rich meal of duck, goose, or game.

BEVERAGE MATCH

Best with full-bodied red wines.

COMMENTS

Invented by Marius Boel, a cheesemaker, in 1914 as an imitation of Roquefort. During World War I, imports of cheeses from various parts of Europe to Denmark were cut off; one of these was Roquefort. At first called Danish Roquefort, its internationally registered name is now Danablu.

Danablu is the best-known Danish cheese and is exported to many countries throughout the world. The greatest quantity of Blue cheese imported to the United States is Danish Blue. It is the least expensive of the imported Blues.

All Danish cheeses that are exported are passed by the Danish State Quality Control, which tests their composition as well as appearance, texture, smell, and taste.

SIMILAR CHEESE

Mycella, Norwegian Blue cheese.

Danbo (also called Dambo)

WHERE MADE

Denmark, in factories.

HOW MADE AND CURED

Type of milk: Pasteurized whole cow's milk.

Method and rind type: Semihard, pressed, ripened by bacteria, with gas holes; washed, thin rind; similar method of manufacture as Swiss cheeses; some flavored with caraway seeds.

Time cured: Three to five months.

Fat content: 45 percent minimum.

AROMA

Fresh and mild.

FLAVOR

Flavor family: Bland and mild.

Taste: Very similar in flavor to Samsoe, but not so distinguished. Very mild and buttery-tasting; becomes stronger with age.

Texture: Firm, smooth texture with some resiliency. Sliceable.

APPEARANCE

Exterior: Dry, yellowish thin rind. Sometimes covered with red or yellow wax.

Interior: Can be whitish-cream color to very yellow; smooth texture with small number of round holes, about size of small cherry. Also comes with caraway seeds in it.

Size and shape: Flat, square shape with slightly convex sides, 10 inches in length and width, 3 inches in height, weighing 13 pounds. Also available in varying weights, from small to very large.

BUYING HINTS

Danish cheeses are extremely reliable; usually, if the cheese looks good, it will be good. The rind or wax should be stamped with the name Danbo and the amount of fat content (45+). Wax coating should adhere closely to cheese and show no cracks; rind should be even and free of blemishes; interior should have no off-color spots and not too many holes.

USABLE LIFE
 About one month, once cut. If uncut, can be aged up to two years.

STORAGE AFTER PURCHASE
 Wrap airtight in plastic wrap or in aluminum foil and then in a plastic bag. Refrigerate.

SERVING AND EATING
 Good eating cheese. Can be eaten at any meal. Good with fruit: the Danes like it with apples, pears, cherries, peaches. Not a good dessert cheese.

BEVERAGE MATCH
 Good with Danish beer, hard cider, and light, fruity red wines.

COMMENTS
 Especially liked by children because of its mild flavor and firm texture. The caraway-seed version ages well and takes on a character similar to Leyden.

SIMILAR CHEESES
 Tybo, Samsoe.

Dauphin

A flavored Maroilles. See *Maroilles.*

Demi-Sel

WHERE MADE
 In the province of Normandy and elsewhere in France; factory-produced.

HOW MADE AND CURED
 Type of milk: Pasteurized cow's milk and cream.
 Method and rind type: Fresh cheese, rindless.
 Time cured: None.
 Fat content: 40–45 percent.

AROMA
 Faint lactic, fresh scent.

FLAVOR
 Flavor family: Fresh.
 Taste: Very mild, creamy; lightly sour and lightly salted. Very simple and attractive.
 Texture: Like a fine cream cheese.

APPEARANCE
 Exterior: White block, foil-wrapped to preserve shape.

Interior: White, creamy, moist, and uniform.

Size and shape: 3-inch square about 1 inch thick, weighing 3 ounces.

BUYING HINTS

Must be fresh and not dried out; try one first before buying in quantity.

USABLE LIFE

Will keep for a week, perhaps a little longer, if refrigerated.

STORAGE AFTER PURCHASE

Best consumed fresh; should be kept in the original wrapper, or rewrapped in foil if not consumed at once, and refrigerated.

SERVING AND EATING

Best for snacks, with crackers of various kinds.

BEVERAGE MATCH

California Emerald Riesling, sparkling cider, or coffee or tea.

COMMENTS

Created about a century ago by M. Pommel; today Gervais is the main producer.

SIMILAR CHEESE

Petit-Suisse.

Derby (also called Derbyshire)

WHERE MADE

Derbyshire, England. Almost all made in factories.

HOW MADE AND CURED

Type of milk: Pasteurized whole cow's milk.

Method and rind type: Hard, uncooked, pressed. Traditionally soaked in brine or salt-rubbed on exterior (the reason for the thinness of this cheese—so the salt can penetrate the interior).

Time cured: Four to six weeks.

Fat content: 45 percent.

AROMA

Fresh, pleasant.

FLAVOR

Flavor family: Mild Cheddar type.

Taste: Clean, tangy, better when aged six months. Not a terribly distinctive cheese. Can occasionally develop undesirable acidity and off-flavors as it matures. Sage Derby has sage flavor to it.

Texture: Flaky when broken; moist, buttery; not as firm and solid as Cheddar.

APPEARANCE

Exterior: Light-yellow rind; now often waxed.

Interior: Pale-honey color with smooth close texture; Sage Derby has two irregular wide horizontal green stripes running through it.

Size and shape: Traditionally flat wheel, 15 inches in diameter by 5 inches high; weight, 30 pounds.

BUYING HINTS

Today this is often an ordinary, unimaginative cheese. It should not have cracks on surface or flecks of white mold; rind should not be cracked or bulging. Taste before buying; it should not have a highly acid, sour taste. Interior should be uniform in color, with no off-color spots.

USABLE LIFE

Can be eaten from four weeks to seven months. Best at about six months.

STORAGE AFTER PURCHASE

Wrap airtight in plastic wrap or damp cloth soaked in water with a bit of vinegar. Refrigerate. Draw flat of knife across cut surface to seal pores and prevent drying out.

SERVING AND EATING

Good eating cheese. Best for sandwiches and snacks, with bread and butter. Not a connoisseur's cheese, but pleasant.

BEVERAGE MATCH

English ale or beer; light, fruity red or white wines.

COMMENTS

In earlier days, the best ones were made in summer months, and were made in farmhouses. Until 1885, cheeses of all sizes, shapes, flavors, and appearances were called Derby, so long as they were made in Derbyshire.

Derbyshire farmers were the first to build a creamery, or cheese factory, in 1870.

At harvesttime and Christmas, Sage Derby is (and was) made. These small 16–18-pound cheeses were flavored with fresh sage leaves, but since the sage adds no color but brown, spinach leaves and corn shoots were added to give it an attractive green color.

SIMILAR CHEESES

Double Gloucester, Leicester.

Double-crème

Double-crèmes are all those cheeses which contain 60-percent butterfat and are ripened for at least a few weeks; many of these 60-percent fat cheeses are also categorized as Brie and Camembert types. See *Triple-crèmes*.

Dunlop (also called Scotch Dunlop and Scotch Cheddar)

WHERE MADE

Scotland, in the counties of Ayrshire, Renfrewshire, and Lanarkshire. Most made in factories, some on farms.

HOW MADE AND CURED

Type of milk: Pasteurized, whole cow's milk.

Method and rind type: Hard, uncooked, pressed with natural rind.

Time cured: Two to four months.

Fat content: 45 percent.

AROMA

Fresh, pleasant, lactic aroma.

FLAVOR

Flavor family: Mild Cheddar type.

Taste: Mild, creamy, sometimes sourish; buttery and rich, similar to young English Cheddar at its best. Little bite.

Texture: Close in texture and moist. Creamier than Cheddar.

APPEARANCE

Exterior: Thin rind, traditionally bandaged; now often waxed.

Interior: Creamy white, between butter and cream color; smooth, moist.

Size and shape: Flat wheel, about 8–10 inches high and 18–20 inches in diameter; sometimes seen in small 1-pound waxed rounds wrapped in paper.

BUYING HINTS

Doesn't travel as well as Cheddar because of higher moisture content; nevertheless, a fairly reliable cheese. Interior should have uniform color and texture. Rind should not be cracked or bulging. Wax should look uniform if wax-coated.

USABLE LIFE

Ready in six weeks to two months, keeps for three to four months beyond that. Best when at least four months old, but some Scotsmen eat them when extremely young.

STORAGE AFTER PURCHASE

Wrap airtight in plastic wrap. Refrigerate.

SERVING AND EATING

Good eating cheese. Best for sandwiches, with homemade whole-wheat bread and butter, toast, or Scotch oatcakes. Excellent when melted; can be used in place of Cheddar.

BEVERAGE MATCH

Good with ale, beer, and light Scotch malt whiskeys. Also nice with light, fruity red and full white wines.

COMMENTS

Dunlop is one of the national cheeses of Scotland. The recipe is supposed to have been brought to Scotland from Ireland about the time of Charles II by a woman named Barbara Gilmour. It was first made by her, it is believed, in 1688 in the town of Dunlop in Ayrshire.

SIMILAR CHEESES

English Cheddar, good Canadian Cheddar.

Edam

WHERE MADE

North Holland; imitations made in the United States and elsewhere. Made primarily in factories.

HOW MADE AND CURED

Type of milk: A blend of whole pasteurized cow's milk and partially skimmed pasteurized cow's milk.

Method and rind type: Semisoft to firm cheese; pressed, uncooked. A natural rind is rubbed with salt (or dipped in salt water), later washed and rubbed with oil, then coated with red wax.

Time cured: Two months. Some aged for longer periods of time—six to twelve months.

Fat content: Not less than 40 percent.

AROMA

Fresh, lactic smell increasing to quite penetrating with age.

FLAVOR

Flavor family: Bland and mild.

Taste: Buttery, mellow taste, slightly tangy and salty; light, clean, "wholesome." Aged versions are much stronger, sharper, and more tangy.

Texture: Slightly rubbery, but firm, close-knit, smooth. No holes. Aged versions are harder and more brittle when sliced.

APPEARANCE

Exterior: Has bright red wax coating over very thin rind, covered with cellophane.

Interior: Straw-yellow with a smooth, even surface. Aged has a more brownish-yellow color and more brittle-looking texture.

Size and shape: Mostly sold in spherical balls weighing 2 or 4 pounds. Also available in 5-pound loaf shapes.

BUYING HINTS

Edam is almost always an extremely reliable cheese and is good all year round. True Edams from the Netherlands have stickers identifying them as Holland Imported Cheese, and the rind under the wax is stamped with a six-sided mark in which the word "Holland" appears as well as the number of the percentage of fat content. The rind should not bulge; the wax should not bulge or show cracks or blemishes; the color of the interior should be uniform. There should be no large holes.

Aged Edam is a rarity in the United States, but it should be hard, even very hard, very light brown in color, and have a strong, lingering flavor.

USABLE LIFE

Edam has a very long life, and if not cut, will continue to age; it will keep up to several years, even in warm climates.

STORAGE AFTER PURCHASE

Keep refrigerated. After cutting, wrap airtight in plastic wrap.

SERVING AND EATING

Cut Edam in long wedges, cutting from center of top of ball to center of bottom. Serve with white or pumpernickel bread or Dutch rusks and butter. Edam is a good eating cheese; in Holland it is eaten for breakfast and in open-faced sandwiches for lunch. It is not good for grating or cooking.

BEVERAGE MATCH

Edam is good with coffee, Dutch or German beer, and light, fruity red and white wines.

COMMENTS

Edam is named for a rural town near Amsterdam. It is the world's only perfectly spherically shaped cheese—possible because it turns firm quickly enough after being made to retain the shape.

Edam is one of the most popular cheeses in the world; it is

exported to most countries and is especially popular in the Caribbean and South America.

Edam was produced in the Middle Ages and exported to other European countries in the thirteenth century. It is thought that Edam was even brought to America on the *May-flower*. Beginning in the thirteenth century Edam rinds were rubbed with vermilion so that they would become red—the reddish rind was supposed to distinguish them from other Dutch cheeses. This practice was eventually established by formal agreement, but now red wax coatings have replaced the vermilion cloth rub.

SIMILAR CHEESES

Gouda, imitations of Holland Edam.

Emmentaler (also called Emmental and Switzerland Swiss)

WHERE MADE

Switzerland, in the central mountain areas; made in valley dairies. Widely copied elsewhere.

HOW MADE AND CURED

Type of milk: Pasteurized or unpasteurized whole cow's milk.

Method and rind type: Hard, pressed, cooked; with natural rind, brushed and oiled.

Time cured: Four-month minimum, usually six to ten months. Strongly flavored ones cured eight to twelve months. Most younger ones come to the United States.

Fat content: 45-percent minimum.

AROMA

Fruity, sweet smell, reminiscent of Alpine pastures.

FLAVOR

Flavor family: Swiss cheeses.

Taste: Fruity, not sharp, with a mellow, sweet aftertaste. Very nutty (some say hazelnut flavor) and zesty; not as rich as Gruyère. Has a high, clean note. The milk from Alpine pastures is supposed to be responsible for its characteristic taste.

Texture: Firm; oily; slightly grainier than Gruyère.

APPEARANCE

Exterior: Golden-yellow to yellow-brown smooth rind that is dry and hard.

Interior: Light ivory-yellow color (though color can vary); smooth, close grain, with many round holes between the size of a cherry and a walnut, according to Simon; holes evenly distributed throughout cheese, not too close together.

Size and shape: Very large wheel shape, with convex sides, 32 to 34 inches in diameter, 9 inches thick, 170 to 220 pounds in weight. The minimum weight by law is 145 pounds.

BUYING HINTS

Swiss cheeses are quite reliable; federal inspectors grade the cheeses according to strict standards. Swiss law prohibits the use of artificial additives, coloring agents, and milk from cows fed on silage. Copies of Emmentaler made in various other countries often have a faintly bitter taste and aftertaste because milk from cows fed on silage is allowed in all of them. Swiss Emmentaler has the word "Switzerland" stamped in red all over the outside of the rind. Quality of the cheese is indicated by the holes; they should be uniform in size (the size of a cherry or walnut), round not oval, and should glisten with the suggestion of moisture. This moisture, known as "weeping," is a sign of full maturity in a quality Emmentaler. There should not be too many holes and the paste should have no fissures or cracks.

USABLE LIFE

Best between four and twelve months, although can age longer. The younger (four-month) cheese will be milder in flavor and aroma. Keeps one month if large piece is correctly wrapped.

STORAGE AFTER PURCHASE

Wrap airtight in plastic wrap; refrigerate.

SERVING AND EATING

Good eating cheese. Serve with just bread and butter, in salads, or with cold meats. Excellent in cooking: one of the main ingredients of Swiss fondue. Good for grating.

BEVERAGE MATCH

Excellent with fruity white wines of Switzerland, Germany, and California.

COMMENTS

Name comes from the valley of the Emme, where the cheese was first and still is made. It is not known when the first Emmentaler was made; it is known that cheese from Switzerland was served in Rome during the reign of Caesar at gourmets' tables, and it is thought that that cheese was one of the ancestors of Emmentaler as we now know it. Legend suggests the first Emmentaler with holes was developed during the sixteenth, seventeenth, or eighteenth century, depending on the version of the legend. It is thought that the holes were developed as a way of making larger and larger cheeses—important when tolls were beginning to be charged for entering towns or using streets and bridges, because the number of cheeses fixed the toll, not the weight or size of them.

Emmentaler is a difficult cheese to make; it needs careful craftsmanship and the highest-quality milk. One wheel of cheese may require as much as 2,500 pounds of milk. Emmentaler is the "Switzerland Swiss" cheese. It has been imitated in all the Scandinavian countries, Germany, France, and the United States. Probably the best copies have been those made by Swiss immigrants who carried on the old Swiss cheese-making traditions in Green County, Wisconsin. Even today some of the cheeses are made the old way, although they are not sold commercially. Danish and Austrian Emmental and Finnish Swiss are also good copies, but have a tendency to be bitter.

SIMILAR CHEESES

Gruyère, Appenzeller, copies of Swiss Emmentaler, Jarlsberg.

Epoisses

WHERE MADE

In the province of Burgundy, France; farm and factory produced.

HOW MADE AND CURED

Type of milk: Cow's.

Method and rind type: Soft; washed rind; traditionally washed in white wine and marc.

Time cured: Up to three months.

Fat content: 45–50 percent.

AROMA

Mild, lactic smell; strong when aged.

FLAVOR

Flavor family: Mild to strong.

Taste: Mild, rich, and creamy to very pungent, spicy, and intense; a very special taste when aged, and when flavored with pepper or fennel, an acquired one.

Texture: Yielding, soft.

APPEARANCE

Exterior: Thin orange mottled rind.

Interior: Smooth and white to yellowish-ivory, fresh cream cheese to pasty consistency.

Size and shape: Flat cylinder 4 inches across by 2½ inches high, and weighing about ½ pound.

BUYING HINTS

Avoid a grayish, overmoldy appearance, foul smell, and overly sharp taste.

USABLE LIFE

Keeps well, but gains in strength.

STORAGE AFTER PURCHASE

Wrap in plastic wrap or foil and refrigerate.

SERVING AND EATING

To end simple meals, to enliven cheese boards. Best with crusty breads.

BEVERAGE MATCH

Inexpensive Burgundies; California Gamay Beaujolais and Pinot Noir.

SIMILAR CHEESES

Strong, flavored cheeses; try Gérômé.

Ermite

A Blue cheese from Canada produced from cow's milk, it has a good reputation.

Esrom

WHERE MADE

Denmark, in factories.

HOW MADE AND CURED

Type of milk: Pasteurized whole cow's milk.

Method and rind type: Semisoft; surface-ripened by bacteria; with gas holes; pressed; thin, washed rind.

Time cured: Matures quickly.

Fat content: 45 to 60 percent.

AROMA

Pronounced aroma, similar to monastery cheeses, emerges as cheese warms. Somewhat barnyardy.

FLAVOR

Flavor family: Monastery cheeses.

Taste: Mild, but with a strong earthy quality. Flavor and aroma vary with age from bland when young to pungent when aged.

Texture: Soft on tongue, sliceable, butterlike, pliable. The best examples cut like butter when room temperature.

APPEARANCE

Exterior: Practically rindless. Thin, yellowish to reddish-brown rind, slightly greasy to the touch; sometimes waxed. Usually wrapped in foil.

Interior: Color can range from pale yellow to white; has many small, irregularly shaped holes in lacy pattern.

Size and shape: Flat, rectangular shape; 8 inches long, 4 inches wide, 2 inches high; weight about 2½ pounds. Also comes in a small size—called Mini Esrom—with same shape, weighing about ½ to 1 pound.

BUYING HINTS

Danish cheeses are extremely reliable; however, because Esrom can be very strong, taste before buying. The packaging (or wax, if waxed) should be stamped with the name "Esrom" and the amount of fat content (45+). Wrapping around cheese should not be sticky. Cheese should not look dried out and should have a mild smell when cold. Often sold as Danish Port-Salut; Danish Saint-Paulin is the actual Danish copy of French Port-Salut.

USABLE LIFE

One month.

STORAGE AFTER PURCHASE

Keeps fresh for a fairly long time. Wrap airtight in plastic wrap. Refrigerate.

SERVING AND EATING

Good eating cheese for lunch or snacks. Danes claim it is delicious with pears and tomatoes; it also melts well. Can be good as a dessert cheese after a rich meal with strongly flavored food to finish a very strong and hearty red wine. Rind can be eaten.

BEVERAGE MATCH

Danish beer, sherry, vermouth, hearty red wines.

COMMENTS

Named for town in which it is made. This is *not* a copy of French Port-Salut, though it is often sold as such.

SIMILAR CHEESE

Tilsit.

Excelsior

A brand name of a French double-crème. See *Double-crème.*

Explorateur

A brand name of a French triple-crème. See *Triple-crème.*

Feta

WHERE MADE

Greece, in farms and factories. Widely copied elsewhere, including Denmark, Bulgaria, and the United States.

HOW MADE AND CURED

Type of milk: Sheep's milk, sometimes with goat's milk or even cow's milk mixed in. Pasteurized if shipped any distance.

Method and rind type: Soft, unpressed, uncooked, rindless cheese macerated in brine.

Time cured: Several days to one month.

Fat content: 40 percent.

AROMA

Fresh and briny; lactic.

FLAVOR

Flavor family: Sheep's milk.

Taste: Very salty, but spicy and tangy, a sort of milky-pickled taste. At best, delicious. Varies in quality.

Texture: Soft, creamy.

APPEARANCE

Exterior: Snow-white chunks, usually kept in brine or milk-and-brine.

Interior: Soft, moist, and crumbly.

Size and shape: Various sizes, from 2-pound chunks to 170-pound kegs packed in brine.

BUYING HINTS

Always taste; some Feta is so salty it makes your skin crawl. It should not be hard and dry, either, but reasonbly moist. It is almost always kept in a brine solution.

USABLE LIFE

Will keep in brine for months, but it is far better when reasonably fresh.

STORAGE AFTER PURCHASE

Keep it packed in original brine, or milk and salt water, or plain salt water. A plastic container is best. A damp cloth or a plastic bag will do if it will be consumed within a day or so. Refrigerate.

SERVING AND EATING

No better cheese could accompany Greek food; it is excellent from beginning to end as a side dish with crusty country breads. For snacks, match with citrus fruits.

BEVERAGE MATCH

An unfussy cheese, try it with any Greek wine or any inexpensive jug wine.

COMMENTS

Wildly popular in Greece, it is practically the national cheese; three-fourths of all cheese consumed in that country is one or another form of Feta. Its quality varies considerably with the maker, and much of it is eaten fresh.

SIMILAR CHEESE

Brinza.

Flotost, see *Gjetost.*

Fol Amour

A brand name of a French-cured double-crème type; rather similar to Caprice des Dieux. See *Caprice des Dieux.*

Fontainebleau, see *Fromage Frais.*

Fontal, see *Fontina.*

Fontina

WHERE MADE

Italy, in the Val d'Aosta of the Piedmont region; mostly in mountain chalets.

HOW MADE AND CURED

Type of milk: Originally made from sheep's milk, now primarily made from whole cow's milk.

Method and rind type: Semihard, cooked, pressed, with natural thin brushed rind.

Time cured: Four months.

Fat content: 45–50 percent.

AROMA

Faint, pleasant, oily.

FLAVOR

Flavor family: Bland and mild/Swiss type.

Taste: Pleasant, mild, yet flavorful and complex; nutty tang, like butternuts. Summer cheeses have a faint smoked flavor. An excellent cheese.

Texture: Plastic texture, firm yet soft, gives to touch, some resilience, creamy in mouth.

APPEARANCE

Exterior: Light-brown smoothish rind covered with thin layer of wax, giving the rind variations of lighter and darker brown. Stamped Italy.

Interior: Light ivory-yellow with a few very small irregular holes.

Size and shape: Flat, wheel shape, 13 to 16 inches in diameter, 3 to 4 inches thick, and weighing around 20 to 22 pounds.

BUYING HINTS

A number of imitations of this cheese are made, called Fontal, Fontinella, Fantina, and so on. The name "Fontina" is protected only in Italy, not in the United States. Only the Italian Fontina from the Val d'Aosta is the authentic Fontina and the best; it has a light-brown rind that looks somewhat like the rind on Gruyère. Imitations often have red rinds. The cheese should not have a bulging or swelling rind, should not be grainy, and should not have many or too large holes. It should look creamy, and the paste should be ivory-yellow, not a bright yellow. The summer-made Fontina, produced from May to September for consumption in September to January, is considered the best.

USABLE LIFE

Keeps creamy for several weeks in large piece. Older grating version keeps for months.

STORAGE AFTER PURCHASE

Wrap airtight in plastic wrap. Refrigerate.

SERVING AND EATING

Good eating cheese; good at end of meals as dessert cheese, especially after veal dishes; melts well, and is basis for fonduta, which is made with truffles and white wine. Old cheeses are grated for use as condiment or in cooking.

BEVERAGE MATCH

Soave for white wines, Bardolino for red wines.

COMMENTS

Name derives from oily nature of cheese. Thought to have been made as early as the eleventh century and to have been

served by the Duke of Savoy in the thirteenth century. Name
protected by law only in Italy.

SIMILAR CHEESES

Fontal, copies such as Danish Fontina.

Fourme d'Ambert   (also called Fourme de Montbrison, Fourme de Pierre-sur-Haute)

WHERE MADE

In the province of Auvergne, France; produced on farms
and in dairies.

HOW MADE AND CURED

Type of milk: Cow's.

Method and rind type: Soft, lightly pressed internal-mold
type with natural rind.

Time cured: Three to five months.

Fat content: 45 percent.

AROMA

A dank, somewhat musty smell.

FLAVOR

Flavor family: Blue.

Taste: A distinct, intense bite; tangy and savory. Sharper
than most French Bleus. A certain slight amount of bitterness is said to be characteristic.

Texture: Creamy, rich.

APPEARANCE

Exterior: White-gray mottled rind with red-brown pigmentation.

Interior: Well-distributed blue marbling against ivory-
white interior; a bit crumbly.

Size and shape: Tall cylinders 4½ inches across and 9
inches high, weighing about 3½ pounds.

BUYING HINTS

Beware of broken or gummy rinds, overcrumbly interiors,
and excessive saltiness or bitterness to the taste.

USABLE LIFE

Keeps well in large pieces if well-wrapped and well-stored.

STORAGE AFTER PURCHASE

Wrap in plastic wrap or damp cloth and refrigerate.

SERVING AND EATING

Simple meals, particularly interesting contrast on cheese
board. Serve with crusty bread, crackers, and sweet butter.

BEVERAGE MATCH

Sturdy, tannic country reds: Cahors, Châteauneuf-du-Pape, Barolo, Barbera, California Ruby Cabernet, Carignane.

COMMENTS

The Fourmes are mountain cheeses named after the shapes into which they are molded. Their distinct character is esteemed by some (not all) turophiles.

SIMILAR CHEESE

Bleu d'Auvergne.

Fromage Fondu (also called French Processed Cheese.)

WHERE MADE

France; factory-produced.

HOW MADE AND CURED

Type of milk: Cow's.

Method and rind type: Processed cheese; no rind.

Time cured: None.

Fat content: Varies from 40 to 60 percent.

AROMA

No smell, except flavoring.

FLAVOR

Flavor family: Bland, mild.

Taste: Extremely bland, uniform, and mild. Some are less boring than others. What interest there is is usually supplied by flavoring.

Texture: Plastic, gummy to vaguely creamy.

APPEARANCE

Exterior: Rindless, unless covered with herbs, nuts, and so forth; simply looks like ivory-white processed cheese.

Interior: Extremely uniform and plastic.

Size and shape: Often foil-wrapped in a variety of shapes, from miniature wedges (*en portions*) to large wheels and mounds. Often covered with grape seeds (*aux raisins*), walnuts (*aux noix*), almonds (burnt or unburnt), currants, pepper, pistachio nuts, hazelnuts, oranges, garlic, various herbs and various combinations of the above; kirsch-flavored types are, in this country, flavored with cherry juice. Flavored types also come in balls and layer-cake-type arrangements.

BUYING HINTS

Fromage Fondu comes plain or spiced under dozens of

brand names; Rambol, Beau Pasteur, Crème de Savoie, Crème de Gruyère, Nec Plus Ultra, Gourmandise, and so on. Perhaps the most famous brand is La Vache Qui Rit (Laughing Cow); all are alike, and almost always reliable, considering that processed cheese is far less perishable than natural cheese types. Nonetheless, be sure the cheese is fresh and hasn't been allowed to sit in a window display or otherwise mishandled. If possible, buy this type of cheese from bulk so that it can be sampled, rather than packaged types, which, due to their ingenious foil wrappings, are impossible to assess without tearing their wrappers.

USABLE LIFE

Forever is a long time, but these cheeses come as close to it as any in their stability; of course, the very creamy flavored types are more perishable than the indestructible little plain wedges and should be consumed within a month.

STORAGE AFTER PURCHASE

Foil-wrapped bite-sized bits need not be refrigerated, but can be left in their original packaging for months awaiting use. They should not be subjected to extremes of heat, however. Bigger portions of creamy and flavored types should be handled like natural cheese; refrigerated, to prevent loss of shape, and wrapped in plastic, to keep them from drying out.

SERVING AND EATING

The prewrapped cubes and wedges are ideal for hikes and picnics without gourmet pretensions. Larger-cut portions of Fromage Fondu are handy for snacks.

BEVERAGE MATCH

Coffee or tea, or for that matter, cocoa.

COMMENTS

Although most American processed cheese is made from a Cheddar base, most European processed cheeses—and this includes the French—are made from Gruyère, Emmentaler, and other Swiss-type cheeses. The highest-quality cheeses of these types naturally do not end up in the processing vats, but then there is nothing questionable about these cheeses; in fact, they are about as reliable, consistent, and uniform a cheese product as you can get. They are simply not very interesting.

SIMILAR CHEESE

Swiss Processed Gruyère.

Fromage Frais

WHERE MADE
France, produced in factories.

HOW MADE AND CURED
Type of milk: Pasteurized cow's milk.
Method and rind type: Fresh, unripened cheese. No rind.
Time cured: None.
Fat content: From 40 to 75 percent.

AROMA
Fresh.

FLAVOR
Flavor family: Fresh.
Taste: Mild and bland, lactic, often deliciously tangy and creamy.
Texture: Soft, curdy, creamy, frothy—texture largely depends on type.

APPEARANCE
Exterior: Rindless and prepackaged; exterior is no different from interior.
Interior: Usually moist, soft, and creamy, and pure white to ivory-white in color.
Size and shape: Depends on size and shape of container.

BUYING HINTS
Simply ensure that the cheese is indeed as fresh as possible and that it has not been mistreated in some fashion.

USABLE LIFE
Best consumed fresh, but will keep for a week or ten days.

STORAGE AFTER PURCHASE
Keep in original container and store in refrigerator.

SERVING AND EATING
Anytime; a delightful snack. Or serve as dessert with fresh fruit or preserves and sugar.

BEVERAGE MATCH
Coffee or tea.

COMMENTS
French fresh cheeses are in general more sour and tangy than fresh cheeses of the United States. There are several loose categories: Fromage Blanc is a sort of sour milk drained of whey, and called Fromage à la Crème when eaten with sugar or Coeur à la Crème when eaten with sugar and cream. Next in complexity is Demi-Sel (see the entry for this), a cream-cheese type with 40–45-percent butterfat, and, richer yet,

Petit-Suisse, a fresh double-crème (60-percent fat; see this entry). There are even fresh triple-crèmes; Fontainebleau is probably the best known of this very rich (75-percent fat) type of Fromage Frais.

SIMILAR CHEESES

All fresh cream-cheese types.

Fromage des Pyrénées

General name for various French cow and sheep-milk mountain cheeses produced in the Pyrenees region. Chiberta is probably the best known of these. See *Chiberta.*

Fromage à Raclette,   see *Raclette.*

Gammelost

WHERE MADE

Norway, mainly in the west country. The best is supposed to be from the counties of Hardanger and Sogn. Most is made in factories.

HOW MADE AND CURED

Type of milk: Sour skim milk.

Method and rind type: Semisoft, both internal-blue-mold ripening and surface ripening. Sometimes packed in straw soaked in juniper extract.

Time cured: Four weeks or longer.

Fat content: 4 percent.

AROMA

Pungent, blue-mold smell.

FLAVOR

Flavor family: Combination blue-veined cheeses and sour-milk cheeses.

Taste: Sharp, potent, lean. Definitely an acquired taste.

Texture: Crumbly, gets harder with age, dry.

APPEARANCE

Exterior: Brownish rind with grainy, rough look; wrapped in foil.

Interior: Brownish-yellow color throughout with blue-green veining distributed fairly evenly throughout. Color of cheese darkens with age.

Size and shape: Cylinder; 5–6 inches thick, 6 inches in diameter, weight 5–9 pounds.

BUYING HINTS

The cheese wrapping should be intact, with no stickiness evident. Although the cheese should be fairly dry, it should not crumble until cut. The mold should be well-outlined; the color of the cheese fairly uniform.

USABLE LIFE

One to two months.

STORAGE AFTER PURCHASE

Wrap in aluminum foil and put in plastic bag or box. Refrigerate.

SERVING AND EATING

Use a very thin sharp knife or fine wire cheese cutter to cut it, drawing it through cheese slowly to prevent crumbling. Serve with Norwegian flatbread or crispbread and butter.

BEVERAGE MATCH

Light Scandinavian beer.

COMMENTS

Gammelost means literally "old-fashioned cheese." The old-fashioned refers to the early method of making cheese with sour milk rather than using rennet to curdle it, a method that predates using rennet. Some claim the tradition of making this cheese dates to the Viking era. It is still made mostly in the western part of the country.

SIMILAR CHEESES

As unusual cheese related vaguely to other sour-milk cheeses, such as those of Germany. But those are not blue-veined, so the resemblance is not very great.

Gaperon (also called Gapron)

WHERE MADE

In the Auvergne province of France by small factories and farms.

HOW MADE AND CURED

Type of milk: Cow's milk, sometimes buttermilk.

Method and rind type: Pressed, uncooked, natural rind cheees flavored with garlic.

Time cured: About two months.

Fat content: 30 percent.

AROMA

Faintly garlicky.

FLAVOR
Flavor family: Spiced.
Taste: Rich, lingering garlic flavor; strong and rustic, but attractive.
Texture: Soft and yielding when mature.

APPEARANCE
Exterior: Blue-gray moldy, knobby rind tied with ribbon.
Interior: Ivory-white paste.
Size and shape: Small slightly flattened balls of about 8 ounces weight, and about 3 inches high.

BUYING HINTS
The rind, although moldy, should not be sticky or give off a rank odor. The feel of the cheese should be somewhat yielding, but not overly soft.

USABLE LIFE
Several weeks to a month or more if uncut. Gains in strength with age.

STORAGE AFTER PURCHASE
Refrigerate; wrap in plastic wrap or foil if cut.

SERVING AND EATING
Use for snacks or as an appetizer; adds drama to a cheese board. Serve with rustic breads.

BEVERAGE MATCH
Serve with strong, simple red wines, such as inexpensive Rhônes or California Ruby Cabernet.

COMMENTS
Although perhaps unappetizing in appearance to the beginning cheese enthusiast, this can be a very tasty and unusual cheese if not too old, and is low in butterfat as well.

SIMILAR CHEESE
Gérômé.

Gérômé

WHERE MADE
In the province of Lorraine, France; produced in dairies.

HOW MADE AND CURED
Type of milk: Cow's, usually pasteurized.
Method and rind type: Soft; washed rind.
Time cured: One to four months, depending on size.
Fat content: 45–50 percent.

AROMA
A strong, redolent, smelly cheese when aged.

FLAVOR

Flavor family: Strong.

Taste: Rather strong, savory taste as well as aroma, something like a Münster, but heavier. Spiced specimens—such as those treated with aniseed or cumin—are correspondingly spicy as well.

Texture: Smooth and pastelike, even unctuous, particularly with age.

APPEARANCE

Exterior: Deep orange-red mottled, washed rind.

Interior: Yellow-ivory paste.

Size and shape: Fat disks 4 to 8 inches across and 1 to 1½ inches thick, weighing from ½ pound to 3½ pounds.

BUYING HINTS

Should not be chalky in consistency or have a hard center, a sign of unripeness; nor should it be overripe to the point of runniness and rank odor.

USABLE LIFE

Keeps well if wrapped and properly stored, but will continue to develop strength, particularly if not cut into.

STORAGE AFTER PURCHASING

Wrap in plastic and refrigerate; to prevent smell from spreading, put into airtight jar or plastic container.

SERVING AND EATING

Géromé is eaten locally, like Münster, before it completely ripens and while it is comparatively mild. In such a condition, it could make, in small amounts, an interesting appetizer with spiced or flavored crackers; in full ripened glory, serve it at the end of a spicy meal, with crusty bread.

BEVERAGE MATCH

Try Alsatian Gewürztraminer when the cheese is young, or sturdy full-bodied red wines when the cheese is ripe.

COMMENTS

One of the oldest cheeses of France, it is named after its place of origin, Gérardmer. The unflavored Géromés are close cousins to Münster (see *Münster*).

SIMILAR CHEESE

Münster.

Gervais

A brand name under which several French fresh and cream cheeses are sold. See *Petit-Suisse*.

Gex, see *Bleu du Haut Jura.*

Gjetost

WHERE MADE
Norway, in factories.

HOW MADE AND CURED
Type of milk: A whey cheese made from 10-percent goat's milk whey and 90-percent cow's milk whey. Formerly and now sometimes made from only goat's milk whey. A version is also made from 100-percent cow's milk whey.

Method and rind type: Hard, cooked whey cheese with milk sugar and fats added; unripened.

Time cured: None.

Fat content: 33 percent.

AROMA
Faint.

FLAVOR
Flavor family: Whey cheeses.

Taste: Sweet, almost like chocolate fudge with butterscotch tang; mild, slightly salty. Doesn't taste at all like what one thinks of as a cheese. For some, an acquired taste; for others, a delight.

Texture: Finely grainy, close, buttery consistency in the mouth. Almost creamy in mouth after it has warmed.

APPEARANCE
Exterior: No rind, exterior is same light-brown color as interior; texture looks the same as interior—looks like small, hard bar of soap; wrapped in foil.

Interior: Light-brown color, similar to the color of caramels, throughout; smooth, close texture.

Size and shape: Small rectangular blocks, usually 8 ounces or 1 pound.

BUYING HINTS
An extremely reliable cheese with good keeping quality if well-stored. Wrapping should be clean, not sticky or brown where in contact with the cheese; cheese should be of a uniform color throughout, with no off-color spots.

When made from 100-percent goat's milk whey, labeled Ekte (genuine) Gjetost; when made only from cow's milk whey, labeled Mysost; when 10-percent whole milk or buttermilk or cream added to whey, cheese is labeled Primost or

Flotost (these are softer than Gjetost). When made by same
method, but from cow's milk rather than whey, called Gomost.

USABLE LIFE

Keeps indefinitely if wrapped well; will dry out if not
wrapped airtight.

STORAGE AFTER PURCHASE

Wrap airtight in aluminum foil and refrigerate.

SERVING AND EATING

Use a cheese slicer when serving; slice in very thin slices.
Serve with butter and slightly sweet crackers, especially En-
glish sweet digestive biscuits. Also good on Norwegian or
Swedish flatbread. Serve for snacks or at end of smorgasbord.

BEVERAGE MATCH

Very good with rich coffee.

COMMENTS

Name comes from words *gjet* (meaning goat) and *ost*
(meaning cheese). For the past one hundred years, it has
been the national cheese of Norway. Name is pronounced
"Yay-toast." Gjetost is very highly nutritious and, because
of the added milk sugar, an extremely good source of energy.
An excellent cheese to take on hikes and backpacking.

SIMILAR CHEESES

The variations Mysost, Flotost, and Gomost.

Glaren Schabzieger, see *Sapsago.*

Glarenkäse, see *Sapsago.*

Gloucester, Double and Single (also called Double and Single Berkeley)

WHERE MADE

Gloucestershire, England, in the vales of Gloucester and
Berkeley; made in factories.

HOW MADE AND CURED

Type of milk: Primarily whole pasteurized cow's milk.

Method and rind type: Hard, uncooked, pressed; natural
rind, traditionally bluish-black, then rubbed with red dyes;
now some wrapped in cloth and waxed, some in rindless
blocks.

Time cured: Three to four months for Double; six weeks for Single.

Fat content: 45 percent.

AROMA

Pleasant, light bouquet when young, gaining intensity with age.

FLAVOR

Flavor family: Mellow Cheddar type.

Taste: Rich, smooth, monotone flavor. Rather like Cheddar; can be slightly acid and pungent when mature; clean and distinctively mellow. Single Gloucester has mild fresh flavor, but is undistinguished.

Texture: Very firm and smooth, moist; satiny.

APPEARANCE

Exterior: Rind is blue with reddish tint; now sometimes waxed.

Interior: Most imported Gloucester is dark orange, darkening toward rind, although it may be a warm yellow-gold. Traditionally it was and is straw-colored. It looks buttery and open in texture. Single Gloucester is cream-colored.

Size and shape: Flat wheel, 14 inches in diameter, 6 inches high, weighing about 30 pounds; also rindless blocks. Single Gloucester is half as high and weighs half as much.

BUYING HINTS

Varies greatly. Taste before buying. Should not look greasy or grainy. Color of interior should be uniform. Rind should not be cracked or bulge or swell. The best is made in August. Single Gloucester is not usually available in this country, as it is consumed when young.

USABLE LIFE

Ready to eat at three to four months; matured to six months, develops a strong flavor; many claim it is at its best between six months and one year. Well-wrapped cheeses keep well. Single Gloucester does not keep well beyond a few weeks.

STORAGE AFTER PURCHASE

Wrap airtight in plastic wrap or damp cloth dipped in water mixed with small amount of vinegar. Refrigerate.

SERVING AND EATING

Good eating cheese. Good with fresh bread and butter; especially good with crisp lettuce and other crispy raw vegetables. Fine for sandwiches, snacks, and so on.

BEVERAGE MATCH

English ale or beer, red Burgundy and Bordeaux for best examples, or even Madeira; traditionally cherry wine.

COMMENTS

Originally made from milk of Gloucester cows, noted for the richness of their milk but small yield. Gloucester cheese is now made from thinner milk, as Gloucester breed has almost died out. In the past, the Single Gloucester was not nearly so fine a cheese as the Double Gloucester. Probably the cheese known today as Double Gloucester is not as rich and distinctive as its predecessor.

Color of Gloucester rinds has changed throughout history. Early on, the curing-room floor was rubbed with herbs twice a month until it was wet and black; as the cheeses sat on this and were turned twice a week, the rind became bluish-black. Later, in the eighteenth century, merchants encouraged dairywomen to find some means of making Gloucester cheese more distinguishable, so the women began staining the surface of the rind reddish-brown. In the past the arrival of spring in the town of Gloucester was celebrated by honoring Gloucester cheese. Flowers were placed on large cheeses that were carried around the streets and rolled three times around the churchyard before eating. Now the festival involves only eating cheese.

SIMILAR CHEESES

Derby, Leicester.

Gomost, see *Gjetost.*

Gomser, see *Raclette.*

Gorgonzola

WHERE MADE

Italy, mainly in areas around Milan, Pavia, and Cremona in Lombardy, and in Piedmont; in factories; also copied in the United States.

HOW MADE AND CURED

Type of milk: Unpasteurized whole cow's milk.

Method and rind type: Semisoft, internal-mold ripened, with natural rind that has been scraped and washed.

Time cured: Three to six months, sometimes one year.

Fat content: 48–50 percent.

AROMA

Strong mold smell and somewhat barnyardy scent.

FLAVOR

Flavor family: Blue.

Taste: Stronger than other Blue cheeses: gamy, spicy, super-savory and tangy, piquant and rich.

Texture: Very soft and creamy texture, almost runny. Spreads better than other Blues, more malleable; becomes firmer with age.

APPEARANCE

Exterior: Reddish-gray, smoothish rind, wrapped in foil.

Interior: Creamy, lightish-yellow paste with well-distributed greenish-blue veins, more pale-greenish than blue; very soft-looking, veins have almost blurry look.

Size and shape: Cylinder with 10- to 12-inch diameter, 6- to 8-inch height, weighing about 14 to 17½ pounds.

BUYING HINTS

The cheese should be a creamy color, not yellow; it should have well-defined veins, although they may have a blurry, not quite distinct, soft look. The cheese near the rind should not be dark, crumbly, or hard. The cheese should not look dry. The texture should not be gummy, and the taste should have no bitterness.

USABLE LIFE

Keeps well, but continues to age and strengthen in flavor, even after being cut. Will keep about two weeks before it begins to turn stronger.

STORAGE AFTER PURCHASE

Wrap in damp cloth and put in plastic box. Refrigerate.

SERVING AND EATING

Cut with any sharp knife. Serve at end of meals, especially after game, duck, or other very richly flavored meal. It is very good with peaches or grapes. Good on plain crackers or Italian bread with butter, especially if it is particularly salty.

BEVERAGE MATCH

Robust reds are best: Barolo, Barbaresco, Barbera, and fine, full-bodied French reds.

COMMENTS

Named for village near Milan where Gorgonzola is thought to have been made first. Legend has it that it was made in Po Valley first in about A.D. 879, and that it was originally a white cheese that accidentally developed mold when stored in a cellar. It is generally considered one of the great cheeses of the world.

SIMILAR CHEESES

Mycella; American imitations made in Wisconsin, especially Stella brand.

Gouda

WHERE MADE

South Holland. Made in factories and on farms.

HOW MADE AND CURED

Type of milk: Pasteurized whole cow's milk is used in factories; unpasteurized whole cow's milk is used on farms.

Method and rind type: Semihard, pressed, uncooked, with a natural thin yellow rind that is brushed.

Time cured: Two to three months. Some are aged longer periods of time, up to six to twelve months, in specially heated drying rooms.

Fat content: By law, at least 48 percent. Sometimes up to 51 percent.

AROMA

Fresh; aged smells slightly oily and stronger.

FLAVOR

Flavor family: Bland and mild.

Taste: Creamy and bland, mellow-tasting; buttery. Gives the impression of solidness, sturdiness, and wholesomeness. The aged has a powerful, tangy, nutty taste; an aged farmhouse Gouda at its best can be a great cheese, with a slightly salty, dry, penetrating, and long-lasting flavor.

Texture: Springy, close-knit, smooth, and soft. Aged is granular and slightly dry and crumbly, yet with a smooth feel in the mouth.

APPEARANCE

Exterior: Coated in red or yellow wax and wrapped in cellophane. Baby Goudas come only in red coating.

Interior: Cheese is light-straw color turning to deeper yellow and hard-looking near rind; texture looks creamy-smooth with irregular small holes scattered evenly throughout. Sides of young Gouda are particularly rounded. Aged Gouda is faded straw-yellow, darkening as it continues to age, and has a more granular, dry, firm texture; sides of aged cheese are more sharply defined.

Size and shape: Flat wheel with rounded, convex edges; comes in varying sizes—large size, 10 to 12 pounds; baby Goudas, 10, 14, and 20 ounces.

BUYING HINTS

True Gouda from Holland is marked under the wax coating; factory Gouda is marked with a circle inside which the words "Holland," "Gouda," "Volvet" (full fat) and percentage of fat, and numbers and letters indicating the factory and date manufactured are stamped. Farmhouse Gouda is stamped with the word "Boerenkaas," meaning "farmer's cheese." There is also a salt-free version that is fairly flavorful. One of the safest cheeses to buy, Gouda is nearly always extremely reliable. If the cheese looks good, it will be good. The wax coating should be intact, with no blemishes or spots showing on it; the cheese should show no off-color spots, no fissures, and should not crumble. The texture should be even. The cheese should show no sweat marks. Summer and autumn are the best seasons for farmhouse cheese.

USABLE LIFE

Gouda is one of the best-keeping cheeses. It has a long life and will continue to age if not cut. It can be eaten from the age of two months to two or three years.

STORAGE AFTER PURCHASE

Wrap airtight in plastic wrap; refrigerate.

SERVING AND EATING

Good eating cheese served in slices at all meals in Holland. It is especially good with rye or pumpernickel bread, in open-faced sandwiches, or plain as a snack. It is not recommended for cooking, but the aged variety can often be grated for a garnish on cooked foods.

BEVERAGE MATCH

Extremely good with coffee, Dutch or German beer, or light and fruity red and white wines.

COMMENTS

Gouda is named for the market town near Rotterdam where the cheese originated. It dates from the Middle Ages and was exported to other European countries as early as the thirteenth century. Gouda cheeses are still, as they were in the past, taken on barges to Alkmaar, a medieval town, where they are sold in the town square. There is a cumin-spiced version and a salt-free version imported as well.

SIMILAR CHEESES

Edam, other nonspiced Dutch cheeses.

Gourmandise

A brand of French processed cheese. See *Fromage Fondu*.

Gournay, see *Neufchâtel*.

Gräddost

WHERE MADE
Sweden, in factories and on farms.

HOW MADE AND CURED
Type of milk: Pasteurized whole cow's milk; some on farms made with unpasteurized milk.
Method and rind type: Semihard, pressed; paraffined.
Time cured: About two months.
Fat content: 60 percent.

AROMA
Fresh, mild.

FLAVOR
Flavor family: Bland and mild.
Taste: Very mild, sweet, buttery, tangy, fresh; best examples have penetrating, complex flavor.
Texture: Very pliable and soft in mouth; sliceable.

APPEARANCE
Exterior: Wax or paraffin or plastic film over very thin yellowish rind with tendency to greasiness.
Interior: Open texture with small, irregularly shaped holes; a light-buttery-yellow color.
Size and shape: Cylinder in varying sizes; also available in rectangular blocks.

BUYING HINTS
A reliable cheese. Look for the amount of fat content stamped on the rind: only cheese with minimum 60-percent-fat content can be called Gräddost in Sweden. The cheese should be of uniform color throughout, the holes should be small, the cheese should look moist and fresh. The taste should be smooth and not bitter.

USABLE LIFE
One month.

STORAGE AFTER PURCHASE
Wrap airtight in plastic wrap. Refrigerate.

SERVING AND EATING

Good eating cheese. Serve on Swedish limpa bread with sweet butter. Excellent with fruit.

BEVERAGE MATCH

Light lager beer; light, fruity red wines; German wines.

COMMENTS

The name means "butter cheese."

SIMILAR CHEESES

American Brick, Maribo.

Grana Padano

Made in Italy in various northern Italian towns, particularly in the Po Valley. Grana is a generic name for a group of hard cheeses that have a special granular texture and are mostly used in grated form. There are two especially good ones in Italy—Grana Padano and Parmigiano-Reggiano (which see). The Grana Padano cheeses are sometimes as good as the Parmigiano-Reggiano cheeses, but not always. They come from a less tightly controlled area and thus the milk they are made from is less uniform; they may be sold before they have been aged as long as the Parmigiano-Reggiano cheeses; they may be made year round; and other than the first-quality cheeses may be exported. In all these ways they differ from the Parmigiano-Reggiano cheeses. Otherwise, they are very similar—very hard, with an intense, sharp flavor and a rough, grainy texture and surface. Padano means "of the Po Valley."

Green Cheese, see *Sapsago*.

Gruyère

WHERE MADE

Switzerland, in the cantons of Fribourg, Vaud, and Neufchâtel; made in Alpine and valley dairies; also made in France (see *Comté*).

HOW MADE AND CURED

Type of milk: Unpasteurized whole cow's milk.

Method and rind type: Hard, pressed, cooked; with a natural rind kept moist with brine; some surface ripening may also occur.

Time cured: Five to twelve months.

Fat content: 47–49 percent.

AROMA

Considerable pleasant nutty bouquet.

FLAVOR

Flavor family: Swiss cheeses.

Taste: Long moist, sweet, nutty flavor; succulent; aged examples have much depth of flavor. Clean, mountain taste, saltier and creamier than Emmentaler. Swiss Gruyère is sweeter than the French. The French is tangier and fruitier than the Swiss. Taste depends greatly on age.

Texture: Firm.

APPEARANCE

Exterior: Light-brown wrinkled rind, although the wrinkles are fairly smooth; rind is slightly greasy, unlike the dry rind of Emmentaler.

Interior: Pale-ivory-yellow color to light-brownish-gold, similar to Emmentaler, with the size varying from pea size to cherrystone size. They are fairly far apart. Sometimes small cracks appear in the paste. The surface has a smooth, oily appearance.

Size and shape: Wheel-shaped, with a 24-inch diameter, 4-inch height, and 70- to 90-pound weight.

BUYING HINTS

Swiss cheeses are fairly reliable; Swiss law prohibits the use of artificial additives, coloring agents, and milk from cows fed on silage. The rind of Gruyère should be even, with no cracks, and although it should be tough, it should not be too thick or have a grayish-yellow subcrust. The rind should be slightly greasy, not dry, but the surface of the paste should not be greasy. Watch out for fissures and cracks beneath the rind, a sandy, grainy texture, and splits in the cheese paste. Holes showing a little moisture in them (called weeping) indicate a fully matured Gruyère of excellent quality. Since strength of flavor depends on age, sample before buying. Young specimens lack character. French Gruyère is very similar to the Swiss and quite as good.

USABLE LIFE

Best between five and ten months, but if uncut will continue to age. If cut, will keep about one month.

STORAGE AFTER PURCHASE

Wrap airtight in plastic wrap; refrigerate.

SERVING AND EATING

Excellent eating cheese. Good with French bread and butter for snacks, lunches, and after a meal of veal or chicken. Melts well; a main ingredient in Swiss fondue and in other dishes, such as quiches.

BEVERAGE MATCH

Delicious with coffee, fruity white wines of Switzerland, and light fruity red wines. Californa Chenin Blanc, Alsatian and California Sylvaners, and German white wines would all be good choices.

COMMENTS

Named after the region of Gruyère in the canton of Fribourg. The earliest mention of a cheese named Gruyère dates from the twelfth century. At that time the Count of Gruyère began taxing each cheese from the area in order to pay for the construction of an abbey, the Abbey of Rougemont. The cheese, however, has changed considerably in character through the centuries.

French Gruyère dates from about the same time as the Swiss; it is not an imitation, but an equal cousin of Swiss Gruyère (see *Comté*).

SIMILAR CHEESES

Comté, Swiss Emmentaler.

Handkäse (also called Hand Cheese)

WHERE MADE

Germany, mainly around area of Mainz and Frankfort and in north central area; in factories. Made in Austria as well. Also made in Pennsylvania in area settled by Germans and in some factories in Wisconsin and New York.

HOW MADE AND CURED

Type of milk: Skimmed sour milk or skimmed milk mixed with buttermilk.

Method and rind type: Soft, surface-ripened, kneaded and molded by hand, pressed, then dried.

Time cured: Six to eight weeks.

Fat content: Low fat; by law must be less than 10 percent.

AROMA

Strong, pungent, increases with age; usually stronger than Limburger.

FLAVOR

Flavor family: Mild to strong/sour milk.

Taste: Taste varies, depending on age, from mild to very pungent and strong, but is milder than aroma would lead one to believe. An acquired taste for most.

Texture: Soft, almost spreadable.

APPEARANCE

Exterior: Smooth, golden-yellow to reddish-brown thin surface rind; some covered with mold that can be eaten.

Interior: Whitish-yellow to pale-yellow color with thick, gelatinous, plastic texture.

Size and shape: There are different shapes and sizes—all are small; most are round and flat; some are shaped like fat fingers.

BUYING HINTS

Sometimes these cheeses are sold too old. They should look good—that is, appetizing—plump, soft, resilient and yielding, not hard or concave and sunken. Although the smell will be very strong, it should not have a rotten odor. The paper in which the cheese is wrapped (if it is packaged) should not be sticky or brown.

USABLE LIFE

Two weeks after purchase.

STORAGE AFTER PURCHASE

Wrap airtight in plastic wrap. To keep smell from spreading throughout refrigerator, put the wrapped cheese into an airtight jar or container.

SERVING AND EATING

Serve strong cheeses together on a plate or board separate from other cheeses being served. Don't serve them on an old wooden cheese board—the wood may absorb the smell of the cheese and it will be hard to scrub off. Marble cheese slabs are best. Good with slices of onion, radishes, pumpernickel bread, and beer. The traditional German way of eating Hand Cheese is to put bits of it in a mug of beer, swirl it around until it melts, and then drink the concoction.

BEVERAGE MATCH

The stronger the cheese, the stronger the beer to accompany it. Serve light, spicy Munich-style beers with milder cheeses and dark, malty beers' with more piquant ones.

COMMENTS

Name derives from the fact that the cheese was shaped by hand-molding. Although most are now made in factories, in some areas the cheese is still shaped by hand.

These cheeses have a very high protein content.

Hand Cheese is made in the United States, especially by Pennsylvanians of German ancestry, and in Latin America, especially in Venezuela.

SIMILAR CHEESES

Limburger, Romadurkäse.

Harzerkäse

A very tiny Hand Cheese made in the Harz Mountains of Germany and named for them. See *Handkäse*.

Havarti   (formerly called Danish Tilsit)

WHERE MADE

Denmark, in factories.

HOW MADE AND CURED

Type of milk: Pasteurized whole cow's milk.

Method and rind type: Semisoft; ripened by bacteria, with gas holes; pressed; thin, washed rind.

Time cured: Two to three months.

Fat content: 45-percent minimum; there is an extra creamy Havarti with 60-percent minimum.

AROMA

Aromatic; with age, monasterylike aroma increases in intensity.

FLAVOR

Flavor family: Bland and mild/monastery.

Taste: Mild and slightly acid when young; full-flavored, sharp and gamy when mature; particularly distinct aftertaste.

Texture: Open texture; moist; firm; sliceable; 60-percent Havarti is creamier and softer.

APPEARANCE

Exterior: Thin, dark-yellowish rind with tendency to be greasy; sometimes rindless. Sometimes waxed. Usually wrapped in foil. Sixty-percent Havarti is rindless, usually vacuum-packed.

Interior: Pure yellow to white in color; numerous irregularly shaped holes of varying sizes. Sixty-percent Havarti has smaller holes and is usually lighter in color.

Size and shape: Various shapes and sizes. Flat, round shape is about 10 inches in diameter, 4 inches high, and weighs about 11 pounds. Rectangular loaf shapes weigh from

½ to 11 pounds. Sixty-percent Havarti comes in rectangular loaf shapes or small cylinders.

BUYING HINTS

Since age determines strength and pungency of flavor, taste before buying. The packaging (or wax or rind) should be stamped with the name "Havarti" and the amount of fat content (45+).

Wrapping around the cheese should not be sticky. Cheese should not look dried out and should have mild smell when cold. Rind should look even and not have blemishes.

USABLE LIFE

One month or longer, but gains in strength with age.

STORAGE AFTER PURCHASE

Keeps well. Wrap airtight in plastic wrap. Refrigerate.

SERVING AND EATING

Good eating cheese; excellent on pumpernickel and other rich, flavorful breads. Danish think it is excellent accompaniment to salads and raw vegetables such as radishes, tomatoes, cucumbers, celery, and olives. Not a dessert cheese.

BEVERAGE MATCH

Best with Danish and German beer.

COMMENTS

Name changed about fifteen years ago at international conference. Named for the farm, Havarti, where Mrs. Hanne Nielson, who pioneered the making of this cheese, lived. Havarti is on the island of Zealand near Copenhagen. Hanne Nielson is actually responsible for the growth of most of the Danish cheese industry. In the mid-nineteenth century she traveled throughout Europe to learn how cheeses were made in various countries. Upon her return, she attempted to copy some of these.

SIMILAR CHEESES

Esrom, German Tilsit.

Herrgärdsost

WHERE MADE

Sweden, in factories.

HOW MADE AND CURED

Type of milk: Pasteurized, partly skimmed cow's milk; sometimes made with whole cow's milk.

Method and rind type: Hard, cooked, pressed cheese with natural rind, usually waxed.

Time cured: Three to four months; four to six months for whole-milk cheese.

Fat content: Ranges from 30 to 45 percent.

AROMA

Pleasant, faint; mild nutty aroma develops as it ages.

FLAVOR

Flavor family: Swiss type.

Taste: Delicate, mild, nutty, sweet when young; gains in sharpness and complexity of flavor as it ages.

Texture: Medium firm, pliable, not as hard as Swiss Emmentaler.

APPEARANCE

Exterior: Thin, yellowish wax coating.

Interior: Pale-yellow-white color with smooth, close-grained texture. Has a few largish round holes, similar to those in Gruyère. Number of holes less numerous than those in Swiss Emmentaler.

Size and shape: Cylinder, about 14 inches in diameter and 4 to 6 inches high, weighing 26 to 40 pounds.

BUYING HINTS

The whole-milk variety is called Herrgård Elite; it resembles Swiss Emmentaler more than the skimmed-milk variety does. When fully aged at about twelve months, the eyes, or holes, will weep when the cheese is cut—a sign of quality. Weeping consists in showing a little moisture in the eyes.

The cheese should have the fat content and date of manufacture stamped on the rind or wax.

A fairly reliable cheese; the surface of it should not have a greasy feel. The texture of an aged cheese may be brittle, but there should not be many small cracks in the cheese paste. The color of the paste should be uniform; the holes should not be oval.

USABLE LIFE

One to two months if cut; up to one and a half years if uncut. Although sold young, the cheese is not truly mature before about twelve months.

STORAGE AFTER PURCHASE

Wrap airtight in plastic wrap and refrigerate.

SERVING AND EATING

Good eating cheese. Excellent in sandwiches with ham and smoked meats, good on flatbread, crispbread, and rye bread. It also melts well.

BEVERAGE MATCH

Serve with Swedish beer or stout, light red or dry white wines.

COMMENTS

One of the most popular cheeses in Sweden, it has been made since the 1890s. Until recently, it was primarily made on farms or in homes—its name means "manor cheese," indicating its origins. It used to be claimed that the best Herrgårdsost was from west Gotland. A copy of Swiss Emmentaler, but with a taste of its own.

SIMILAR CHEESES

Danish Emmental, Jarlsberg.

Jarlsberg

WHERE MADE

Norway, in factories.

HOW MADE AND CURED

Type of milk: Pasteurized whole cow's milk.

Method and rind type: Hard, cooked, pressed, ripened by bacteria, with gas holes; thick, natural rind.

Time cured: Three to six months.

Fat content: 45 percent.

AROMA

Sweetish, lactic aroma.

FLAVOR

Flavor family: Swiss type.

Taste: Fairly bland, mild, nutty. Sharpens somewhat as ages, but not much. Does not have the complex taste of Swiss Emmentaler.

Texture: Firm, somewhat elastic, sliceable; softer in mouth than Swiss Emmentaler.

APPEARANCE

Exterior: Thick natural rind, waxed with yellow wax.

Interior: Pale-whitish-yellow color; many rounded holes of varying sizes, mostly fairly large, Smooth, close texture.

Size and shape: Flat wheels and blocks weighing about 20 pounds.

BUYING HINTS

Fairly reliable cheese. The rind should be tough and thick, but not too thick, and it should not have a yellow-gray subcrust. The surface of the cheese should not have a greasy feel or look.

USABLE LIFE

Keeps one or two months in large piece if properly wrapped. If uncut, keeps a year or two.

STORAGE AFTER PURCHASE

Wrap airtight in plastic wrap; refrigerate.

SERVING AND EATING

Good eating cheese. Especially good for sandwiches and snacks, with ham, smoked meats, and sausages. Serve in thin slices with Norwegian flatbread or whole-wheat bread. Also good for cooking.

BEVERAGE MATCH

Scandinavian beer; fruity red and white wines.

COMMENTS

The name "Jarlsberg" comes from that of an old estate where cheesemaking began supposedly hundreds of years ago. The estate is located on the western shore of the Oslo Fjord.

Extremely popular, and now imitated in other countries, Jarlsberg is often the cheese Americans think of when they think of Swiss cheese, and is closer to American Swiss than to Switzerland Swiss.

SIMILAR CHEESES

American Swiss, Finnish Swiss, Danish Emmental.

Kashkaval (also called Kaskaval)

WHERE MADE

Bulgaria and Romania; widely copied elsewhere, particularly in Yugoslavia and Greece; both farm- and factory-produced.

HOW MADE AND CURED

Type of milk: Sheep, and occasionally cow's milk.

Method and rind type: Hard, drawn-curd cheese with very thin natural-rind cheese.

Time cured: One to three months.

Fat content: 30 percent.

AROMA

Pronounced, attractive, sour, sheep smell; vaguely like Provolone.

FLAVOR

Flavor family: Sheep-Cheddar type.

Taste: Unusual peppery-tangy taste; attractive.

Texture: Creamy Cheddar texture; soft in mouth, faintly mealy.

APPEARANCE

Exterior: Negligible cream-colored rind.

Interior: Cream-colored, moist-looking, faint granular quality.

Size and shape: Comes in various sizes, commonly fat wheels 5 to 8 inches across and 3 inches thick, weighing from 4½ to 6½ pounds.

BUYING HINTS

Taste first for flavor and to ensure that it is neither too dried out or too crumbly. Some examples are also too salty.

USABLE LIFE

Will keep for weeks if properly stored.

STORAGE AFTER PURCHASE

Wrap securely in plastic wrap and refrigerate.

SERVING AND EATING

Particularly good with spicy cuisines of Eastern Europe, but makes a fine snack and adds interest to a cheese board. Serve with dark breads.

BEVERAGE MATCH

Try it with spicy Hungarian white wines or good European beers.

COMMENTS

A similar cheese is called Katschkawalj in Bulgaria and Zomma in Turkey. All these are distantly related to Caciocavallo by method and style, though not milk type.

SIMILAR CHEESE

Kasseri.

Kasseri

WHERE MADE

Greece; copied in the United States and elsewhere. Farm- and factory-produced.

HOW MADE AND CURED

Type of milk: Sheep's or goat's milk.

Method and rind type: Hard, pressed, uncooked; thin, natural rind.

Time cured: Two months.

Fat content: 40 percent.

AROMA

Milky-sour; savory.

FLAVOR

Flavor family: Mild sheep.

Taste: Rather pronounced sheep-milk flavor; oily; attractive.

Texture: Moist, light, slightly mealy in mouth.

APPEARANCE

Exterior: Smooth ivory rind with faint pinkish blotches.

Interior: Cream-colored, with occasional tiny irregular holes. Fairly firm to touch.

Size and shape: Flat round wheels averaging 20 pounds in weight.

BUYING HINTS

Sample first; beware of overly sour taste and smell, which can be unpleasant. Watch out for excessively dry and crumbly texture.

USABLE LIFE

Will keep for weeks if properly stored. Best when young and moist.

STORAGE AFTER PURCHASE

Wrap in plastic wrap and refrigerate.

SERVING AND EATING

With Greek meals and plenty of crusty bread, or to add interest to cheese tray.

BEVERAGE MATCH

Not a fussy cheese; try it with Greek wines, even Retsina.

COMMENTS

The U.S. version is considered quite good.

SIMILAR CHEESE

Kashkaval.

Katschkawalj, see *Kashkaval.*

La Grappe (also called Grape Cheese or Fromage Fondu aux Raisins)

A French processed cheese covered with a hard inedible rind of grape pips and skins.

See *Fromage Fondu.*

Lancashire

WHERE MADE

Lancashire, England; best from the Fylde, an area bordering the Irish Sea. Almost all made in factories.

HOW MADE AND CURED

Type of milk: Whole or partly skimmed pasteurized cow's milk.

Method and rind type: Hard, uncooked,, pressed; natural rind. Traditionally bathed in whey butter.

Time cured: One to two months.

Fat content: About 40 percent.

AROMA

Faint, pleasant, increasing with age.

FLAVOR

Flavor family: Mild Cheddar type.

Taste: Stronger, sharper flavor than Cheddar or Cheshire, but still mild.

Texture: Crumbly, softer, and moister than Cheddar or Cheshire, spreads easily when three months old. Hardens with age, but retains loose texture.

APPEARANCE

Exterior: Natural rind, uncolored.

Interior: Some colored orange, some yellow-white; buttery, open texture.

Size and shape: Flat wheel, 8 inches high by 14 inches across; weight, 40 pounds.

BUYING HINTS

Lancashire travels poorly, so few good examples are seen. Taste before buying. Should not be dried out or uneven in texture or color. Rind should not bulge or swell or be cracked.

USABLE LIFE

Matures rapidly. Use between one and four months; best eating when two to three months old. Does not keep well long once cut.

STORAGE AFTER PURCHASE

Wrap airtight in plastic wrap or damp cloth dipped in mixture of water and small amount of vinegar. Seal pores by running flat of knife across cut surface. Refrigerate.

SERVING AND EATING

The best cheese to use for cooking and in Welsh rarebit. When cooked, has consistency of hot custard; toasts to a rich brown color. Its soft texture and sharp flavor make it excellent for all melting purposes. Good, for example, for Sauce Mornay. Also good eating cheese with bread, butter, and sweet pickles.

BEVERAGE MATCH

Ale goes best with Welsh rarebit; beer; fruity red wines; traditionally cherry wine.

COMMENTS

Most is consumed locally. Called Leigh Toaster in old cookery books, this is the cheese most writers meant when they talked about "toasted cheese."

SIMILAR CHEESES

Cheshire, Leicester.

La Vache Qui Rit

A brand of French processed cheese. See *Fromage Fondu.*

Leicester

WHERE MADE

Leicestershire, England; almost all made in factories.

HOW MADE AND CURED

Type of milk: Pasteurized whole cow's milk.

Method and rind type: Hard, uncooked, pressed; natural rind.

Time cured: Ten to twelve weeks; fully ripe at six months.

Fat content: About 45 percent.

AROMA

Pleasant, light aroma.

FLAVOR

Flavor family: Medium Cheddar type.

Taste: Mild when young; strong, rich, and tangy yet mellow and creamy when aged, with a hint of lemon in the flavor.

Texture: Loose and flaky, yet creamy in the mouth.

APPEARANCE

Exterior: Thin, smooth natural rind; can be waxed or paraffined.

Interior: Brilliant to dark orange in color, depending on age. No holes, but it has what looks like fine lines or cracks through it when aged. Darkens near edge of rind.

Size and shape: Flat wheel, of varying sizes from 7 to 40 pounds; usually diameter is three times height.

BUYING HINTS

Leicester sometimes develops unevenly; watch out for white marks on the interior surface that indicate unpleasant, strong patches of flavor. There should not be white-mold dots on surface; color should be uniform throughout. Rind should not bulge, swell, or be cracked. A true farmhouse-quality Leicester should be soft and crumbly, and leave a smudge on the knife when it is cut. Don't buy too much at one time, because it doesn't keep well. Once cut, it deteriorates rapidly.

USABLE LIFE

Short life span due to high moisture content. Best between three and nine months old. Overripe when one year old.

STORAGE AFTER PURCHASE

Wrap airtight in plastic wrap. Seal pores by running flat of knife across cut surface. Refrigerate. If it seems to be drying out, wrap in damp cloth dipped in water with small amount of vinegar in it.

SERVING AND EATING

Good eating cheese for lunches and snacks. Supposed to be especially good with watercress and scallions and when eaten outside. Leicester also melts well and can be used in cooking. Cut slowly, carefully, and easily, drawing the knife through the cheese so it does not crumble.

BEVERAGE MATCH

Good with ale, beer, hard cider, red wine, and in winter, Madeira. Traditionally served with red-currant wine.

COMMENTS

The origins of this cheese are not known, but it was named for the county in which it is made. The cheese has been made for centuries in various towns in Leicestershire and these cheeses were exhibited regularly at cheese fairs. Quality control was handled by dealers at the fair who sampled a few of each farmer's cheeses before they were exhibited. The whole wagonload was sent home if the samples were not good. To further put fear into the hearts of those who tried to sell inferior cheese or short-weighted cheese, the town crier called out the list of penalties for these lawbreakers on the day of the fair.

Supposedly those aging young cheeses at home made a hole in the top, poured old ale in it, and wrapped it in a damp cloth.

At one time, Leicester was considered the second-best cheese in England, but it is no longer as good as it once was.

SIMILAR CHEESES

Lancashire, Cheshire, Double Gloucester, Derby.

Levroux, see *Valençay.*

Leyden (also called Liedse Kaas—Dutch name; a

variation of this cheese is called Liedse Nagelkaas; also Frie-
sian cheese).

WHERE MADE

South Holland. Almost all made in factories.

HOW MADE AND CURED

Type of milk: There are two grades of Leyden; one made
with partially skimmed cow's milk with a fat content of 20
percent; another made with whole cow's milk with a fat content of 40 percent.

Method and rind type: A semihard, pressed cheese flavored
with cumin seeds and caraway seeds and coloring added. The
Nagelkaas version has cloves added to it. The cheese has a
thin brushed and washed rind covered with red wax.

Time cured: Three months.

Fat content: 20–40 percent.

AROMA

Fresh spicy smell; examples of Nagelkaas have a pronounced clove smell.

FLAVOR

Flavor family: Spiced cheeses.

Taste: Mild but spicy, with a dry, nutty flavor. Interesting
and delicious; one of the more distinguished of the spiced
cheeses. Tangy.

Texture: Firm, slightly supple, but also dry and brittle when
sliced.

APPEARANCE

Exterior: Smooth grayish-yellow rind covered with red wax.

Interior: Cheese is pale brownish-yellow, similar to aged
Gouda, with cumin seeds and caraway seeds distributed evenly
throughout cheese. Has a slightly granular, dry, brittle appearance.

Size and shape: Cylindrical, 14 to 16 inches in diameter, 3
to 4 inches thick, weighing 11 to 22 pounds.

BUYING HINTS

Available and good throughout the year. An extremely reliable cheese. The wax coating should be intact with no blemishes or cracks; the cheese should show no interior fissures or
off-color spots. The seeds should be evenly distributed. To
determine authenticity, check for government of Netherlands
mark on rind under wax.

USABLE LIFE

Very long-lasting cheese. Will keep several years, if not cut, and will continue to age. Good for several months to several years in age.

STORAGE AFTER PURCHASE

Wrap airtight in plastic wrap; refrigerate.

SERVING AND EATING

Good eating cheese. Cut thin slices with a cheese plane—one of those stainless-steel cheese slicers with a thin slit in the middle. Good on crackers, with bread and butter, and in open-faced sandwiches. Not recommended for cooking.

BEVERAGE MATCH

Good with Dutch and German beer particularly; also nice with light, fruity red and white wines.

COMMENTS

Named for the city of Leyden, from which it was originally shipped.

SIMILAR CHEESES

Other spiced cheeses such as spiced Gouda, Norwegian Nokkelost.

Lezay

Brand name for various French chèvres. See *Chèvres.*

Liederkranz

WHERE MADE

Van Wert, Ohio, United States; factory-produced.

HOW MADE AND CURED

Type of milk: Pasteurized cow's milk.

Method and rind type: Soft, surface-ripened cheese.

Time cured: Three to four weeks.

Fat content: 50 percent.

AROMA

Pungent to full monastery smell.

FLAVOR

Flavor family: Strong.

Taste: When fully ripe, delicious and pungent; rather mild and delicate for a strong cheese; very attractive.

Texture: Soft, creamy, satiny.

APPEARANCE

Exterior: Orange-ocher surface crust.

Interior: Soft, yellow-ivory spreadable paste.

Size and shape: Marketed in four-ounce foil-wrapped bars.

BUYING HINTS

Liederkranz is a brand name used by Borden, Inc., which markets this cheese some six weeks before it reaches its peak and stamps the expected date of last sale on the package. The cheese is expected to be fully ripened one to two weeks before date stamped, so that there should be no problem in finding a good one. It can be enjoyed young, when the center of the interior is still rather firm, but full flavor emerges when fully ripened and completely soft inside. Young ones are firm to the touch; ripe ones somewhat soft. Although quite reliable, beware of foul, acrid-smelling ones (as opposed to faint monastery-smelling ones), which may be overaged. Buy where there is a good turnover.

USABLE LIFE

Since it reaches a peak of ripeness and then rapidly declines, eat when ripe.

STORAGE AFTER PURCHASE

Keep in original packaging and refrigerate until used. Unused portions can be rerefrigerated, but use the same day if possible.

SERVING AND EATING

Never better than when matched with a cold stein of beer, crackers or dark bread, and onions for lunch. But it deserves a place on the cheese board as well. The rind is usually edible.

BEVERAGE MATCH

This is a beer cheese par excellence, with light lagers, pale ales, and even dark beers.

COMMENTS

An American invention, Liederkranz was discovered by Emil Frey, a cheesemaker in Monroe, New York, in the 1880's, who was attempting to duplicate a popular German cheese and instead invented one of his own. Considered similar to Limburger, it became especially popular with cheese lovers in a New York singing society, Liederkranz Hall, and was thus named after them. Borden's purchased the rights to produce the cheese, and it has since became one of America's best-appreciated contributions to the world of cheese.

SIMILAR CHEESES

Limburger, fully aged Brick.

Limburger

WHERE MADE

Germany, in Algäu area; in factories. Originally and still

made in Belgium, but most is now made in Germany. Also made in the United States and Austria.

HOW MADE AND CURED

Type of milk: Pasteurized or unpasteurized whole cow's milk.

Method and rind type: Semisoft, surface-ripened, lightly pressed, with thin rind.

Time cured: Two weeks to eight weeks; sixty-day minimum if made from unpasteurized milk.

Fat content: 30–40 percent.

AROMA

Highly developed smell, redolent, sometimes overwhelming and almost rank-smelling with spicy overtones.

FLAVOR

Flavor family: Strong.

Taste: Strongly flavored, but not as potent as the smell. Not usually as strong as Hand Cheese.

Texture: A butter-soft texture, almost spreadable.

APPEARANCE

Exterior: Covered with a reddish-yellowish-brownish skin; often wrapped in wax paper and then in foil.

Interior: Pale-yellow color; smooth texture with a few small irregular holes; when cut, surface of cheese looks shiny.

Size and shape: Various sizes, including a 3-inch cube, a 6-inch square, and a rectangular brick shape.

BUYING HINTS

Unfortunately, most Limburger cheese from Europe is liable to be overripe; it should not be runny. The rind should not be cracked; the texture of the paste should not be grainy or hard; the cheese, though strong-smelling, should have no hint of ammonia odors. The wrappings around the cheese should look fresh and should not be stuck to the cheese. The cheese should be plump and resilient. There is a Limburger that is processed and sold in jars: it has nothing in common with true Limburger.

USABLE LIFE

Two weeks after purchase.

STORAGE AFTER PURCHASE

Wrap airtight in plastic wrap. To prevent odor from spreading in refrigerator, put wrapped cheese in airtight jar or container.

SERVING AND EATING

Good for snacks and lunches with dark-brown bread, pumpernickel, and other strongly flavored breads and crackers, onions, radishes, pretzels, and beer. Serve strong cheeses on separate plates or boards, away from other cheeses; use marble or plastic slabs rather than old wood boards—the wood may absorb the smell of the cheese and be difficult to clean.

BEVERAGE MATCH

Good with spicy light German beer as well as dark, heavy, malty beers.

COMMENTS

First made in Liège, Belgium, and sold in markets in Limburg, for which it was named. Now it is made more extensively in many parts of Germany and has become a popular German cheese. It is a difficult cheese to make as the various steps are quite delicate and require perfect timing and temperature assessment. Many anecdotes concern Limburger's smell. One is about the Limburger Rebellion that occurred in Green County, Wisconsin, when residents of a town protested that the wagonload of hundreds of Limburger cheeses parked in front of the bank was causing the entire town to stink. A party of concerned citizens even threatened to hold a "Boston Tea Party" and remove the cheeses.

SIMILAR CHEESES

Limburger imitations from the United States, Maroilles, Romadurkäse, and Liederkranz.

Livarot

WHERE MADE

In the province of Normandy, France; produced by both farms and factories.

HOW MADE AND CURED

Type of milk: Cow's milk.

Method and rind type: Soft, surface-ripened; washed rind.

Time cured: Three to four months.

Fat content: 40–45 percent.

AROMA

Very strong and redolent monastery smell.

FLAVOR

Flavor family: Strong.

Taste: Like an intensified Pont-L'Évêque; a very strong yet complex, fine cheese.

Texture: Elastic and yielding.

APPEARANCE

Exterior: Sometimes described as a terra-cotta color, its slightly sticky mottled rind is traditionally marked by a band of sedge or marsh grass wrapped around its outer edge.

Interior: Yellow-ivory, almost spreadable when ripe.

Size and shape: A flat disk about 5 inches across and 2 inches thick, weighing a little over a pound.

BUYING HINTS

Despite the fact that Livarot is a strong cheese, beware of signs of excessive age: extreme stench, runniness, a dry, hard, crusty rind, and if boxed, a sticky wrapper or shrunken cheese. Quality is not as good during summer months as it is the rest of the year.

USABLE LIFE

Will last for weeks if properly wrapped and stored, but gains in strength.

STORAGE AFTER PURCHASE

Leave in original box or wrap in plastic wrap and refrigerate; to prevent spread of smell, enclose wrapped cheese in airtight jar or plastic container.

SERVING AND EATING

Excellent as a cheese to accompany the last of a very sturdy red dinner wine at the end of a meal, although it may be too strong and smelly for some palates. Serve with crusty Italian or French bread.

BEVERAGE MATCH

Any really substantial red wine, but a fine wine is a waste, as the cheese will overwhelm it. Androuët recommends Normandy hard cider or even a shot of Calvados.

COMMENTS

One of the oldest cheeses of Normandy, it was named for the town of Livarot where it is still made. The fine reed bands traditionally seen around Livarot have caused it to be nicknamed The Colonel after the five-band cuff for this rank on the French army officer's uniform.

SIMILAR CHEESES

Pont-L'Évêque, Maroilles.

Mainzerkäse (also called Mainzer Handkäse)

A Hand Cheese made in the area of Mainz, Germany, for which it is named. It is often sold in jars. See *Handkäse.*

Manchego

WHERE MADE

Central plateau of La Mancha, Spain. Principally produced on farms.

HOW MADE AND CURED

Type of milk: Sheep's.

Method and rind type: Hard, pressed, uncooked cheese with natural rind.

Time cured: Varies; about one month.

Fat content: 57 percent.

AROMA

Full sheep aroma.

FLAVOR

Flavor family: Sheep.

Taste: Comes in a great range of quality; best is very rich, tangy, and attractive; aged specimens rather Swiss-like in texture and somewhat peppery.

Texture: Creamy rich when young.

APPEARANCE

Exterior: Thin yellow-ocher rind.

Interior: White to yellowish with or without small eyes; moderately firm to the touch.

Size and shape: Cylinders up to 50 inches in length, but 8-pound sizes are seen here.

BUYING HINTS

Sample for good flavor and lack of defects; watch out for rank overage smell, rancid flavor, and rubbery texture.

USABLE LIFE

Will last for weeks if well-stored.

STORAGE AFTER PURCHASE

Wrap in plastic wrap or foil and refrigerate.

SERVING AND EATING

Enjoy with Spanish food or on its own with rustic breads.

BEVERAGE MATCH

Excellent with good red Rioja wine.

COMMENTS

The most popular cheese of Spain, it is of considerable antiquity. The best is said to come from Ciudad Real.

SIMILAR CHEESES

Serra da Estrella, Kasseri.

Maribo

WHERE MADE

Denmark, in factories.

HOW MADE AND CURED

Type of milk: Pasteurized whole cow's milk.

Method and rind type: Semihard, pressed, ripened by bacteria, with gas holes; washed thin rind.

Time cured: Several months.

Fat content: 45-percent minimum.

AROMA

Mild, fresh aroma.

FLAVOR

Flavor family: Bland and mild.

Taste: Mild, fresh, clean, slightly acid; pronounced aftertaste; cross between Emmentaler and Port-Salut in flavor.

Texture: Firm, sliceable, open texture, moist.

APPEARANCE

Exterior: Dry, yellowish, thin rind; sometimes rindless.

Interior: Darker, purer yellow than Samsoe; very compact but with many irregularly shaped, close-together holes about the size of rice kernels.

Size and shape: Flat, circular, with rounded edges and sides; 16 inches in diameter, 4 inches in height, 27 to 30 pounds in weight. Also made in rindless and with-rind rectangular blocks.

BUYING HINTS

Danish cheeses are extremely reliable; usually, if it looks good, the cheese will be good. The rind or packaging should be stamped with the name "Maribo" and the amount of fat content (45+). The rind should be even and without blemishes; the interior should look moist and firm and have no off-color spots. Maribo is often sold as "King Christian IX cheese" because of its historical association with that monarch.

USABLE LIFE

About one month.

STORAGE AFTER PURCHASE

Wrap airtight in plastic wrap or in aluminum foil and then in plastic bag. Refrigerate.

SERVING AND EATING

Good eating cheese. Can be eaten for any meal. Good with vegetables and salads; the Danes particularly like it with radishes, tomatoes, green peppers, and celery. Not a dessert cheese.

BEVERAGE MATCH
Good with Danish beer and fruity, light red wines.

SIMILAR CHEESES
Tybo, Samsoe.

Maroilles (also called *Marolles*)

WHERE MADE
Nord Département, France; produced by farms and factories.

HOW MADE AND CURED
Type of milk: Cow's.
Method and rind type: Soft, surface-ripened; washed rind. Said to be rinsed frequently in beer.
Time cured: Two to seven months.
Fat content: 45–50 percent.

AROMA
Very strong, penetrating smell.

FLAVOR
Flavor family: Monastery/strong.
Taste: Strong, potent, very tangy—close to Livarot or a very strong Pont-L'Évêque.
Texture: Creamy and yielding.

APPEARANCE
Exterior: Reddish-brown, textured, slightly sticky rind.
Interior: Soft, yellow, almost spreadable when ripe.
Size and shape: Like a large Pont-L'Évêque; a square 5 by 5 inches and about 2½ inches thick, weighing 1 pound 12 ounces. Mignon, Sorbais, Quart, and Baguette Laonnaise are names given to Maroilles prepared in slightly different sizes and thicknesses. Maroilles Gris is the stronger, longer-aged version.

BUYING HINTS
If boxed, be sure the wrapper is not sticky or the cheese shrunken within; beware of dry crusty rinds or ammoniated stench. Avoid buying during summer months, as quality falls off.

USABLE LIFE
Lasts for weeks if well wrapped and stored; gains in strength, however, with time.

STORAGE AFTER PURCHASE
Wrap carefully in plastic wrap or leave in original wrap-

ping; enclose wrapped cheese in airtight jar or plastic container to prevent spread of smell. Refrigerate.

SERVING AND EATING

This potent, smelly cheese can be used to end a meal with understanding and appreciative guests, or could be offered as an adventuresome snack on a cheese board (be sure to segregate from other cheeses until serving) with rustic breads.

BEVERAGE MATCH

Strong, sturdy, but not fine red wines are called for, or else strong, bitter-spicy European beers.

COMMENTS

This venerable French cheese is named for the Abbey of Maroilles near Avesnes. It is thought to have originated a thousand years ago, and has been long appreciated by the French, who (according to Marquis and Haskell) nickname it Vieux Puant—Old Stinker. There are two other cheeses made in the Nord Département that Simon lists as Maroilles types: Dauphin, a crescent-shaped (sometimes fish-shaped) washed-rind cheese seasoned with herbs and spices (tarragon, parsley, bay leaves, pepper, powdered cloves), a sort of deluxe Maroilles; and Boulette d'Avesnes, produced from "imperfect" Maroilles that are mashed with parsley, pepper, and tarragon and shaped into fearsome-looking brick-red half-pound cones. Both are strong to very strong, spicy cheeses.

SIMILAR CHEESES

Pont-L'Évêque, Livarot.

Middelbare

An especially large version of Dutch Edam, weighing ten to fourteen pounds; it tastes, looks, and is made just like Edam.

Mimolette

WHERE MADE

Northern France, in factories. According to Androuët, Mimolette is a French imitation of Dutch cheese.

HOW MADE AND CURED

Type of milk: Pasteurized cow's milk.

Method and rind type: Pressed, uncooked cheese, heavily colored with annatto. Thin natural rind.

Time cured: Six to eighteen months.

Fat content: 45 percent.

AROMA
    A rather Cheddar-like scent.

FLAVOR
    Flavor family: Bland and mild.
    Taste: Good eating cheese, rather like Edam; slightly salty, slightly nutty; a simple, pleasant cheese.
    Texture: Firm, oily, close-textured; like a very dense Cheddar.

APPEARANCE
    Exterior: Thin wax over grayish to brownish thin natural rind.
    Interior: Uniform deep bright-orange color, slight darkening near rind, with a smooth waxy appearance.
    Size and shape: Big fat Edam-type ball, about 8½ inches in diameter and weighing about 6½ pounds.

BUYING HINTS
    An unfussy and usually reliable cheese. One should nonetheless watch out for cracked rind, large or frequent holes in the cheese interior, a sharp bitter taste, and waxy texture.

USABLE LIFE
    Will last for months if properly wrapped and stored.

STORAGE AFTER PURCHASE
    Wrap tightly in plastic wrap (wrap again in foil if keeping for a long period) and refrigerate.

SERVING AND EATING
    Snacks, or for lunches, with various breads and crackers.

BEVERAGE MATCH
    Goes well with a variety of beverages: coffee, inexpensive red wines, medium-dry sherries, tawny ports, and beer.

SIMILAR CHEESES
    Edam, Gouda.

Mondseer

WHERE MADE
    Mond Lake district, Austria; factory-produced.

HOW MADE AND CURED
    Type of milk: Cow's, either skimmed or whole.
    Method and rind type: Semisoft, pressed, washed-rind cheese.
    Time cured: Three to six months.
    Fat content: 40–50 percent.

AROMA

Monastery, earthy; attractive, and not overly strong.

FLAVOR

Flavor family: Monastery.

Taste: Full, spreading, complex, and lingering; reminiscent of Münster, although the texture is different—rather more like Brick Cheese. Its flavor has been described as a cross between Münster and Limburger.

Texture: Soft on the palate, but not particularly creamy.

APPEARANCE

Exterior: Reddish-yellow-ocher rind often crisscrossed with slat marks.

Interior: Yellow-gold and somewhat resilient to the touch, with occasional small irregular holes.

Size and shape: Fat small wheels, 6 inches across by 2 inches thick, weighing about 2¼ pounds. Also smaller sizes.

BUYING HINTS

Buy from bulk sizes, and taste for oversaltiness and flavor development. A reliable cheese; nonetheless, watch out for dried-out specimens.

USABLE LIFE

Will last for several weeks in large pieces if well-stored; it gains somewhat in strength, however.

STORAGE AFTER PURCHASE

Wrap in plastic wrap and then again in foil if keeping for more than a few days; to prevent smell from spreading, place enclosed cheese in airtight jar or plastic container. Refrigerate.

SERVING AND EATING

An excellent choice for those who do not want an overly strong cheese, but like a monastery flavor in a nonspreadable cheese. Try it with rye bread or rye crackers for lunch.

BEVERAGE MATCH

Mondseer is particularly nice with spicy Munich-style beers.

COMMENTS

Some varieties of Mondseer are said to be monastery-produced. Skimmed-milk versions are called Mondseer Schachtelkäse; whole-milk cheeses are called Mondseer Schlosskäse.

SIMILAR CHEESES

Münster, Esrom.

Monsieur-Fromage

A brand name for a French cured double-crème, rather Camembert-like. See *Double-crème*.

Monterey Jack (also called Jack Cheese or California Jack)

WHERE MADE

Monterey County and elsewhere in California; elsewhere in the United States; factory-produced.

HOW MADE AND CURED

Type of milk: Pasteurized cow's milk.

Method and rind type: Semisoft; pressed, uncooked, surface-ripened; thin natural-rind cheese.

Time cured: Three to six weeks.

Fat content: 50 percent.

AROMA

Faint, lactic, fresh, buttery aroma.

FLAVOR

Flavor family: Mild Cheddar.

Taste: Bland and mild; best examples have a light sweet-sour tang.

Texture: Soft and yielding to the palate.

APPEARANCE

Exterior: Thin natural rind, or none at all if cured in rindless block form.

Interior: Close-grained, springy to the touch; pale-yellow-white (no coloring added); numerous small irregular holes.

Size and shape: Rindless 10-pound loaves, 40-pound wheels, smaller wheels in various sizes.

BUYING HINTS

The best examples of Monterey Jack come from California, but good versions of it are made in Wisconsin and elsewhere. If possible, buy from large bulk sizes so that it can be sampled before purchase. Some specimens are quite boring in taste and exhibit little character. There is a hard Jack Cheese, rarely seen, that is aged six months for grating purposes, and flavored Jacks (caraway seeds, fennel, and so on).

USABLE LIFE

Several weeks if properly stored.

STORAGE AFTER PURCHASE

Wrap carefully in plastic wrap and refrigerate.

SERVING AND EATING

Monterey Jack is an excellent luncheon cheese, mild enough to go well with a great variety of breads, cold cuts, and pickles and other condiments. It is particularly nice with fresh fruit and very tasty on San Francisco sourdough bread.

BEVERAGE MATCH

A fine Monterey Jack is superb with fine California Chardonnay, Sauvignon Blanc, Pinot Blanc, and even Grey Riesling, although it goes well with light, fruity red wines, and, for that matter, with coffee or tea.

COMMENTS

Considered a Cheddar relative by some, it strikes most people as closer in character to very mild, bland cheeses. At any rate, it is not a great cheese, but a very attractive and agreeable one. One of the oldest dairy products of California, it is said to derive from the cheese made by Spanish padres and to have acquired its name from David Jacks, a Scots dairy farmer active in Monterey County in the late nineteenth century.

SIMILAR CHEESES

Mild American Cheddar, Muenster.

Montrachet   (also called Chèvre du Montrachet)

WHERE MADE

In the province of Burgundy, France; produced in dairies.

HOW MADE AND CURED

Type of milk: Goat's milk, usually pasteurized.

Method and rind type: Soft, very thin natural-rind cheese.

Time cured: From one week to two months.

Fat content: 45 percent.

AROMA

Light and goaty; attractive.

FLAVOR

Flavor family: Goat.

Taste: Mild, sourish taste, distinctively goaty; not buttery but very rich and attractive. The ash-covered versions have an additional sharp, salty note.

Texture: Creamy and very soft.

APPEARANCE

Exterior: Comes packed in small containers or ash-covered logs; otherwise exterior looks like interior.

Interior: Snow-white, soft-packed moist cheese, somewhere between fine-curd cottage cheese and cream cheese in appearance.

Size and shape: May be in the form of a leaf-wrapped 4-inch-tall cylinder, comes packed in a container, or in an ash-dusted log about 7 inches long.

BUYING HINTS

Montrachet is most delicious when fresh; look out for old, tired, or mishandled cheeses.

USABLE LIFE

Will keep for a week or more in the refrigerator.

STORAGE AFTER PURCHASE

Keep in original container or wrap carefully in plastic wrap or foil and refrigerate.

SERVING AND EATING

Makes a sophisticated appetizer with a variety of crackers, but also good at the end of meals with light French bread.

BEVERAGE MATCH

Try it with Beaujolais or Beaujolais-Villages, or California Gamay or Gamay Beaujolais.

COMMENTS

A brand of goat cheese named after the great white wine of Burgundy.

SIMILAR CHEESES

Fresh French chèvres.

Morbier

WHERE MADE

In the province of Franche-Comté, France; produced in dairies.

HOW MADE AND CURED

Type of milk: Cow's.

Method and rind type: Semisoft, pressed, uncooked, with brushed rind.

Time cured: Two to three months.

Fat content: 45 percent.

AROMA

Faint earthy, lactic scent.

FLAVOR

Flavor family: Monastery, mild.

Taste: Bland, buttery, and mild; older specimens show a more pronounced and attractive flavor.

Texture: Firm, but resilient and supple.

APPEARANCE

Exterior: Light-brown-and-gray rind with faint crisscrossings.

Interior: Light-creamy-ivory with thick dark-gray streak

of cinders running through cheese horizontally; occasional tiny irregular holes.

Size and shape: Flat wheels with rounded sides from 8 to 16 pounds in weight and about 12 to 16 inches across and 3 to 4 inches thick.

BUYING HINTS

Beware of an unyielding feel to a whole cheese and a bitter aftertaste to the flavor. Otherwise, this is a fairly reliable cheese.

USABLE LIFE

Lasts for weeks if well-stored and wrapped.

STORAGE AFTER PURCHASE

Wrap airtight in plastic wrap and refrigerate.

SERVING AND EATING

Although it can be served at the end of a meal, it is best as a snack with bread and crackers. It also looks interesting on a cheese board.

BEVERAGE MATCH

Light, fruity red wines of all kinds.

COMMENTS

Morbier is described by some authorities as having a smoky flavor, but this is not apparent in contemporary examples, probably due to a change in manufacturing methods.

SIMILAR CHEESES

Tomme de Savoie, Beaumont.

Mozzarella

WHERE MADE

Italy and the United States; in small and large factories.

HOW MADE AND CURED

Type of milk: Pasteurized whole or skimmed cow's milk; in past (and still made in southern Italy) from buffalo's milk.

Method and rind type: Semisoft, drawn-curd, molded cheese; uncured.

Time cured: None.

Fat content: 40–45 percent.

AROMA

Faint lactic smell.

FLAVOR

Flavor family: Fresh, uncured.

Taste: Delicate, mild, creamy, milky, sweet.

Texture: Soft, tender, pliable, elastic, moist.

APPEARANCE

Exterior: Very white, moist-looking.

Interior: Very white, creamy-looking, smooth.

Size and shape: Various sizes and shapes; usually a slightly irregularly shaped sphere weighing 4 ounces to 2 pounds.

BUYING HINTS

Those available in small Italian stores will be better and fresher; the packaged supermarket variety will not be so juicy and tender and sweet—it will be good for cooking, but not to eat fresh. Overaged examples may show a slight yellowing and may taste bitter.

USABLE LIFE

Short—a few days to a week.

STORAGE AFTER PURCHASE

Wrap in plastic wrap, airtight, and refrigerate.

SERVING AND EATING

Used primarily in cooking, especially on pizza. In Italy also eaten fresh with salt and pepper on Italian bread.

BEVERAGE MATCH

Coffee or light white wine.

COMMENTS

If aged, Mozzarella resembles a Provolone.

SIMILAR CHEESES

Scamorza, Ricotta.

Muenster (also called American Münster)

WHERE MADE

All over the United States, particularly Wisconsin and Midwest states; factory-produced.

HOW MADE AND CURED

Type of milk: Pasteurized cow's milk.

Method and rind type: Semisoft; pressed, washed-rind type.

Time cured: One week to one month.

Fat content: 45 percent.

AROMA

Negligible.

FLAVOR

Flavor family: Mild.

Taste: Bland but not particularly buttery cheese, very pleasant, unassertive, sweet and simple.

Texture: Soft, resilient, a trace gummy.

APPEARANCE

Exterior: Light-orange, very thin faint rind.

Interior: Light-yellow-white; occasional small irregular holes; soft, springy-to-touch interior.

Size and shape: Small fat wheel 2 inches thick and 5 inches across, weighing about 1½ pounds; also larger wheels and loaves.

BUYING HINTS

Very reliable, but variations in quality exist; sample for flavor interest, as some examples are nearly flavorless. There are spiced examples (caraway-seed versions, for instance) as well.

USABLE LIFE

Will last for a week or so if well-stored.

STORAGE AFTER PURCHASE

Wrap airtight in plastic wrap and refrigerate.

SERVING AND EATING

Mild enough for breakfast, it is mild enough to serve as a foil to other foods at lunch and goes well with almost any sort of bread or cracker.

BEVERAGE MATCH

Wines are not really called for; cider, perhaps, or coffee or tea.

COMMENTS

Bears no resemblance whatever to European Münster—see Münster. Nonetheless, enjoyable for its own light, simple taste.

SIMILAR CHEESES

Mild Monterey Jack, very mild Brick cheeses.

Münster

WHERE MADE

In the province of Alsace, France; produced principally in factories; some farm production. Also produced in Germany.

HOW MADE AND CURED

Type of milk: Cow's milk, usually pasteurized.

Method and rind type: Soft, surface-ripened, washed-rind cheese.

Time cured: From one month to three months, depending on size.

Fat content: 45–50 percent.

AROMA

Rich, penetrating, redolent aroma, varying in intensity according to age; often a bit barnyardy.

FLAVOR

Flavor family: Monastery; strong.

Taste: The aroma of the rind suggests a stronger cheese inside; actually, the cheese is delicate, complex, and lingering; its flavor is a bit earthy, mushroomy, and herby. A noble, dramatic, delicious cheese whose pungency varies with age.

Texture: Creamy, oily-rich.

APPEARANCE

Exterior: Rough, reddish-orange mottled rind with browny-yellow pigmentation.

Interior: Straw-yellow, creamier toward rind as it ripens; occasional small irregular holes; nearly spreadable when ripe.

Size and shape: Fat disks 10 ounces to 3½ pounds in weight, 4½ to 8 inches across and 1 to 2 inches thick.

BUYING HINTS

Münster should always be moist; the interior of young examples does not show the uniform, soft, pastelike texture of fully ripe cheeses, but is also very attractive in its own way and is particularly enjoyed that way locally. Watch out for saltiness and peculiar odors; Münster should not be dominantly barnyardy. German Münsters are highly regarded, though not as commonly seen as the French Alsatian.

USABLE LIFE

Will keep for a week or perhaps a little longer if not overly ripe to begin with, if properly wrapped and stored, but it gains in strength as it ages.

STORAGE AFTER PURCHASE

Wrap tightly in plastic wrap and, to prevent smell from spreading, store wrapped cheese in airtight jar or plastic container. Refrigerate.

SERVING AND EATING

Münster is very rich; a little goes a long way, which makes it ideal as the cheese to end a meal, particularly an Alsatian dinner. Serve with crusty bread. It also makes a sophisticated snack.

BEVERAGE MATCH

When not too old, match it with Alsatian Gewürztraminer; when fully ripe, try it with spicy Munich-style German beers with plenty of hop character.

COMMENTS

Considered one of France's greatest cheeses, it has been produced for a thousand years in the Vosges Mountains and today is produced all over Alsace (and Germany as well). Münster bears no resemblance to American Münster, which is a very mild cheese with a very different taste.

SIMILAR CHEESES

Géromé.

Mycella

WHERE MADE

Denmark, in factories.

HOW MADE AND CURED

Type of milk: Pasteurized whole cow's milk.

Method and rind type: Semisoft, internal-mold-ripened cheese; thin, washed rind, packaged in foil.

Time cured: Several weeks.

Fat content: 50-percent minimum.

AROMA

Mild moldy scent.

FLAVOR

Flavor family: Blue cheeses.

Taste: Distinctive yet mild flavor, piquant but not sharp; very fat; not so salty as Danablu and creamier-tasting.

Texture: Softish, spreadable; creamy in mouth.

APPEARANCE

Exterior: Rind is off-white to brown in color; dry but sometimes a little greasy. Wrapped in foil.

Interior: Cream-colored paste with considerable greenish-blue veining throughout. Where Danablu veins are very blue, verging on blue-gray, Mycella veins are very greenish, even lightish green in spots. Veining is evenly spaced, but with occasional thick pockets of mold.

Size and shape: Usually cylinder 11 inches in diameter, 8 inches high, weight 11 to 13 pounds; also extra large version and individually wrapped consumer packets of 4 ounces and 8 ounces.

BUYING HINTS

Should not be too old; watch for dried-out interior with unattractive look to cheese near rind. Taste should not be sharp or bitter. Wrapping should look clean and fresh; veins should be clearly defined; color of cheese should be creamy yellowish, not grayish. The texture of the cheese should be creamy, not hard. The wrapping should be marked with the name and percentage of fat.

USABLE LIFE

Two weeks, if carefully stored.

STORAGE AFTER PURCHASE

Wrap airtight in foil and put in plastic bag or box. Refrigerate or keep in cool cellar with temperature not higher than 46°F.

SERVING AND EATING

Cut with any very sharp knife. Serve as a snack, in salads, or after dinner. The Danes think it is particularly good with green grapes and fresh strawberries. A good ending to a rich meal.

BEVERAGE MATCH

Best with full-bodied red wines, especially those of Italy.

COMMENTS

Named for the mold *mycelium,* which causes the greenish-blue veins in it. Invented as a copy of Gorgonzola, it is not as rich and savory as the original.

SIMILAR CHEESE

Gorgonzola.

Mysost, see *Gjetost.*

Nantais, see *Curé de Nantais.*

Nec Plus Ultra

A brand of French processed cheese. See *Fromage Fondu.*

Neufchatel

WHERE MADE

In the province of Normandy, France; in factories. Widely copied elsewhere.

HOW MADE AND CURED

Type of milk: Pasteurized cow's milk.

Method and rind type: Soft, bloomy-rind cheese.

Time cured: About three weeks.

Fat content: 45 percent.

AROMA
   None to faintly mushroomlike.
FLAVOR
   Flavor family: Mild.
   Taste: Varies from extremely mild to slightly pungent and crèmelike.
   Texture: Smooth, soft, creamy, velvety; pastelike and firmer with age.
APPEARANCE
   Exterior: White velvety down, tinged with pink-brown pigmentation in longer-aged examples.
   Interior: Smooth ivory-colored paste.
   Size and shape: Most Neufchâtels are about 4 ounces in weight and come in various shapes; a square is the most common, but a small cylinder about 2½ inches high is known as a Bondon, a heart-shaped cheese is known as a Coeur de Bray, whereas Briquette and Gournay are names for variants of the usual square shape.
BUYING HINTS
   Neufchâtel should be enjoyed young; consequently, freshness is a prime consideration. Watch out, therefore, for grayish rind and excessively salty taste.
USABLE LIFE
   About a week, but can be enjoyed longer than that.
STORAGE AFTER PURCHASE
   Uneaten portions should be tightly wrapped in plastic wrap and refrigerated.
SERVING AND EATING
   Can be enjoyed as a simple dessert or snack.
BEVERAGE MATCH
   Can be enjoyed with fruity, light red wines, but goes very well with coffee or tea.
COMMENTS
   Said to have a thousand-year history in Normandy, but delicious as it is, is rather a simple cheese. There are fresh, uncured versions of Neufchâtel consumed locally; these resemble cream cheese or Petit-Suisse, but are not so rich.
SIMILAR CHEESE
   Carré de l'Est

Neufchatel, American

The only difference between American cream cheese and

Neufchâtel is that the latter is lower in fat (as little as 20 percent) and consequently lacks the richness of American cream cheese. See *Cream Cheese, American.*

Niolo

A sharp Corsican goat or sheep's milk cheese produced on farms. Comes in a grayish-pink square. Not commonly seen.

Nökkelost (also called Nögelost)

WHERE MADE

Norway, in factories; also copied in the United States.

HOW MADE AND CURED

Type of milk: Pasteurized, partly skimmed cow's milk.

Method and rind type: A semihard, pressed cheese flavored with cumin or caraway, or both, with cloves added too. Thin rind covered with red wax, or rindless.

Time cured: About three months.

Fat content: Varying fat content from about 20 percent to 45 percent.

AROMA

Faint caraway, clove scent.

FLAVOR

Flavor family: Spiced.

Taste: Moist, spicy, pleasant when young, does not age as well as Leyden. Fairly mild.

Texture: Firm, fairly pliable, and supple, can have a tendency to turn rubbery as warms.

APPEARANCE

Exterior: Very thin rind with tendency to slight greasiness; sometimes rindless; usually covered with red wax.

Interior: Pale yellow in color, smooth, with cumin (light brown, thin) seeds, caraway (dark brown, thicker) seeds, and cloves (or any combination of the three) distributed evenly through cheese.

Size and shape: Cylinder weighing 18 to 32 pounds, or rectangular block-shaped.

BUYING HINTS

This cheese is much imitated in the United States. The true Norwegian Nökkelost is labeled "Cheese from Norway," is marked with the fat content and the name "Nökkelost," and has the Tine symbol on it signifying it has been approved by the Royal Ministry of Agriculture. The Tine symbol looks like the Viking bows on top with two horizontal heavy red stripes divided by a thinner blue stripe below it.

An extremely reliable cheese. The wax coating should show no cracks; the cheese should have no off-color spots; the seeds should be evenly distributed.

USABLE LIFE

Until about one year old, if not cut. Keeps about a month once cut.

STORAGE AFTER PURCHASE

Wrap airtight in plastic wrap; refrigerate.

SERVING AND EATING

Good eating cheese; also good in cooking. Cut thin slices with cheese plane—one of those stainless-steel cheese slicers with a thin slit in the middle. Good with rye bread, Scandinavian flatbread, and butter. Good for sandwiches and snacks.

BEVERAGE MATCH

Good with light beer; also nice with coffee.

COMMENTS

Originated as a copy of the Dutch Leyden. Name comes from symbol that used to be branded on the cheese rind—St. Peter's crossed keys, the arms of the city of Leyden, *Nökkel* means "key."

SIMILAR CHEESES

Leyden, Spiced Gouda, Spiced Danbo or Tybo.

Oka

WHERE MADE

Fromagerie de la Trappe, in Oka, Quebec, Canada. Monastery-produced.

HOW MADE AND CURED

Type of milk: Pasteurized cow's milk.

Method and rind type: Semisoft, pressed, uncooked, washed-rind cheese.

Time cured: About two months.

Fat content: 45–50 percent.

AROMA

Mild monastery scent sometimes barnyardy.

FLAVOR

Flavor family: Monastery.

Taste: Creamy and delectable, with a fairly strong tang

and complex, nutty overtones. A superb cheese, a worthy cousin to the best Saint-Paulin and Port-Salut types.

Texture: Creamy and smooth, melting in the mouth.

APPEARANCE

Exterior: Russet-brown rind with whitish and pink pigmentation.

Interior: Pale creamy yellow, very uniform and smooth and somewhat resilient to the touch; soft, but keeps its shape when cut.

Size and shape: Fat wheels about 8 inches across by 2 inches high, weighing about 5 pounds; also comes in 1-pound disks.

BUYING HINTS

Oka is a scarce item, so be sure it is authentic; when buying the smaller prepackaged wheels, examine the paper wrapping to make sure it is clean and the cheese does not give off a strong stink or have a shrunken tough rind. The cheese should feel plump and softly springy. If possible, buy pieces from larger wheels and taste for bitterness.

USABLE LIFE

Will keep for weeks in large pieces if properly stored.

STORAGE AFTER PURCHASE

Wrap in plastic wrap, airtight, and store in refrigerator.

SERVING AND EATING

Excellent after meals; adds interest to cheese board; can even be used as an appetizer (sparingly). Serve with crusty bread and plain crackers.

BEVERAGE MATCH

Serve with good red wines with body and character: fine Beaujolais, Châteauneuf-du-Pape, Saint-Emilion, Pomerol, red Burgundy, California Pinot Noir, and fine Zinfandel.

COMMENTS

First made in the nineteenth century as a Canadian version of Port-Salut, utilizing the same methods employed by French Trappists, Oka today is still monastery-produced. It has its own characteristic flavor and quality, and is considered by some superior to the original; demand always exceeds supply. For a time in the 1960s, production ceased, but it has now resumed.

SIMILAR CHEESES

Port-Salut, Saint-Paulin.

Olivet

This French Camembert-type cheese is produced with a soft, bluish bloom (Olivet Bleu) or coated with ashes (Olivet Cendré). Both come from the area around Orléans; not common.

Parmesan, see *Parmigiana-Reggiano* and *Grana Padano*.

Parmigiano-Reggiano (also called Parmesan)

WHERE MADE

Italy, in strictly controlled area including Modena, Parma, Reggionell'Emilia, on right bank of the Po River in Mantua, and left bank of the Reno in Bologna; in factories. Widely made and copied in the United States in factories.

HOW MADE AND CURED

Type of milk: Unpasteurized, partly skimmed cow's milk.

Method and rind type: Very hard, cooked, pressed; with thick brushed rind, rubbed with oil and dark earth.

Time cured: Very slow to mature. Two to three years.

Fat content: 32–38 percent.

AROMA

Faint, sharp aroma that strengthens with age; becomes pungent.

FLAVOR

Flavor family: Grana type.

Taste: Subtle, yet sharp; complex with depth of flavor. Granular character is almost part of taste, giving it an almost crunchy flavor. Can also be eaten as a table cheese when more white and moist.

Texture: Granular, but delicately so; soft and melting in the mouth, though cheese, when aged, is too hard to cut with knife. Table cheese will be moist and crumbly.

Exterior: Thick, brownish, smooth rind.

Interior: Pale-gold to light-brownish-gold color; surface of aged cheese resembles grainy texture of granite; hard, brittle. Even when young has grainy appearance.

Size and shape: Cylinder with convex sides; 14 to 18 inches in diameter, 7½ to 9½ inches high, weighing 52 to 88 pounds.

BUYING HINTS

The cheese is highly regulated; the area in which Parmigiano-Reggiano can be produced is tightly controlled and thus milk is very uniform. The cheeses must be made from April 15 to November 11, thus no cheeses are made with poorer-quality winter milk. It must be two years old before it is sold, and only the first-quality cheeses may be exported. Parmigiano-Reggiano is the best-quality Grana cheese made in Italy; the Grana Padano cheese (which see) is not so tightly controlled. In buying, look for the words "Parmigiano-Reggiano" stenciled on rind. The rind should not have cracks; the interior should show no cracks and should not be too grainy. Italian Parmesan (Parmigiano-Reggiano and Grana Padano) are far superior to American imitations. Check to make sure the Parmesan you are being offered is Italian. Well-aged cheese is pale yellow; whitish Parmesan is too young. Although the cheese may have white marks here and there, it should not have white dotlike formations on it or be dried out and mealy in texture. Sample before buying; the cheese should be mild but tangy, not too salty, and not bitter (Pecorino Romano looks similar, but is much stronger).

It is best to buy Parmesan in a piece and grate your own; however, if you must buy pregrated Parmesan, make sure it is Italian. Read labels on containers of pregrated Parmesan carefully—they should say Italian Parmesan or Imported Italian Parmesan. Those that say, simply, imported Parmesan are not Italian.

American Parmesan, although it must be aged fourteen months, is not as good as the Italian, but the Stella product made in Wisconsin is fairly good.

USABLE LIFE

Very durable. The cheese lasts indefinitely in a large, well-wrapped piece.

STORAGE AFTER PURCHASE

Wrap airtight in plastic wrap. Refrigerate or keep in some cool place.

SERVING AND EATING

When younger, makes a good table cheese, especially with fruit such as cantaloupe at the end of a meal. It is traditionally eaten in Italy with ripe figs. It is good on Italian bread with butter.

The very old Parmesan cannot be cut with a knife; instead a small instrument like a chisel with a pointed blade is used to break off small chunks to be grated. Freshly grated Parmesan has the most flavor—and it fades quickly, within a few hours. Parmesan is used grated in cooking and as a condiment.

The well-aged cheese dissolves in soup, and never becomes gummy.

BEVERAGE MATCH

Full-bodied red wines: Barolo, Chianti, Barbera, and Barbaresco.

COMMENTS

First made in Parma, from which the name "Parmesan" ("Parmigiano") derives. The cheese has a very long history, and is thought to date as far back as the eleventh or twelfth century. Parmesan is probably the oldest Grana-type cheese in Italy. It is mentioned by Boccacio in the *Decameron,* was supposedly Leonardo da Vinci's favorite cheese, and was introduced to the French by Catherine de' Médici, who truly established the cooking of France.

Parmesan is now used in many Italian foods, from soup and hors d'oeuvres to dessert; it is used with most pasta, but never with seafood sauces.

In 1954, it was legally established that only cheeses from a certain area would be called Parmigiano-Reggiano.

The Japanese import more Parmesan than any other cheese.

SIMILAR CHEESES

Grana Padano, American Parmesan, Sbrinz.

Pecorino Romano

WHERE MADE

Italy, primarily in area around Rome; much still made in shepherd's huts, some in factories. Pecorino from Sardinia is called Pecorino Sardo. It is very close to Pecorino Romano.

HOW MADE AND CURED

Type of milk: Sheep's milk, partly skimmed.

Method and rind type: Two varieties: some salted in brine like Feta; some very hard, cooked, pressed, with a thick hard rind that is rubbed with oil.

Time cured: From very short time to one year for grating cheese.

Fat content: 36–38 percent.

AROMA

Very young has a clean, fresh, milky, buttery scent. Aged has a slightly smoky, lactic odor, with characteristic sheep tang.

FLAVOR

Flavor family: Sheep's milk/Grana type.

Taste: When young, has a milky, tangy, very mild flavor similar to Feta, but with an unusual note. When aged, has a strong, very assertive sharpness and piquancy. It is not as subtle and complex as Parmesan and has a characteristic sheep's milk flavor.

Texture: When young, soft and crumbly, moist, yielding, yet granular. When aged, hard, compact, brittle.

APPEARANCE

Exterior: When young, very white and moist. When aged, has a shiny white or ocher-yellow smooth rind.

Interior: When young, looks very white and very crumbly. When aged, is white to straw-colored, looks very compact, and has a certain grainy quality, though not so grainy-looking as Parmesan.

Size and shape: When aged, cylindrical with a diameter of 5½ to 8½ inches and weighing 12 to 44 pounds.

BUYING HINTS

The aged variety shouldn't be extremely grainy or have a bitter or unpleasant taste. It is often sold grated as Parmesan; check label to make sure. There are many Pecorino cheeses from Italy, but Pecorino Romano is considered the best.

USABLE LIFE

Aged variety keeps indefinitely; the young version remains moist and milky for two weeks. Once cut, it cannot be aged.

STORAGE AFTER PURCHASE

Wrap airtight in plastic wrap; refrigerate or keep in cool place.

SERVING AND EATING

Eat the fresh version on dark bread or with salads; the aged version is used grated instead of, or together with, Parmesan.

BEVERAGE MATCH

For foods with the grated version or slices of partly aged cheese, serve robust, strong reds such as Chianti.

COMMENTS

Pecorino is a generic name for all Italian cheeses made from sheep's milk—and derives from *pecora,* the word for sheep. The original is supposedly Pecorino Romano, so named because it was first made near Rome. It is one of the oldest Italian cheeses, mentioned by Pliny. Various other versions are Pecorino degli Abruzzi, Pecorino Toscano (a small Pecorino Romano), Pecorino Siciliano (also called Canestrato). All are somewhat similar.

SIMILAR CHEESES
Pecorino Sardo, other sheep's cheeses.

Persillés

A French term used to indicate a Blue cheese, as is *bleu*. Persillés are often goat's or sheep's milk (but not always), whereas the Bleus are mostly (but not invariably) cow's milk cheeses.

Petit-

As a prefix, indicates a smaller than usual version of whatever French cheese follows it. Petit versions of cheeses are not listed separately here; for example, Petit Pont-L'Évêque is listed under Pont-L'Évêque. The exception is Petit-Suisse, which is commonly used as the name of the cheese.

Petit-Suisse

WHERE MADE
All over France, by factories.

HOW MADE AND CURED
Type of milk: Pasteurized cow's milk and cream.
Method and rind type: Fresh, uncured cheese; no rind.
Time cured: None.
Fat content: 60–75 percent.

AROMA
Fresh.

FLAVOR
Flavor family: Fresh.
Taste: Exquisite, mild, sourish, creamy flavor.
Texture: Spreadable like cream cheese, without elasticity.

APPEARANCE
Exterior: No rind; foil-wrapped or packed in container; exterior looks like interior.
Interior: Snow-white or ivory-white cheese; extremely soft.
Size and shape: Small cylinders; squares of various sizes wrapped in plastic, foil, or paper; most run 1 to 2 ounces.

BUYING HINTS
Freshness is sole criterion, but make sure cheese has not been mishandled. Try one first before buying in quantity.

USABLE LIFE

A week or longer if properly stored, but best enjoyed immediately.

STORAGE AFTER PURCHASE

Keep in original container and refrigerate.

SERVING AND EATING

Best enjoyed as a dessert with fruit (particularly fresh strawberries) and a little sugar. Can also be spread on digestive biscuits for a snack. With fresh herbs, makes a superlative dip.

BEVERAGE MATCH

Delicious with fine, rich coffee or tea.

COMMENTS

The name "Petit-Suisse" is said to have arisen because of a Swiss worker on a small farm north of Paris owned by Madame Héroult about 1850. He suggested that cream should be mixed with the curd of the fresh cheese that the farm sold. His bright idea was a success, and the cheese became popular through the efforts of a Monsieur Gervais, Madame Héroult's eventual partner, whose name is now a well-known brand (Gervais), practically synonymous with this sort of cheese. Another common brand is Pommel.

SIMILAR CHEESES

Cream cheese, American.

Pipo Crem

WHERE MADE

In the Department of Ain, France; factory-produced.

HOW MADE AND CURED

Type of milk: Pasteurized cow's milk.

Method and rind type: Soft, internal mold; thin, natural rind.

Time cured: Varies; about three months.

Fat content: 50 percent.

AROMA

Moldy, but pleasant.

FLAVOR

Flavor family: Blue.

Taste: Creamy; delicious; rich. Milder than most French Bleus.

Texture: Very creamy.

APPEARANCE

Exterior: Mottled thin rind, pinkish-brown in color.

Interior: Well-distributed light-blue internal mold against ivory-white cheese.

Size and shape: Large log about 4 inches in diameter and about 5½ pounds in weight. Pipo Nain is a smaller version.

BUYING HINTS

Sold by the slice. Be sure to sample first to ensure that the taste is not uncharacteristically bitter or dry and crumbly in texture.

USABLE LIFE

Will last for weeks if properly stored, particularly in large pieces, but it is best consumed within a week.

STORAGE AFTER PURCHASE

Wrap in plastic wrap, airtight, or foil, or a damp cloth, and refrigerate.

SERVING AND EATING

After meals or as a snack; good choice for a cheese board. Try dark bread, crusty breads, and flavored crackers (but not salted ones).

BEVERAGE MATCH

Rich red wines; try Italian Gattinara, fine California Zinfandel, California Grignolino, Saint-Emilion, Pomerol. Try also medium-dry sherries and tawny port.

COMMENTS

According to Marquis and Haskell, Pipo Crem also goes by the name "Grièges" in France. Simon classes it as Bleu de Bresse type. It is a deservedly popular Bleu.

SIMILAR CHEESES

Bleu de Bresse, Bleu du Haut Jura.

Poivre-d' Ane, see *Banon.*

Pommel

A brand name of French Petit-Suisse. See *Petit-Suisse.*

Pont-L'Evêque

WHERE MADE

In the province of Normandy, France; on farms and in factories.

HOW MADE AND CURED

Type of milk: Cow's.

Method and rind type: Soft, surface-ripened; washed rind, sometimes brushed.

Time cured: About six weeks.

Fat content: 45 to 50 percent.

AROMA

Earthy, vegetative, odiferous but attractive.

FLAVOR

Flavor family: Monastery.

Taste: Complex, not quite intense enough to belong to the strong class, but rich and tangy with a lingering flavor; a splendid cheese if properly ripened.

Texture: Soft, yielding, melting in the mouth.

APPEARANCE

Exterior: Smooth golden rind with crisscross impressions from straw mats, slightly sticky.

Interior: Pale-ivory-yellow color with infrequent, tiny, irregular holes and a resilient, elastic, almost-spreadable quality.

Size and shape: Commonly 4 by 4 inches by 1 inch thick and weighing 12 ounces, and a petit size of about 7 ounces.

BUYING HINTS

Pont-L'Évêque is available year round, but quality falls off in the summer. Since Pont-L'Évêque comes boxed, it is important to examine the wrapping and feel the cheese carefully. A sticky, unclean wrapper is a poor sign, as is a cheese shrunk down inside the box.

One should not assume that a hard, stiff Pont-L'Évêque is merely underripe; on the contrary, it is almost assuredly one too old, or one that may have never ripened properly at all. It should feel plump, supple, and moist in its wrapper, and not be plagued with odd, rank, or barnyard odors. Since it is extremely doubtful one will have a chance to taste Pont-L'Évêque before purchase, there is no way to screen out those that have an unfortunate bitter aftertaste. In short, it isn't easy to find a good example of Pont-L'Évêque, but it is certainly worth looking for.

USABLE LIFE

One in prime condition should not be allowed to pass its peak; it is true, however, that the genuinely young specimen will develop slowly in the refrigerator for a week. But watch it carefully.

STORAGE AFTER PURCHASE

Keep it in its original box, as it is easier to feel the cheese in its wrapper; unused portions (if there be any) can be returned to the refrigerator if wrapped tight in plastic wrap, but this should be done only if it will not be finished off by the next meal, or in a heat wave. It will rarely be as good if rerefrigerated after ripening properly.

SERVING AND EATING

Pont-L'Évêque is a superb choice (presuming you have your hands on a superb specimen) with which to end a meal. It is neither so strong that it will overpower the dinner wine (although it is powerful enough that a fine wine should be introduced early enough in the dinner to be appreciated on its own before coming into competition with the cheese) nor so mild that serving it would be an anticlimax. It offers complexity, tanginess, and savoriness in abundance, as well as a delightful, sensual texture. Crusty French bread and the last of a bottle of good red wine are all that are needed to provide the capstone to a fine meal.

BEVERAGE MATCH

Full-bodied, tannic red wines are needed here—Médoc, Saint-Emilion, Pomerol, fine California Cabernet Sauvignon are excellent choices, although a fine Normandy hard cider is not a bad choice either.

COMMENTS

Named after a small Calvados town in northwestern France, it is one of France's best. According to Androuët, it is referred to in the thirteenth-century *Roman de la Rose*.

SIMILAR CHEESES

Saint-Paulin (milder), Livarot (stronger).

Port-Salut (also called Port-du-Salut)

WHERE MADE

Western France; factory-produced. Widely imitated everywhere, including France.

HOW MADE AND CURED

Type of milk: Cow's milk, pasteurized.

Method and rind type: Soft, pressed, uncooked, washed-rind type.

Time cured: Two months.

Fat content: 40–50 percent.

AROMA

Mild, faint lactic scent.

FLAVOR
Flavor family: Mild monastery.

Taste: Mild, creamy flavor with slight tang; not a terribly interesting cheese. Layton describes the taste as a cross between Bel Paese and Camembert.

Texture: The most seductive thing about Port-Salut is its enticing texture: very creamy-smooth and melting in the mouth.

APPEARANCE
Exterior: Characteristic orange wax-papery thin fabric with brand name over very thin, matte-finish washed orange rind.

Interior: Pale creamy yellow, extremely uniform and smooth and elastic-looking; springy to the feel.

Size and shape: Fat disk about 9 inches across and 4 inches thick, weighing 4½ pounds.

BUYING HINTS
The authentic Port-Salut is referred to as "S.A.F.R."—the initials of the firm that has the rights to produce and market the cheese. Reliable and unfussy, it should be in fine shape unless mishandled. Examine its appearance, however, and sample the taste to avoid infrequent bitter specimens.

USABLE LIFE
Port-Salut keeps very well, for weeks and probably longer, particularly in large pieces—at least under good conditions.

STORAGE AFTER PURCHASE
Wrap airtight in plastic wrap and refrigerate.

SERVING AND EATING
An excellent choice when a mild cheese is called for to help finish off the dinner wine; an agreeable cheese, it serves on a variety of occasions and is a fine snack.

BEVERAGE MATCH
It perhaps calls for red more than white wine, but it goes well with all sorts of fruity wines.

COMMENTS
In 1815 a group of Trappist monks returning from exile during the Napoleonic era took over a twelfth-century priory at Laval in the Mayenne Département and renamed it the Abbey of Notre-Dame de Port-du-Salut (*port du salut,* "port of safety"). The monks made cheese, at first for their own consumption and, by 1850, for local sale. About 1875 the cheese was first sold in Paris and became an immediate sensation. For all intents and purposes, Port-Salut is now a brand name for a Saint-Paulin-type cheese originated by the monks of the Mon-

astery of Port-du-Salut. Several court decisions have restricted
the use of the names "Port-Salut" and "Port-du-Salut" by
other cheesemakers (at least in France). The cheese itself,
however, is imitated successfully by a number of countries and
is very close to a number of French Saint-Paulins.

SIMILAR CHEESES

Oka, Saint-Paulin, U.S. "Port-Salut," particularly Lion
brand.

Primost, see *Gjetost.*

Provolone

WHERE MADE

Italy, mainly in the southern part; in the United States made
mainly in Wisconsin and Michigan; in factories, primarily.

HOW MADE AND CURED

Type of milk: Whole cow's milk.

Method and rind type: Hard, drawn curd, uncooked, salted,
dried, smoked, then paraffined or oiled.

Time cured: Two to three to six months; depends on size—
some larger cheeses still appropriate for table cheese at fourteen months.

Fat content: 44–47 percent.

AROMA

Faint, lactic, gaining strength as ages; sometimes has mildly
smoky smell.

FLAVOR

Flavor family: Cheddar type/Grana type.

Taste: There are two types made: 1) *Dolce* is milder, but
still strong, with a more delicate flavor; 2) *Picante* is stronger,
with a very pronounced but mellow flavor (rennet used to
coagulate the milk comes from a kid's stomach); piquant and
sharp; sometimes has a faintly smoky taste.

Texture: Hard, compact, somewhat flaky, but still smooth.

APPEARANCE

Exterior: Light-golden-yellow to light-golden-brown color;
surface is glossy and smooth; all have grooves left by cords
from which it was hung, some still have cord on it.

Interior: Creamy-yellow-white color; solid, compact texture;
doesn't crumble when cut.

Size and shape: Comes in many shapes and sizes, including

pear, sausage, cylinder, melon, and truncated cone. Typical is pear-shaped, weighing about 8 to 14 pounds.

The cheese should not have surface cracks or discoloration; the interior shouldn't have holes or be grainy. Taste before buying to determine strength and creamy taste. Cheese should feel soft in mouth.

USABLE LIFE

Keeps well. If well-wrapped, will keep for several months in large piece.

STORAGE AFTER PURCHASE

Wrap airtight in plastic wrap; refrigerate.

SERVING AND EATING

Good eating cheese with Italian bread and sausages. Also good at end of meals, especially with pears. When very old, makes an interesting grating cheese.

BEVERAGE MATCH

Chianti is supposed to be the best; try it with a Chianti Riserva.

COMMENTS

Name derives from the word "prova," which refers to fresh, round cheeses from Naples, and the suffix "-one," which denotes a larger version. American-made Provolone is made differently from the Italian and tastes very different.

SIMILAR CHEESE

Caciocavallo.

Pyramide

A French chèvre of pyramidal shape. These come from various areas of France. See *Valençay*.

Quargel

A German cheese considered similar to Harzerkäse, which is a type of Hand Cheese. See *Handkäse* and *Harzerkäse*.

Queso Blanco (also called Latin American White Cheese)

WHERE MADE

Throughout Latin America and Puerto Rico; farm-, dairy-, and factory-produced.

HOW MADE AND CURED

Type of milk: Cow's, sometimes skimmed, sometimes whole.

Method and rind type: Fresh, pressed, rindless cheese; co-agulated by organic acid, sometimes lemon juice, sometimes vinegar. The entire process takes but a few hours.

Time cured: Usually unripened, but sometimes cured for two weeks to two months.

Fat content: About 15–20 percent.

AROMA

Fresh, lactic.

FLAVOR

Flavor family: Fresh, mild.

Taste: Bland and somewhat acidy; quite tasty.

Texture: After a month, the texture resembles a soft Cheddar.

APPEARANCE

Exterior: Rindless, like interior.

Interior: Light, whitish, soft-looking, lightly springy.

Size and shape: Various; commonly 1-pound or larger blocks.

BUYING HINTS

Freshness principal criterion of quality.

USABLE LIFE

Keeps well for several weeks if well-stored.

STORAGE AFTER PURCHASE

Wrap airtight in plastic wrap; refrigerate.

SERVING AND EATING

Usually eaten with fruit, even guava paste, this light mild cheese can be enjoyed with meals, as a snack, or even as breakfast.

BEVERAGE MATCH

Particularly good with coffee.

COMMENTS

Quesos—literally, "cheeses"—are vast in number and are usually given local place-names to identify local variations in manufacture.

SIMILAR CHEESES

Various fresh cheeses.

Raclette (also called Bagnes, Gomser, Valais Raclette, and Fromage à Raclette)

WHERE MADE

Switzerland, primarily in canton of Valais; most made on farms.

HOW MADE AND CURED

Type of milk: Unpasteurized, whole cow's milk.

Method and rind type: Hard, pressed, cooked; with brushed, natural rind.

Time cured: Three to six months.

Fat content: 50 percent.

AROMA

Earthy, pleasant smell.

FLAVOR

Flavor family: Swiss cheeses.

Taste: Mild and delicious when served at room temperature; soft and nutty; heating unlocks extra flavors and aroma.

Texture: Very firm.

APPEARANCE

Exterior: Resembles Gruyère; has a slightly rough, light-brown rind.

Interior: Pale-ivory-yellow to light-brown color with more holes than Gruyère.

Size and shape: Wheel shape, weighing 12 to 16 pounds.

BUYING HINTS

Swiss cheeses are quite reliable; federal inspectors grade the cheeses according to strict standards. Swiss law prohibits the use of artificial additives, coloring agents, and milk from cows fed on silage. The rind should be even and have no cracks. The cheese should not be sharp. The texture should not be grainy.

USABLE LIFE

Best is between four and six months old; if uncut, will continue to age. If cut, keeps about one month if well-wrapped.

STORAGE AFTER PURCHASE

Wrap airtight in plastic wrap. Refrigerate.

SERVING AND EATING

Primarily used in preparing Raclette, a Swiss specialty. A thick slice is cut across the surface of the whole cheese and toasted until runny and bubbling. It is usually eaten with a roasted potato. Another method is to put the slice of cheese in front of a fire and then scrape it onto bread. Also served unheated as a table cheese at the end of meals.

BEVERAGE MATCH

Good with light German beer and white Swiss wines, such as Fendant.

COMMENTS

Name comes from the French word *racler,* meaning "to scrape." There are a number of Raclette-type cheeses in Switzerland; among these are Belsano and Belalp.

SIMILAR CHEESES

Belsano, Belalp; Gruyère is somewhat similar.

Ragnit, see *Tilsiter.*

Rambol

A brand of French processed cheese; often flavored or covered with nuts, it is high in butterfat (60 percent). See *Fromage Fondu.*

Reblochon

WHERE MADE

In the province of Savoy, France; produced on farms and in factories.

HOW MADE AND CURED

Type of milk: Cow's.

Method and rind type: Soft, pressed, washed-rind type.

Time cured: About one month.

Fat content: 45 to 50 percent.

AROMA

Slightly musty-moldy.

FLAVOR

Flavor family: Mild monastery.

Taste: Mild, creamy, rather nutty, and with some depth. A very fine cheese.

Texture: Creamy, elastic, yielding.

APPEARANCE

Exterior: Dappled white, brown-yellow, and pink rind.

Interior: Soft, ivory-hued thick paste, spreadable when ripe.

Size and shape: Disk, 5 inches across by 1 inch thick, weighing a little over a pound. A Reblochonnet is a small Reblochon.

BUYING HINTS

Reblochon has a very supple texture when ripe and felt

through the rind. Packaged on thin boards in loose paper wrapping, it is easy to examine to see if the cheese is a hard disk or a plump beauty. If possible, however, taste first to ensure that the taste is creamy and not bitter.

USABLE LIFE

Will continue to develop in the refrigerator, particularly if whole, so do not let it overripen.

STORAGE AFTER PURCHASE

Wrap in plastic wrap and refrigerate.

SERVING AND EATING

A popular choice to end a meal for those who do not care for the developed monastery odor and flavor, but would like something more interesting than simple Saint-Paulin. Also good on cheese boards and as snacks. Best with very rustic breads.

BEVERAGE MATCH

Beaujolais is an excellent choice here, as is California Gamay and Gamay Beaujolais, although almost any fruity wine will do.

COMMENTS

A very popular cheese, it is very old and originated as the cheese produced from milk held back for the personal use of the herdsman. The name derives from the word *reblocher,* meaning to milk a second time. An Alpine cheese.

SIMILAR CHEESES

Tomme de Savoie, Beaumont.

Ricotta

WHERE MADE

Italy, in all areas; in the United States, mainly in Wisconsin and New York; also in most countries in central and southern Europe.

HOW MADE AND CURED

Type of milk: Whey from cow's milk, cow's milk, or a mixture of whey and cow's milk.

Method and rind type: Fresh cheese made from whey left over from making Provolone. In the United States, almost always made from whole milk or a combination of milk and whey.

Time cured: Uncured.

Fat content: 4–10 percent.

AROMA

Fresh, lactic smell.

FLAVOR

Flavor family: Fresh cheeses/whey cheeses.

Taste: Bland, sweet; U.S. varieties thicker, creamier, and sweeter than the all-whey version.

Texture: Smooth with slightly grainy quality, satiny; all cow's milk variety smoother and creamier, but not so silky-tasting.

APPEARANCE

Exterior: Very white, smooth; packaged in paper or plastic container.

Interior: Very white; smooth.

Size and shape: Various sizes and shapes.

BUYING HINTS

Cheese should be very white—yellowish color indicates overaging. There is a dry version, sort of like pot cheese, used for grating, but most recipes call for the moist Ricotta.

USABLE LIFE

Short life—keeps a few days.

STORAGE AFTER PURCHASE

Wrap in aluminum foil to maintain maximum freshness; refrigerate.

SERVING AND EATING

Used primarily in cooking and in desserts. Sometimes it is eaten alone with sugar. It is the major ingredient in Italian cheesecake and is used to stuff cannelloni, manicotti, and ravioli.

BEVERAGE MATCH

Depends on dish in which Ricotta was used—from Barolo to coffee.

SIMILAR CHEESE

Mozzarella.

Ricotta-Pecorina   (also called Ricotta Salata)

Sometimes called Pina Ricotta, this white, solid, moist sheep's milk cheese resembles a young *Pecorino Romano*. Do not confuse it with *Ricotta*.

Rollot

WHERE MADE

In the Department of Somme, France; produced in dairies.

HOW MADE AND CURED

Type of milk: Cow's.

Method and rind type: Soft, washed-rind type.

Time cured: Two months.

Fat content: 45 percent.

AROMA

Monastery scent.

FLAVOR

Flavor family: Monastery.

Taste: Tangy, full-flavored, redolent, close to Pont-L'Évêque in character.

Texture: Soft and pastelike.

APPEARANCE

Exterior: Ocher to reddish rind, slightly sticky.

Interior: Soft, yellow, resilient and spreadable when ripe.

Size and shape: Fat round disks about 3 inches across by 1 inch thick. There is also a heart-shaped version. Both shapes weigh about ½ pound each.

BUYING HINTS

Examine wrappers for excessive stickiness, rank odors, and hard, bricklike, or shrunken feel—all poor signs. It should look and feel plump and moist.

USABLE LIFE

Will keep for week or more, but best if consumed at peak period of ripeness.

STORAGE AFTER PURCHASE

Rollot should be wrapped in plastic wrap and refrigerated.

SERVING AND EATING

Serve at the end of meals or to add interest to a cheese board; best with crusty breads.

BEVERAGE MATCH

Sturdy, inexpensive red wines.

COMMENTS

According to Layton, Louis XIV was so delighted by the Rollot presented to him by M. DeGources on May Day, 1678, that he bestowed sixty-six livres a year on him and his descendants.

SIMILAR CHEESE

Pont-L'Évêque.

Romadurkäse

WHERE MADE

Germany, especially in Bavaria and southern Germany; also in Austria and Eastern Europe; made in factories.

HOW MADE AND CURED

Type of milk: Pasteurized whole or skimmed cow's milk.

Method and rind type: Soft, surface-ripened, with thin rind.

Time cured: Less time than Limburger, three to five weeks.

Fat content: 47 percent.

AROMA

Pleasant, strong, but much milder than Limburger.

FLAVOR

Flavor family: Mild to strong.

Taste: Similar to Limburger, but not so pungent. Contains less salt than Limburger. Can range from mild when young to stronger when matured.

Texture: Very creamy.

APPEARANCE

Exterior: Smooth yellowish-brown to reddish-brown skin; usually wrapped in paper and then in foil.

Interior: Pale-yellow color, smooth texture with a few small holes.

Size and shape: Various sizes and shapes, usually either bars or squares smaller than those of Limburger. Often available in bars 2 inches square and 4½ inches long, weighing 1 pound.

BUYING HINTS

Sometimes sold overripe; the cheese should not be runny. The rind should not be cracked; the texture of the paste should not be grainy or hard. The wrappings around the cheese should look fresh; they should not be stained or be stuck to the cheese. The cheese should be soft and plump but not mushy.

USABLE LIFE

Two weeks after purchase.

STORAGE AFTER PURCHASE

Wrap airtight in plastic wrap. If a strong sample, prevent odor from spreading through the refrigerator by putting wrapped cheese in airtight jar or container.

SERVING AND EATING

Good for snacks and lunches with pumpernickel, wheat bread, and flavored crackers. Milder examples are good after a meal of duck or venison. Best to eat in winter months from November to April.

BEVERAGE MATCH

Good with light, Munich-style beer and very spicy Gewürztraminers from Alsace, Germany, or the United States.

SIMILAR CHEESES

Liederkranz, Limburger.

Roquefort

WHERE MADE

Aquitaine, France.

HOW MADE AND CURED

Type of milk: Sheep's milk.

Method and rind type: Soft, internal mold; thin, natural rind.

Time cured: Three months.

Fat content: 45 percent.

AROMA

Sheep's milk scent, light mold overtones.

FLAVOR

Flavor family: Blue.

Taste: Intense sheep flavor and tangy, pungent, lingering taste. Very creamy and all too often very salty. At its best, a superb cheese.

Texture: Very creamy and buttery.

APPEARANCE

Exterior: Foil-wrapped, smooth white natural rind (if whole).

Interior: White with delicate blue marbling.

Size and shape: Fat cylinders about 7 inches across by 4 inches high, weighing about 5½ pounds. Also comes prepackaged in smaller pieces.

BUYING HINTS

Buy Roquefort from bulk cheeses if possible, so that it can be sampled before purchase. This famous cheese does not always live up to its reputation. Often too salty to be appreciated on its own, it is too expensive to be relegated to salads. A fine Roquefort, however, is worth looking for; its flavor is unique among the Blue cheeses of the world. Other than tasting for oversaltiness, look over the cheese for other signs of poor condition: a gray color, lack of veins, and a dried-out, excessively crumbly or chalky character (a little crumbling is natural).

Roquefort is a highly protected name, however, both here and in France, and as long as one sees the official red oval symbol with the sheep in it, one is reasonably assured it's the genuine article. Occasionally one sees specific producers mentioned. Société Bee brand has the best reputation, but others produce fine Roquefort as well.

USABLE LIFE

Well-wrapped and stored, Roquefort will keep for several weeks, especially in large portions. One should eat it before it loses moisture, however, since the cheese appears even sharper and saltier the more dried out it becomes.

STORAGE AFTER PURCHASE

Wrap carefully in plastic wrap or foil (or first plastic followed by foil for several days' storage) or wrap in a damp cloth.

SERVING AND EATING

Eating Roquefort with sweet butter is frowned on by its producers, but then they presumably don't eat the oversalty specimens usually exported. Serve with crusty French bread or thin plain crackers and fine sweet butter, which can be added or not as the palate requires. (Some people go so far as to add in Petit-Suisse to their Roquefort.) If feeling extravagant, go right ahead and use it in salad dressings, although a fine one should await the end of a fine meal, when it can be savored with a fine wine or sweet pears.

BEVERAGE MATCH

The finest red wines of Burgundy and Bordeaux are often listed as proper companions to Roquefort, but this is probably done simply because this venerable and patrician cheese would seem to call for an equally noble wine. Actually, this is almost always a mistake, because the Roquefort is simply too intensely savory to marry well with subtle, complex wine. Far better to match it to Hermitage, fine Barolo, and robust California reds or even ports, sherries, and brandies than to impose it on a truly superlative wine.

COMMENTS

Often considered the greatest of the French cheeses, Roquefort has an enormous reputation to live up to, and, frankly, even the French will admit this cheese is rarely as superb as its press. That does not mean that it is not a fine cheese; it *can* be superb. It's just that superb specimens are not easily found. For tradition and historical background, however, no cheese can match Roquefort. It is generally claimed that Roquefort was

known in some form to the Romans, and there is an oft-
repeated story about Charlemagne that has the emperor being
offered a Roquefort during his travels through Aquitaine. At
first disgusted with the looks of the cheese, the ruler decided
to make the best of it and began picking out the bits of mold
with the point of his knife. Told that the blue mold was the
best part, he tried it, and the cheese gained one of its staunch-
est supporters. Since that time the French have continued to
protect the integrity of this cheese. Charles VI, Henry IV,
Louis XII, and Louis XIV all signed charters granting to the
inhabitants of the village of Roquefort-sur-Soulzon the mo-
nopoly of curing sheep's milk cheese in the humid natural
caves of Cambalou near the village; current French law codi-
fies the traditional methods that have been used for centuries.
It should be noted that though all Roquefort has been aged in
the caves of Cambalou, the sheep's milk cheeses may come
from as far away as Corsica.

SIMILAR CHEESES

The fact that Roquefort is a sheep's milk Blue cheese and
has been cured in the unusually humid caves of Roquefort
makes it a unique cheese; nonetheless, there are many fine
Blue cheeses in France: Bleu des Causses, Bleu du Haut Jura,
Pipo Crem.

Saanen

WHERE MADE

Switzerland, in cantons of Bern and Valais, particularly
around areas of Saanen and Gruyère in the Bernese Alps; made
primarily in chalets, not in factories.

HOW MADE AND CURED

Type of milk: Unpasteurized, whole cow's milk.

Method and rind type: Hard, pressed, cooked; natural
brushed and oiled rind.

Time cured: Five to seven years, longer if possible.

Fat content: 40–45 percent.

AROMA

Strong, but pleasant.

FLAVOR

Flavor family: Swiss/Grana type.

Taste: Very fruity, interesting flavor, similar to very hard,
long-aged Gruyère.

Texture: Brittle when sliced, very hard and granular.

APPEARANCE

Exterior: Light-brown to darker-brown, slightly rough rind.

Interior: Dark yellow with few or no holes; texture looks granular.

Size and shape: Large wheel with straight sides, 24 inches in diameter, 5½ inches high, and weighing 50 to 100 pounds.

BUYING HINTS

Very reliable; available all year. Swiss law prohibits the use of artificial additives, coloring agents, and milk from cows fed on silage.

USABLE LIFE

If uncut, lasts indefinitely. If cut, keeps for several months.

STORAGE AFTER PURCHASE

Wrap airtight in plastic wrap. Refrigeration is preferable, but cheese will keep in cool place without it for some time.

SERVING AND EATING

Used as a grating cheese; also shaved into very thin slices with special cheese plane. Thin slices are good on rustic breads with butter and on Scandinavian flatbreads. In Switzerland, served at special family feasts and ceremonies.

BEVERAGE MATCH

Fruity red and white wines, especially those of Switzerland.

COMMENTS

Named for the Saanen Valley, which is the center of production for this cheese. In earlier times, a Saanen cheese was selected on the birth of a child, a small amount eaten at his or her christening, brought out to eat from again at the person's wedding and anniversaries, and finished after the person's death at his or her funeral. It is believed that some Saanen cheeses have kept well for over a hundred years.

SIMILAR CHEESES

Sbrinz, Parmesan.

Sage

Sage cheese is a spiced or flavored American Cheddar (or less often, a cream cheese) with a green mottled appearance. Most are now flavored artificially, but some authentic sage cheeses are still made in Vermont.

Saint-André

A brand of French triple-crème. See *Triple-crème.*

Saint-Benoît

WHERE MADE

In the province of Orléanais, France; produced on farms and by factories.

HOW MADE AND CURED

Type of milk: Cow's milk, either whole or partly skimmed.

Method and rind type: Soft, bloomy-rind, surface-ripened cheese.

Time cured: Twelve days to one month.

Fat content: 40–60 percent.

AROMA

Somewhat earthy smell.

FLAVOR

Flavor family: Brie and Camembert type.

Taste: An herby tang can be found in this Camembert-type cheese; farm examples are said to be rather fruity. Interesting but not exciting or complex.

Texture: Spreadable and creamy when ripe.

APPEARANCE

Exterior: Snow-white rind, with a trace of pigmentation.

Interior: Creamy ivory with a few tiny, infrequent holes in a uniform pastelike body.

Size and shape: Small flat disk 3 inches across by 1¼ inches high, weighing about 5 ounces. It also comes in larger sizes.

BUYING HINTS

As the cheese comes boxed, examine the wrapper for signs of stickiness and whether the cheese gives off an ammoniated smell—both poor signs. The cheese should be soft and yield under gentle pressure but not be firm or shrunken in its box. An overpigmented rind is also cause for caution.

USABLE LIFE

Saint-Benoît, particularly the 60-percent-fat version, will keep for a week or ten days properly stored.

STORAGE AFTER PURCHASE

Keep in its original packaging and refrigerate until use; then wrap unused portions in plastic wrap and refrigerate as well.

SERVING AND EATING

End of meals; snacks, particularly with flavored crackers. Small whole bloomy-rind cheeses look attractive on cheese boards; Saint-Benoît is no exception.

BEVERAGE MATCH

Any simple fruity wine; reds, particularly Beaujolais, and

whites, notably Vouvray and Chenin Blanc, are especially nice, as is Grenache Rosé.

SIMILAR CHEESE

Coulommiers.

Sainte-Maure (also called *Chèvre Long*)

WHERE MADE

Anjou, Charentes, Poitou, Touraine, France; on farms and in factories.

HOW MADE AND CURED

Type of milk: Goat's.
Method and rind type: Soft, bloomy, natural rind.
Time cured: One month.
Fat content: 45 percent.

AROMA

Goaty; fresh to strong, depending on age.

FLAVOR

Flavor family: Goat.
Taste: Full, goaty tang; can be excellent.
Texture: Soft and creamy to pasty.

APPEARANCE

Exterior: Farm-produced cheeses have bluish rinds dotted with brown pigmentation; factory-produced cheeses have a light, downy, white rind dotted with brownish-pink pigmentation.
Interior: May or may not have a traditional straw in the center of the cheese, but should be white to ivory in color and moist-looking.
Size and shape: Log shape, about 6½ inches long by 1½ inches in diameter, weighing about 7 to 10 ounces.

BUYING HINTS

Beware of overage specimens (unless that is to your taste) showing excessive pigmentation and giving off a powerful odor. If sampling is possible, be sure the cheese is not overly salty, bitter, or crumbly.

USABLE LIFE

Will last for several weeks, but gains in strength.

STORAGE AFTER PURCHASE

Wrap in plastic wrap or foil (or first plastic and then foil) and refrigerate.

SERVING AND EATING

At the end of meals with crusty French bread or very sparingly as an appetizer with assorted crackers and breads.

BEVERAGE MATCH

Lively, fruity white or red wines: Beaujolais, Vouvray, California Gamay or Chenin Blanc, and so forth.

SIMILAR CHEESES

Saint-Saviol, various French chèvres.

Saint-Marcellin

WHERE MADE

In the Departments of Isère and Savoy, France; produced in factories and on farms.

HOW MADE AND CURED

Type of milk: Formerly goat's and cow's milk combined, now entirely cow's milk.

Method and rind type: Soft, surface-ripened; blue mold is cultivated on surface, but does not penetrate the interior; thus it is not classified as a Blue cheese.

Time cured: One month.

Fat content: 50 percent.

AROMA

Fresh, tangy.

FLAVOR

Flavor family: Mild.

Taste: Tangy, creamy, very attractive; very close in character to young chèvres.

Texture: Soft, rather cream cheeselike.

APPEARANCE

Exterior: Often leaf-wrapped, with blue-mold spores on rindless surface of ivory-colored cheese.

Interior: Soft, white; cheese the consistency of cream cheese.

Size and shape: 6 inches across by 2 inches high, usually seen wrapped in chestnut leaves and tied with raffia like a Banon. Small ones may be pepper- or *sariette*-covered.

BUYING HINTS

Saint-Marcellin should be enjoyed fresh; beware of dried-out-looking leaf wrappings and mold growth on the leaves, signs of overage. If possible to sample, watch out for a dirt flavor, as if the cheese had been buried underground.

USABLE LIFE

Will keep for a week or longer, but best enjoyed while fresh and moist.

STORAGE AFTER PURCHASE

Will keep in its leaf wrappings, but wrap again in plastic wrap to preserve moisture if cheese will not be consumed immediately. Refrigerate; unused portions keep well for a few days if well-wrapped.

SERVING AND EATING

Very attractive looking in its leaf wrappings, it makes an excellent appetizer served with a variety of breads and crackers. Unfortunately, some attention to the wrapping and rind must be paid; the leaves are difficult to cut through without creating a mess, and the mold can be bitter-tasting. Stripping the cheese of its rustic wrapping removes much of its interest, however, so compromise by cutting a generous wedge out of it and cleaning that up as an example.

BEVERAGE MATCH

Simple fruity red wines: Côtes du Rhône; California Gamay and Zinfandel; Italian Valpolicella and Bardolino; Beaujolais.

SIMILAR CHEESES

Mild Epoisses, Banon.

Saint-Nectaire

WHERE MADE

In strictly delimited areas of the Departments of Puy-de-Dôme and Cantal, France; principally produced on farms.

HOW MADE AND CURED

Type of milk: Cow's.

Method and rind type: Semisoft, pressed, uncooked; natural rind.

Time cured: Two months.

Fat content: 45 percent.

AROMA

Very moldy.

FLAVOR

Flavor family: Monastery.

Taste: Tangy and lingering, rather unique delicate nutty flavor, perhaps something like aged Saint-Paulin.

Texture: Yielding, melting in the mouth.

APPEARANCE

Exterior: White-yellow-and-red pigmented, moldy crust.

Interior: Soft, ivory-yellow, firm paste.

Size and shape: Flat disk about 8 inches by 1½ inches, weighing about 3 pounds.

BUYING HINTS

Watch out for gummy rinds or a dried-out, hard-looking rind; sample for bitter taste. Look for mark of origin.

USABLE LIFE

Will last for weeks, but gains somewhat in strength.

STORAGE AFTER PURCHASE

Wrap in plastic wrap and refrigerate.

SERVING AND EATING

Excellent choice to end a meal of provincial French cooking; serve with crusty French bread. Also adds interest to a cheese board.

BEVERAGE MATCH

French country wines: Chinon, Bourgueil, or Mercurey. But any fruity red wine will go well.

COMMENTS

Highly esteemed by French turophiles.

SIMILAR CHEESE

Saint-Paulin.

Saint Otho

WHERE MADE

Switzerland.

HOW MADE AND CURED

Type of milk: Unpasteurized skimmed milk.

Method and rind type: Hard, pressed, cooked, with natural rind.

Time cured: Three to four months.

Fat content: 9 percent.

AROMA

Mild, sourish scent.

FLAVOR

Flavor family: Bland and mild cheeses.

Taste: Nutty and waxy, but somewhat flavorless. Lacks salt to give it tang. Not bad for a fat-free cheese, though boring compared to high-fat cheeses.

Texture: Soft, almost Cheddar-type texture; waxy.

APPEARANCE

Exterior: Thin, orangish rind similar to that of Münster.

Interior: Yellow-ivory in color with very small irregularly shaped holes. Firm and resilient in texture.

Size and shape: Small flat wheel, weighing about 15 pounds.

BUYING HINTS

Very reliable. Should not be dried out. Good flavor in comparison to other fat-free cheeses, probably because of Swiss laws that prohibit artificial additives, coloring agents, and milk from cows fed on silage.

USABLE LIFE

Skim-milk cheeses do not keep as well as whole-milk cheeses; keeps about three weeks when well-wrapped.

STORAGE AFTER PURCHASE

Wrap airtight in plastic wrap; refrigerate.

SERVING AND EATING

An eating cheese; good with interesting, rustic breads and crackers. Primarily for those who cannot eat full-fat cheeses.

BEVERAGE MATCH

Fruity red and white wines.

COMMENTS

The lowest-fat natural cheese available.

SIMILAR CHEESES

Appenzeller Rass, other low-fat cheeses.

Saint-Paulin

WHERE MADE

All over France; factory-produced. Copied elsewhere, particularly in Denmark.

HOW MADE AND CURED

Type of milk: Pasteurized cow's milk.

Method and rind type: Soft, pressed, uncooked, washed-rind type.

Time cured: About two months.

Fat content: 45–50 percent.

AROMA

Faint to light and lactic to pleasantly fruity; intensifies and sharpens with age and according to example and producer.

FLAVOR

Flavor family: Mild monastery.

Taste: Mild, sourish, tangy to deep, lingering, complex and very attractive and characterful. Complexity and intensity depend on age and producer.

Texture: Tender, smooth, and melting in the mouth, velvety; poorer examples rather gummy.

APPEARANCE

Exterior: Smooth thin orange-colored rind.

Interior: Light-yellow-ivory, uniform, springy soft paste that holds shape when cut.

Size and shape: Fat wheels 8 inches across by 2 inches thick, weighing about 4½ pounds. There are smaller sizes as well.

BUYING HINTS

A usually reliable cheese, it keeps well and only tired or mishandled examples show signs of damage. But there are a great many brands of Saint-Paulin, so buy from large wheels and sample; look for one that has depth, character, and fine texture. Avoid bitter, gummy examples.

USABLE LIFE

This cheese will keep well for weeks if properly stored and wrapped.

STORAGE AFTER PURCHASE

Simply wrap in plastic wrap and refrigerate.

SERVING AND EATING

A fine choice with which to end a meal and to accompany the last of the dinner wine, it is mild enough to accompany substantial white wines but really goes best with excellent red wines. An unfussy cheese, it is always popular on the cheese board and is an excellent snack. Goes well with a variety of breads and crackers.

BEVERAGE MATCH

Complements fine red wines very well, including better Beaujolais, Bordeaux, and Burgundies, and for that matter, Châteauneuf-du-Pape; California reds like Pinot Noir, Cabernet Sauvignon, and better Zinfandel, and the best Spanish Riojas. It is usually mild enough to go with most dry fruity wines, however, and is excellent with coffee.

COMMENTS

Saint-Paulin is the cheese type of which Port-Salut is probably the most famous example; Port-Salut can be considered a brand name of Saint-Paulin, and there are Saint-Paulins as good as or better than Port-Salut. See *Port-Salut.*

SIMILAR CHEESES

Port-Salut, Danish Saint-Paulin, Oka.

Saint-Saviol

WHERE MADE

In the province of Poitou, France; by local dairy.

HOW MADE AND CURED

Type of milk: Goat's.

Method and rind type: Soft, bloomy-rind cheese.

Time cured: About one month, depending on size.

Fat content: 45 percent.

AROMA

Sharp, goaty aroma.

FLAVOR

Flavor family: Goat.

Taste: Intense, peppery, sharp, and savory, a penetrating and spicy cheese and a very attractive one.

Texture: Soft, creamy texture.

APPEARANCE

Exterior: White, bloomy, pebbly rind with brown-pink pigmentation.

Interior: Creamy interior ripens from rind in; young examples have light cream-cheese texture, older examples soft, spreadable, pastelike texture.

Size and shape: 7-ounce truncated pyramids about 2½ inches tall, and various other shapes, including large logs (Bucherons).

BUYING HINTS

Beware of overage, shrunken-looking, heavily pigmented, moldly specimens (unless you have acquired a taste for aged chèvres). Buy from bulk if possible to sample; watch out for oversaltiness.

USABLE LIFE

Lasts well but gains in strength from week to week.

STORAGE AFTER PURCHASE

Wrap in plastic wrap or foil; to keep smell from spreading, put wrapped cheese into airtight jar or plastic container.

SERVING AND EATING

At the end of a meal with crusty French bread or as an appetizer.

BEVERAGE MATCH

The stronger the chèvres, the stronger, sturdier, and less sophisticated the wine should be. Alsatian Gewürztraminer and the yellow wines of the Jura might stand up well, but reds are better: Rhône wines, California Petite Sirah, Ruby Cabernet, Zinfandel, and northern Italian reds are good choices.

COMMENTS

Saint-Saviol is a brand name as well as a source of these cheeses.

SIMILAR CHEESES

Various French chèvres.

Samsoe (also formerly called Danish Swiss)

WHERE MADE

Denmark, in factories.

HOW MADE AND CURED

Type of milk: Pasteurized whole cow's milk.

Method and rind type: Semihard, pressed, ripened by bacteria, with gas holes; washed, thin rind; similar to method of manufacture used for Swiss cheese.

Time cured: About five months.

Fat content: 45 percent minimum.

AROMA

Mild but distinctive aroma.

FLAVOR

Flavor family: Bland and mild.

Taste: Rich, buttery, mild, with nutlike, sweet flavor; with age acquires greater pungency and distinction.

Texture: Firm, yet soft and moist in mouth; suitable for slicing.

APPEARANCE

Exterior: Dry, yellowish, thin rind. Sometimes wax-covered. Also available rindless. "Mini" versions covered with red or yellow wax and wrapped in cellophane.

Interior: Yellow, buttery color; smooth texture sprinkled with a few small round holes of varying sizes from pea size to cherry size.

Size and shape: Flat round wheel, about 17 inches in diameter, 4 inches high, weighing about 30 pounds. Also "mini" versions of seven ounces.

BUYING HINTS

Danish cheeses are extremely reliable; usually, if it looks good, it will be good. The rind, wax, or packaging should be stamped with the name Samsoe and the amount of fat content (45+).

Wax or paraffin coating should adhere closely to cheese and show no cracks; interior should have no off-color spots.

USABLE LIFE

About one month.

STORAGE AFTER PURCHASE

Wrap airtight in plastic wrap or in aluminum foil and then in a plastic bag. Refrigerate.

SERVING AND EATING

Good eating cheese. Can be eaten for any meal. Good with fruit and nuts; the Danes particularly like it with apples, pears, bananas, pineapple, celery. It would also be good after a meal of fish, poultry, or veal.

BEVERAGE MATCH

Good with Danish beer, white wines, light, fruity red wines.

COMMENTS

Named for island of Samsö, where it was first made and has been made for generations. The staple cheese of Denmark, it is the most popular Danish cheese in Denmark. Although called Danish Swiss at one time, it is not a copy of Swiss cheese. It was called that simply to identify it as similar to Swiss.

SIMILAR CHEESES

Danbo, Tybo.

Sapsago (also called Glaren Schabzieger, Glarenkäse, and Green Cheese)

WHERE MADE

Switzerland, in the canton of Glarus; also in southern Germany; made in factories.

HOW MADE AND CURED

Type of milk: Slightly sour, skimmed cow's milk with added buttermilk.

Method and rind type: Very hard, cooked, pressed; flavored with blue melilot, a kind of clover grown for hay; no rind.

Time cured: Three to five months.

Fat content: 5–9 percent.

AROMA

Strong, grassy, herby smell.

FLAVOR

Flavor family: Grana/spiced type.

Taste: Very sharp flavor, pungent; tastes very unlike a cheese.

Texture: Hard, dry.

APPEARANCE

Exterior: Light green similar to sage in color; wrapped in foil. No rind.

Interior: Same color and texture as exterior; grainy, pressed-looking texture.

Size and shape: Small, flat-topped cone, 2 inches in diameter at the base, 3 inches high, weighing 3 ounces.

BUYING HINTS

Extremely reliable cheese.

USABLE LIFE

Keeps indefinitely.

STORAGE AFTER PURCHASE

Wrap in foil; can be but doesn't have to be refrigerated.

SERVING AND EATING

Usually grated and used as a condiment on potatoes, spaghetti, macaroni, or soups. Grated Sapsago is also mixed with butter and used as a spread on plain or rye or wheat crackers.

BEVERAGE MATCH

Very spicy Gewürztraminer wines from Alsace or the United States.

COMMENTS

Has been made in exactly the same way since the fifteenth century; probably introduced from the Orient into Russia and brought into Switzerland for commercial purposes by Russians.

SIMILAR CHEESES

None, quite unique.

Sbrinz

WHERE MADE

Switzerland, in cantons of Schwyz, Unterwalden, and Uri; made in small dairies.

HOW MADE AND CURED

Type of milk: Unpasteurized whole cow's milk.

Method and rind type: Very hard, pressed, cooked, with washed, brushed, and oiled rind.

Time cured: Eighteen months to three years.

Fat content: Usually between 47 and 50 percent.

AROMA

Light, rancid odor.

FLAVOR

Flavor family: Grana type/Swiss cheeses.

Taste: Sharp, nutty flavor, similar in some ways to Gruyère, but tending toward a soapy taste. Rich flavor, with pronounced tang.

Texture: Hard, brittle, compact, grainy.

APPEARANCE

Exterior: Dark-yellow rind, darker than Gruyère and dry.

Interior: Darkish-yellow, dense, and compact with close texture; very small pinhead-size holes, sometimes no holes.

Size and shape: Large wheel, 24 inches in diameter, 4 to 6 inches thick, weighing 50 to 100 pounds.

BUYING HINTS

A reliable cheese. Cheese stores are supposed to store the cheese vertically, not horizontally. The cheese should not be excessively crumbly or grainy, or have a rancid tang.

USABLE LIFE

Keeps uncut for many years. Cut, keeps several months.

STORAGE AFTER PURCHASE

Wrap in aluminum foil; can but does not have to be refrigerated.

SERVING AND EATING

Used primarily as grating cheese; thin slices are also cut with a cheese plane and served at the end of meals. When the cheese is not quite hard, the thin slices are eaten with bread.

BEVERAGE MATCH

Serve with full-bodied wines, either red or white.

COMMENTS

To prevent evaporation from the cheese, the rind is rubbed with linseed oil when the cheese is a year old.

According to Simon, Sbrinz may be the *caseus helveticus* mentioned by Columella, a Roman writer. Other writers have felt it is the *caseus helveticus* mentioned by Pliny the Elder as popular in Rome.

Spalen, named for the wooden containers in which it is shipped, is a younger, soft-cutting version of Sbrinz. Only the aged cheeses can be sold as Sbrinz.

SIMILAR CHEESES

Saanen, Parmesan.

Scamorza

A fresh, drawn-curd, uncured cheese made primarily in central Italy and not exported. It is very mild, sometimes lightly smoked, with delicate nutty overtones. It is very like Mozzarella. First made from buffalo's milk, it is now mostly made from cow's milk. In Italy the cheese is sometimes fried with an egg or toasted on bread. It is available in Italy mostly in the autumn.

Selles-sur-Cher

WHERE MADE

In the provinces of Orléanais and Berry, France; produced in dairies.

HOW MADE AND CURED

Type of milk: Goat's.

Method and rind type: Soft, natural rind covered with powdered charcoal.

Time cured: Three weeks.

Fat content: 45 percent.

AROMA

Fresh, goaty.

FLAVOR

Flavor family: Goat.

Taste: Mild, nutty-sweet, and very attractive.

Texture: Soft and creamy.

APPEARANCE

Exterior: Gray-blue moldy rind.

Interior: White, smooth; like a light cream cheese.

Size and shape: Fat, little, flattened balls, 3 inches across by 1 inch thick, weighing about 5 ounces.

BUYING HINTS

Beware of saltiness and graininess; as it is unlikely you'll be able to sample before purchasing, try one before buying in quantity. Best fresh, so watch out for odiferous examples.

USABLE LIFE

Will last for a week or more, but gains in strength.

STORAGE AFTER PURCHASE

Wrap in plastic wrap and refrigerate.

SERVING AND EATING

Delightful as a sophisticated appetizer or snack served with flavored crackers and crusty bread. Also nice with which to end a meal.

BEVERAGE MATCH

Try it with fruity white or red wines: Sancerre, dry Graves, California Sauvignon Blanc, Grey Riesling, Alsatian whites; Mercurey or Mâcon.

COMMENTS

Highly esteemed for its nutty flavor. Named for the town in which it was first made.

SIMILAR CHEESES

Banon and other French chèvres.

Septmoncel, see *Bleu du Haut Jura.*

Serra da Estrella

WHERE MADE

Serra da Estrella Mountains, Portugal. Farm- and factory-produced.

HOW MADE AND CURED

Type of milk: Sheep's (or sheep's and goat's) milk; sometimes cow's.

Method and rind type: Semisoft to semihard natural-rind cheese. Said to be coagulated by extract from thistle flowers.

Time cured: Two to three weeks.

Fat content: 40 percent.

AROMA

Fresh sheep scent if young; more assertive and pungent if aged.

FLAVOR

Flavor family: Mild when young; sheep.

Taste: Piquant, distinctive; acidy and oily.

Texture: Particularly attractive velvety-creamy texture.

APPEARANCE

Exterior: Varies; typical yellow thin rind.

Interior: Uniform ivory color with occasional irregular holes. Usually firm to the touch.

Size and shape: Fat wheels or disks, 6 to 10 inches across and some 2 inches thick, weighing 5 or more pounds; also cylinders 2 to 3 inches in diameter, weighing 2 to 5 pounds.

BUYING HINTS

Taste for excessive saltiness and flavor defects.

USABLE LIFE

Will last for weeks if well-stored.

STORAGE AFTER PURCHASE

Wrap in plastic wrap or foil and refrigerate.

SERVING AND EATING

Makes a very different luncheon cheese; enjoy the texture on plain crackers as well as breads. Interesting on a cheese board.

BEVERAGE MATCH

Match it with a Portuguese Dão; barring that, any sturdy red wine, perhaps a red Rioja from Spain.

COMMENTS

Serra cheeses are mountain cheeses, and Serra da Estrella

is considered the best of these. It is highly prized in Portugal and commands a high price.

SIMILAR CHEESES

Sheep's milk Tommes, Queso Blanco, Manchego.

Spalen A younger version of Sbrinz, see *Sbrinz*.

Stilton

WHERE MADE

Leicestershire, Huntingdonshire, and Rutlandshire in England; made primarily on farms. Center is around main towns of Melton Mowbray, Hartington in the Dove Valley, and in the Vale of Belvoir.

HOW MADE AND CURED

Type of milk: Unpasteurized whole cow's milk enriched with additional cream; some manufacturers use only milk from Shorthorn cows.

Method and rind type: Semisoft, ripened by interior mold; natural, brushed rind. Matured without refrigeration.

Time cured: Four to six months (best at at least eight months).

Fat content: 55 percent.

AROMA

Rich, strong, spicy mold smell.

FLAVOR

Flavor family: Blue type.

Taste: Rich, mellow, intense, salty, creamy, penetrating, lingering. Touch of Cheddar in its tang. Very distinct flavor.

Texture: Open and flaky, but with a velvety and silky consistency; moist and creamy.

APPEARANCE

Exterior: Ridged or wrinkled brownish-gray rind resembling the rind of a melon; gives when pressed.

Interior: Creamy color with blue-green mold; fairly dense veins of mold; thin brown line below rind and slightly brownish edges. Narrow veins. Looks firm, not crumbly or soft.

Size and shape: Cylinder, 8-inch diameter by 9-inch height, 12 to 15 pounds in weight.

BUYING HINTS

Those made from May to late September are best; these are usually available from fall to spring.

Often sold too young, when it is hard, sour, and chalky. When unripe, Stilton is dry and white.

The rind should be well wrinkled, brown-gray, and free from cracks. The interior should look moist, not granular, dry, or cakey. The color should not be yellow; the mold should be clearly defined; the cheese near the rind should look pleasant. There should not be pronounced interior crevasses. The taste should not be excessively sharp or bitter.

USABLE LIFE

Six months to two years; some say it should be aged at least eight months, and that it is at its best at about nine months. Once cut, however, the cheese will stay moist only a few weeks, even when stored optimally.

STORAGE AFTER PURCHASE

Wrap in damp cloth and keep in plastic box or under plastic bell; the cheese needs air around it. While supposedly doesn't need refrigeration, most houses are too warm for it to be stored at room temperature. Keep refrigerated. Whole cheese, uncut, can be kept in cellar until needed, but rind will need brushing.

SERVING AND EATING

Cut whole cheese in half horizontally. Then cut line from center to edges down about one-half inch from exposed surface. Using knife horizontally, cut around entire cheese, so that a half-inch top cut layer is formed. Cut wedges from this layer first; then proceed to cut another one-half-inch-thick layer. It was tradition for many years to wrap Stilton in a linen napkin, spoon out the cheese from the center with a silver cheese scoop, and then pour port in the hole when the cheese was put away. Because this way the cheese will dry out quickly and its flavor will be spoiled, this is *not* the way to eat Stilton. If an entire half-cheese will be consumed at once, however, you may want to use a cheese scoop. Serve as an after-dinner cheese. Some people like it with apples, grapes, apple pie, or celery. Serve with plain crackers. If you have a small bit of slightly dried-out cheese left, mix it with butter and a small amount of brandy and use as a spread.

BEVERAGE MATCH

Traditionally served with vintage port. Also good with tawny port, Madeira, sherry, full-bodied red wines. For a country wine, pick elderberry wine.

COMMENTS

Stilton is considered the finest English cheese. The cheese

has a cloudy history, but it is named for the town in which it was probably first sold publicly: Stilton, in Huntingdonshire at the Bell Inn. Exactly where it was first made is unknown, though it seems likely it was first made in Leicestershire. It was made in or about 1730, since it was mentioned in documents and books of that time. Various authorities attribute its discovery to Mrs. Paulet of Wymondham, Mrs. Orton at Little Dalby, and Mrs. Stilton, head dairymaid to the fifth Duchess of Rutland. The most likely of these is Mrs. Orton, since the dates attributed to her discovery are similar to the dates of publications first mentioning Stilton as a cheese by name.

Popular throughout its history, Stilton is mentioned by Daniel Defoe, Alexander Pope, Jane Austen, and Charles Lamb in letters or in books and poems.

The name Stilton is controlled. There is a society to which Stilton makers *must* belong in order to sell the cheeses they make (at least in England).

SIMILAR CHEESES

Blue Wensleydale, Gorgonzola, Bleu du Haut Jura.

Stracchino

A soft, uncooked, fast-ripening (ten to fifteen days) cheese with hardly any rind. Made in Italy, primarily in Lombardy, it is too fresh to travel and is not made in the United States. There are several varieties of this cheese, of which the best is supposed to be Crescenza, a very rich (over 50-percent fat), creamy, slightly tart, glistening cheese that spreads like butter.

Stracchino is also a generic name for cheeses that were once made from milk from cows that were tired, passing through Lombardy on their way south for the winter. Supposedly the cows' tiredness affected the taste of the milk. However, cows no longer travel to southern Italy for the winter, and Stracchino as a generic name refers to cheeses made on the Lombardy plains such as Gorgonzola, Bel Paese, and Taleggio, as well as the soft, fast-ripening cheeses such as Crescenza.

Suisse, see *Petit-Suisse.*

Sveciaost

WHERE MADE

Sweden, in factories.

HOW MADE AND CURED

Type of milk: Pasteurized whole cow's milk, or (more usually) partly skimmed cow's milk, or skimmed cow's milk.

Method and rind type: Semihard, pressed, sometimes flavored with caraway seeds or caraway seeds and cloves; usually waxed.

Time cured: Six weeks to four months; sometimes as much as twelve months.

Fat content: Made with varying fat contents, from 30 to 60 percent.

AROMA

Faint; aged smells stronger.

FLAVOR

Flavor family: Bland and mild.

Taste: Mild and pleasant, fresh like Gouda when young; increases in complexity, pungency, and interest when aged about twelve months.

Texture: Open texture, firm, pliable, and almost rubbery and sticky when young.

APPEARANCE

Exterior: Smooth. Or waxed or wrapped in plastic film.

Interior: Very white, but not snow-white. Smooth. Contains small, irregularly shaped holes the size of rice grains.

Size and shape: Flat wheel with 15-inch diameter, 5–6-inch height, 25–30-pound weight.

BUYING HINTS

The taste of Sveciaost varies considerably depending on fat content and time the cheese has been aged. Look for the amount of fat content and date of manufacture stamped on the wax coating, rind, or other covering. A fairly reliable cheese. The cheese should show no off-color spots; the holes should not be too big; the cheese should not appear dried out or show small cracks and fissures.

USABLE LIFE

Uncut, the whole-milk cheeses can improve for some time, up to twelve months; the part-skimmed-milk cheeses and skimmed-milk cheeses for a shorter time. Cut, the cheese keeps for about two months.

STORAGE AFTER PURCHASE

Wrap airtight in plastic wrap. Refrigerate.

SERVING AND EATING

Good eating cheese. Serve on dark breads and Scandinavian flatbread and crispbread. Excellent with raw vegetables. Not recommended for cooking.

BEVERAGE MATCH

Swedish beer or stout.

COMMENTS

The name means simply "Swedish cheese." There are many different varieties of this cheese manufactured in different parts of the country. Intended as a copy of Gouda, it has its own taste.

SIMILAR CHEESE

Tilsit.

Swiss Finnish

Finnish Swiss cheese is probably the best copy of Swiss Emmentaler; it regularly wins various international competitions as the best copy. It is cured one hundred days, rather than the minimum sixty-day curing period of other copies, giving it a much more pronounced and interesting flavor. Finnish Swiss is often sold as the "real" imported Swiss from Switzerland in American stores, but the wrappings show it to be from Finland. See also *Emmentaler.*

Taleggio

WHERE MADE

Italy, in Lombardy, mostly around Bergamo.

HOW MADE AND CURED

Type of milk: Pasteurized whole cow's milk.

Method and rind type: Semisoft, pressed, uncooked, surface-ripened cheese.

Time cured: About seven weeks.

Fat content: 48 percent.

AROMA

Mild, pleasant.

FLAVOR

Flavor family: Bland and mild.

Taste: Smooth, round, creamy, with slightly tart, cheddary edge; sharpens as it ages.

Texture: Soft, creamy, tender.

APPEARANCE

Exterior: Pinkish-gray rind; slightly rough, like sandpaper.

Interior: Creamy-ivory-white to pale-straw color; smooth and luscious-looking.

Size and shape: Square, 8 inches on each side, 2 inches thick, weighing 2 to 3 pounds.

BUYING HINTS

The cheese should not have a strong Brie-like smell—or it is overripe. It should look plump, the rind should not be slightly shrunken, and the wrappings should not seem glued to the surface of the rind. When pressed, the cheese should feel resilient and springy.

USABLE LIFE

Keeps a very short time—about one week.

STORAGE AFTER PURCHASE

Wrap airtight in plastic wrap. Refrigerate.

SERVING AND EATING

Primarily a dessert cheese to serve at end of meals. Especially good after a fairly light meal of chicken, fish, veal. Serve with juicy, sweet, but tangy fruit such as sweet cherries and with bread.

BEVERAGE MATCH

Light, fruity white wines.

COMMENTS

Named for town and valley in Lombardy where it supposedly originated. Although reputed to have been made for fifty years, now made and marketed by one of the largest cheesemaking companies in Italy.

SIMILAR CHEESE

Bel Paese.

Tête-de-Moine

WHERE MADE

Switzerland, in the canton of Bern, especially in the area around Bellelay and the Jura Mountains; made in small traditional dairies.

HOW MADE AND CURED

Type of milk: Unpasteurized whole cow's milk.

Method and rind type: Hard, pressed, uncooked; natural, washed rind.

Time cured: Three to five months.

Fat content: 45–50 percent.

AROMA

Definite, fruity bouquet.

FLAVOR

Flavor family: Swiss type/monastery cheese.
Taste: Spicy, fruity, zingy, crisp, clean taste.
Texture: Firm, smooth.

APPEARANCE

Exterior: Slightly sticky, yellowish rind; wrapped in foil.
Interior: Pale-ivory-yellow, with a smooth, close texture.
Size and shape: Cylinder 5 inches high, 5 inches in diameter, between 2 and 4 pounds in weight.

BUYING HINTS

Best seasons are autumn and winter. The cheese should not have a coarse grain. The rind should not have excessive mold on it; the color of the cheese should be regular with no off-color spots or sections. Age determines the sharpness and pungency. Taste before buying.

USABLE LIFE

If uncut, keeps a year or two. Cut, keeps about one to two months.

STORAGE AFTER PURCHASE

Wrap airtight in plastic wrap; refrigerate.

SERVING AND EATING

Serve for snacks or at the end of a meal with rustic bread or French bread and butter. Scrape with cheese slicer.

BEVERAGE MATCH

Light, zingy, fruity red wines.

COMMENTS

The name originates with the custom of giving one cheese to each monk—or did the cheese resemble a monk's head? Made originally only in the Abbey of Bellelay, near Moutiers; now it is made elsewhere in that area.

SIMILAR CHEESES

Appenzeller, Raclette.

Tillamook

American Cheddar cheese made in a cooperative dairy at Bandon, Oregon, in Tillamook County. An excellent, medium-sharp, very toothsome Cheddar.

Tilsiter (also called Ragnit)

WHERE MADE

Germany, especially in areas of east Prussia and northern Germany; made in factories; also made in central Europe, Switzerland, Scandinavia, and the United States.

HOW MADE AND CURED

Type of milk: Pasteurized or unpasteurized whole or skimmed cow's milk.

Method and rind type: Semihard, bacteria-ripened; washed rind.

Time cured: Five to six months.

Fat content: 10–30 percent.

AROMA

Pleasant, pronounced aroma, similar to monastery cheeses such as Pont-L'Évêque. Aroma strengthens with age of cheese.

FLAVOR

Flavor family: Monastery cheeses.

Taste: Mild to slightly piquant; medium sharp. Stronger than Port-Salut; full-bodied, not elegant. Has a pleasant, slightly sourish tang.

Texture: Medium firm, but supple, sliceable.

APPEARANCE

Exterior: Dry, yellowish rind, slightly darker than paste.

Interior: Ivory to pale yellow in color with small irregular holes, some of which may be round.

Size and shape: Available in both brick and cylindrical shapes.

BUYING HINTS

Fairly reliable cheese. Should not be dried out; interior should not have cracks in cheese. Texture should look creamy and rich. The Swiss version of Tilsiter is called Glarus.

USABLE LIFE

Three weeks after purchase.

STORAGE AFTER PURCHASE

Wrap airtight in plastic wrap. Refrigerate.

SERVING AND EATING

Good for snacks and lunches. Serve with crisp vegetables; whole-wheat, pumpernickel, or rye bread; and beer.

BEVERAGE MATCH

Light, spicy Munich-style beer or dark, malty beer. Also good with fruity, spicy red wines.

COMMENTS

Named for town in Prussia (now in U.S.S.R.) where first made. Brought by Dutch immigrants who settled in Tilsit,

Prussia. Subsequently copied in all Scandinavian countries, Eastern Europe, Switzerland (where it was brought in eighteenth century), and the United States. The Swiss copy is often considered superior to the original.

SIMILAR CHEESES

Esrom, Havarti, aged American Brick.

Tommes (also called Tomes)

These semihard to semisoft French mountain cheeses—dozens in number—often take the name of the specific producing district or village of their home, the Savoy Mountains. However, Tomme may be stuck, confusingly enough, in front of other cheese names (Tomme de Saint-Marcellin, for example) which are not usually thought of as Tommes (this is probably because "tomme" means "cheese" in the dialect of the Haute-Savoie). Tommes are typically unsophisticated, mild, and tasty, and have good keeping qualities. While there is some variation, they all show a strong family resemblance and belong to the same flavor family. The goat's milk Tommes are sold as Tommes de Chèvres. See *Tomme de Savoie.*

Tomme de Pyrénées, see *Fromage des Pyrénées.*

Tomme de Savoie (also called Tome de Savoie)

WHERE MADE

Savoy Mountains, France; produced on farms and in factories.

HOW MADE AND CURED

Type of milk: Cow's, usually, partly skimmed.

Method and rind type: Pressed, uncooked, natural-rind cheese.

Time cured: Two months.

Fat content: 20–40 percent.

AROMA

The rind has a pronounced moldy scent; the interior cheese has a buttery-sweet earthy scent.

FLAVOR

Flavor family: Mild monastery.

Taste: Mild, nutty-earthy flavor when young; stronger flavors in older specimens. An attractive cheese.

Texture: Soft.

APPEARANCE

Exterior: Reddish-orangy rind with gray-mold pigmentation.

Interior: Yellow-ivory, uniform; resilient and bouncy.

Size and shape: Fat wheels, 8 inches by 2½ to 5 inches high, and weighing 4 to 6½ pounds.

BUYING HINTS

A usually reliable cheese, but beware of cracked rind, a dry or heat-damaged saggy interior, and a bitter aftertaste.

USABLE LIFE

In large pieces, would last for weeks if well-wrapped and stored.

STORAGE AFTER PURCHASE

Wrap in plastic wrap (for long storage wrap again in foil) and refrigerate.

SERVING AND EATING

Particularly good as a luncheon cheese or for use as snack. Serve with various breads and crackers.

BEVERAGE MATCH

An unfussy cheese; any inexpensive dry red or white wine.

COMMENTS

Tomme de Savoie is the most widely seen name; there is a Tomme au Marc de Raisins, which is a strong, sharp, macerated cheese often confused in print with the ubiquitous Fromage Fondu aux Raisins (La Grappe), which is a processed cheese. See *La Grappe.* These days a number of cheeses are called Tommes, including downy-rind Camembert types.

SIMILAR CHEESES

Beaumont, Reblochon.

Trappist

A term used for monastery-type cheeses, because of the historical association of these cheeses with Trappist monks. See *Saint-Paulin, Port-Salut, Oka.* Also the specific name for an Austrian cheese originally made by monks, now produced commercially, and similar to Port-Salut.

Triple-crème

WHERE MADE

France, elsewhere in Europe and rest of world. Factory-produced.

HOW MADE AND CURED

Type of milk: Cow's milk and cream.

Method and rind type: Soft, bloomy-rind, surface-ripened cheese.

Time cured: About three weeks.

Fat content: 75 percent.

AROMA

Fresh, creamy and lactic; pleasant moldy scent to rind.

FLAVOR

Flavor family: Crème.

Taste: Exceptionally rich, unctuous, and delicious; however, it is a simple taste.

Texture: Soft, like whipped butter or cream.

APPEARANCE

Exterior: Downy white rind, with slight pink-brown pigmentation.

Interior: Creamy ivory, and spreadable.

Size and shape: Typically a small fat cylinder about 7 ounces in weight, measuring 3 inches by 1½ inches thick, although there are square shapes and larger wheels.

BUYING HINTS

Small ones come boxed; inspect the wrapper for signs of stickiness and mold growth, strong ammoniated or other sharp smell (all signs of overage). Pigmentation should be in evidence, but not dominant on the rind. Some triple-crèmes come in bulk sizes and can be sampled for excessively moldy flavor. They are usually sold by brand names—Boursault, Explorateur, Saint-André, Boursin, and so forth.

USABLE LIFE

Will last for a week or so if properly stored.

STORAGE AFTER PURCHASE

Leave in original wrapper until use; wrap unused portions or cut pieces in plastic wrap or foil; refrigerate.

SERVING AND EATING

Triple-crèmes are the cheeses to serve at the end of meals when dessert is not called for, since they are extraordinarily rich themselves. Serve with plain crackers. They are never better than when served at a light, elegant luncheon or as a self-indulgent snack.

BEVERAGE MATCH

The heavy-cream content of triple-crèmes makes them ideal with coffee, and they are among the few cheeses that go well with sweet wines, in particular the sweetish Spätleses and

Ausleses of the Rhine and Moselle. They will not be out of place with fruity red wines, however.

COMMENTS

One of the most popular cheese types, and instantly likable; simple, but delicious. Triple-crèmes also come in a great number of flavored versions—with herbs, spices, pepper, and so forth.

SIMILAR CHEESE

Crema Dania.

Tybo

WHERE MADE

Denmark, in factories.

HOW MADE AND CURED

Type of milk: Pasteurized whole cow's milk.

Method and rind type: Semihard, ripened by bacteria, with gas holes; pressed; washed, thin rind; similar in method of manufacture to Swiss cheese. Sometimes flavored with caraway seeds.

Time cured: Three to five months.

Fat content: 45 percent minimum for some; 40 percent minimum for others.

AROMA

Mild, fresh aroma.

FLAVOR

Flavor family: Bland and mild.

Taste: Mild, fresh, buttery; similar to Danbo. Becomes stronger with age.

Texture: Firm, smooth texture; sliceable.

APPEARANCE

Exterior: Dry, yellowish, thin rind; usually covered by red wax coating.

Interior: Usually butter-yellow; smooth surface with small number of round, pea-size holes; some have caraway seeds in them.

Size and shape: Rectangular loaf, about 8 inches long, 4 inches high and wide, weight 4 to 5 pounds.

BUYING HINTS

Danish cheeses are extremely reliable; usually, if the cheese looks good, it will be good. The rind or wax should be stamped with the name "Tybo" and the amount of fat content (40+ or 45+). Wax coating should adhere closely to cheese and show no cracks; rind should be even and free of blemishes; interior should have no off-color spots and not too many holes.

USABLE LIFE

One month, or longer, if uncut.

STORAGE AFTER PURCHASE

Wrap airtight in plastic wrap or in aluminum foil and then in a plastic bag. Refrigerate.

SERVING AND EATING

Good eating cheese. Can be eaten at any meal. Also good in cooking. The Danes like it with fruit and salads, particularly with apples, pears, and bananas. Not a dessert cheese.

BEVERAGE MATCH

Good with Danish beer, hard cider, and light, fruity red wines.

COMMENTS

Especially liked by children because of its mild flavor. Gains in character if aged.

SIMILAR CHEESES

Danbo, Samsoe.

Vacherin

WHERE MADE

Switzerland, in the cantons of Vaud and Fribourg; also made in the Savoy Mountains in France; made in small dairies and chalets.

HOW MADE AND CURED

Type of milk: Whole cow's milk, to which skimmed milk is sometimes added.

Method and rind type: Soft, lightly pressed, uncooked; washed, brushed rind.

Time cured: Two to four months, depending on the variety.

Fat content: 45–50 percent.

AROMA

Faint moldy scent, with hint of resin.

FLAVOR

Flavor family: Monastery type.

Taste: Most taste very creamy and have a faint sour flavor and a sappy, balsamy tang.

Texture: Supple, creamy, smooth; some can be runny.

APPEARANCE

Exterior: Thin, smooth rind, yellowish-gray to light pink. Sometimes wrapped with birch, wild cherry, or fir bark.

Interior: Creamy-white with very small holes and smooth, creamy appearance.

Size and shape: Varies. Usually a small wheel, weighing from 1½ to 20 pounds.

BUYING HINTS

In general, the rind should be moist and pink. Taste before buying. The cheese should not have a bitter aftertaste. The texture should be smooth and creamy, not grainy.

USABLE LIFE

Does not keep well once cut, as peak of ripeness lasts only a few days.

STORAGE AFTER PURCHASE

Wrap in damp cloth and keep in cool place until ripe or consumed.

SERVING AND EATING

Serve at end of meal with French bread. Vacherin de Fribourg is also used in Fribourg fondue.

BEVERAGE MATCH

Fruity and light Swiss wines, both red and white; German Rieslings; California Gamay.

COMMENTS

There are a number of Vacherin cheeses. Vacherin de Fribourg is an ancient cheese, thought to be similar to the cheeses made with unheated milk made before the Gruyère and Emmentaler cheeses. Vacherin Mont D'or from Switzerland is perhaps the most commonly seen in the United States. All are consumed young and held in high esteem by turophiles. Some are semisoft; others are so runny they are eaten with a spoon. Some names that might be seen: Vacherin d'Abondance, Vacherin des Aillons, and Vacherin des Beauges.

SIMILAR CHEESE

Reblochon.

Valais Raclette, see *Raclette.*

Valençay (also known as Pyramide)

WHERE MADE

Touraine, Anjou, Charentes, and Poitou, France; farm- and factory-produced.

HOW MADE AND CURED

Type of milk: Goat's.

Method and rind type: Soft, bloomy-rind cheese.
Time cured: Three to four weeks.
Fat content: 45 percent.

AROMA

Moldy-goaty.

FLAVOR

Flavor family: Goat.
Taste: Strongly goaty; nongoat enthusiasts are liable to find aged specimens rather overblown, an acquired taste.
Texture: Creamy, pasty.

APPEARANCE

Exterior: Downy white rind; others dusted with charcoal.
Interior: Ivory, creamy, smooth, and soft.
Size and shape: Truncated pyramid, 3 inches square at the base, 2½ inches high.

BUYING HINTS

Beware of overage specimens (unless that is to your taste) exhibiting excessive mold growth and a dry, shrunken appearance. Some examples have an oversalty taste.

USABLE LIFE

Will last for weeks, but gains considerable strength.

STORAGE AFTER PURCHASE

Wrap in plastic wrap or foil and, to keep smell from spreading, place wrapped cheese in airtight jar or plastic container.

SERVING AND EATING

At the end of meals, or to add interest to the cheese board. Serve with rustic, crusty breads.

BEVERAGE MATCH

Serve with fruity red or white wines, particularly sturdy reds with aged examples.

COMMENTS

Called Pyramide after its most characteristic shape. Levroux is a variant local name of this cheese.

SIMILAR CHEESES

French chèvres.

Weisslackerkäse

(also called Bierkäse and Beer Cheese).

WHERE MADE

Germany, mostly in Bavaria; in factories.

HOW MADE AND CURED

Type of milk: Pasteurized whole cow's milk.

Method and rind type: Soft, surface-ripened, with a thin rind.

Time cured: Four months.

Fat content: 2.8 percent.

AROMA

Mild, pleasant; increases in pungency as cheese ages until it has a fairly strong, smelly aroma reminiscent of Limburger.

FLAVOR

Flavor family: Mild to strong cheeses.

Taste: Milder than but similar to Limburger. Pungent, almost sharp taste in aged examples.

Texture: Semisoft, sliceable.

APPEARANCE

Exterior: Lustrous, smeary white crust that is more like a thin skin. Looks shiny.

Interior: Very white and smooth with few holes.

Size and shape: Square, 4 to 5 inches on each side, 3½ inches thick, weighing 2½ to 3½ pounds.

BUYING HINTS

Strength determined by age; taste before buying. Should look moist and pleasant, not dried out with cracks or large holes. Surface rind of cheese should be shiny.

USABLE LIFE

Three weeks after purchase.

STORAGE AFTER PURCHASE

Wrap airtight in plastic wrap; refrigerate. To keep odor from permeating refrigerator, put wrapped cheese in airtight jar or plastic container.

SERVING AND EATING

Good for snacks and sandwiches with pumpernickel, sour rye, rye, and dark breads, onions, sausages, and beer or ale.

BEVERAGE MATCH

Especially good with light, spicy Munich-style beer.

COMMENTS

Name comes from words "white," *weiss,* and "lacquer," *lacker,* which describe the surface of the cheese. The cheese is called Bierkäse when it is well-ripened and has a strong flavor. American Beer Cheese is milder.

SIMILAR CHEESE

Aged American Brick.

Wensleydale

WHERE MADE

Yorkshire, England; also in Lancashire.

HOW MADE AND CURED

Type of milk: Pasteurized whole cow's milk.

Method and rind type: Uncooked, pressed (very lightly pressed), with natural rind; less acidity developed if intended to turn blue.

Time cured: Three weeks for white; six months for blue (rarely seen).

Fat content: 45 percent.

AROMA

Fresh, pleasant; blue has mold smell.

FLAVOR

Flavor family: Mild, Cheddar type; blue-veined cheeses.

Taste: Acidic, creamy, delicious, honeyed aftertaste; younger ones often have buttermilk tang reminiscent of Caerphilly, but more creamy. Blue version is rich, creamy, sweet; milder and more mellow than Stilton, yet tangy with touch of honey.

Texture: Soft and flaky, crumbly, moist, creamier than Caerphilly. Blue version is soft, nearly as spreadable as butter, very creamy.

APPEARANCE

Exterior: Thin, grayish-white natural rind, usually bandaged; often waxed; now also sold in rindless blocks. Blue has very wrinkled surface rind that looks almost corrugated.

Interior: Snow-white, moist, and creamy-looking, with a close texture. Blue is creamier color with blue veins and a closer, creamier-looking texture.

Size and shape: Cylinder, 7 inches high by 9 inches across, weighing 10 to 12 pounds. Also made in small size: 3 inches in diameter by 3¾ inches high.

BUYING HINTS

Often sold too old: should not be dried out or yellowish, should have uniform color and texture. The surface of the cheese should not look greasy. Rind should not bulge or swell. Blues are not usually imported into the United States, but should be extremely creamy with very pleasant honeyed aftertaste, not bitter.

USABLE LIFE

Short-lived; best is young, around three to five weeks; keeps a few weeks when wrapped well. Blue is best at about six to eight months old and keeps well if uncut. Cut, keeps only a few weeks before drying out.

STORAGE AFTER PURCHASE

Wrap in airtight plastic wrap or in a damp cloth dipped in water with small amount of vinegar. Refrigerate. Keep blue wrapped in damp cloth inside plastic box or under plastic bell. Refrigerate.

SERVING AND EATING

Good eating cheese. Good with bread and butter, lettuce, and celery; in sandwiches and for snacks. Blue is dessert cheese.

BEVERAGE MATCH

English ale and beer; light fruity red wines; Rhine wines when sweet; traditionally, vintage sweet apple wine.

COMMENTS

Originated in and named for the town of Wensleydale in the valley of the Ure River. Local tradition suggests that it has been made for the past thousand years in Yorkshire dales. Some kind of cheese has been made in Yorkshire since the days of the great abbeys of Fountains, Jervaulx, Kirkstall, and Bolton. Wensleydale is believed to have originated primarily as a Blue cheese, introduced to the abbots of Jervaulx Abbey by the Normans. It is thought that it was originally made from ewe's milk; cow's milk began to be used in the eighteenth century. Throughout the eighteenth and the nineteenth centuries, cheeses made on farms were traded and bartered for flour and other provisions. Today Blue Wensleydale is rarely seen, even in Britain, and practically all Wensleydale sold in the United States is white.

SIMILAR CHEESES

Caerphilly is closest to the white in flavor, texture, and appearance. Stilton is closest to the blue.

Wilstermarschkäse

A German cheese made mostly in area of Schleswig-Holstein from cow's milk. It has a slightly sour, mildly acid taste and resembles Tilsiter, although it ripens more rapidly. See *Tilsiter.*

York (also called Cambridge)

A soft, delicate cream cheese made in England in various

locales. It is shaped like a small brick and the interior shows alternate layers of firm white cheese and buff cream. It has a creamy, tangy taste. After ripening for thirty hours on a straw mat, it was (and is) sold on the same mat and is eaten two to thirty days after being made.

Yorkshire-Stilton, see *Cotherstone.*

Zomma, see *Kashkaval.*

FURTHER READING

The following brief list of recommended books omits excellent but technical works consulted for this book, such as Lucius L. Van Slyke's *Cheese: A Treatise, etc.*, and Frank V. Kosikowski's *Cheese and Fermented Milk Foods,* as well as wholly anecdotal collections or historical studies, very brief treatments of the subject, and out-of-print texts.

The Complete Encyclopedia of French Cheese. Pierre Androuët. Harper's Magazine Press. New York, 1973.

This translation of M. Androuët's *Guide du Fromage* gives the English-speaking cheese lover an impressive amount of authoritative information on French cheese. Androuët's categorizations can be confusing to the American buyer, however, since many of the cheeses he distinguishes differ only slightly from one another, and a good many are scarce and obscure even in France. Useful for the advanced turophile, particularly one going abroad.

Dictionnaire des Fromages. Robert J. Courtine. Librairie Larousse. Paris, 1972.

For those who read French, this excellent, concise text complements Androuët's, although here too, much of it concerns cheeses not available in the United States.

Cheeses of the World. U.S. Department of Agriculture. Dover Publications. New York, 1972.

A reprint of the 1969 reissue of the Department of Agriculture's 1953 bulletin "Cheese Varieties and Descriptions." This work lists hundreds of cheeses, many very obscure, and goes into considerable detail on their manufacture. Taste descriptions are not usually given. Dated, and thus not always reliable, but interesting reading for the technical-minded.

The International Wine and Food Society's Guide to Cheese and Cheese Cookery. T. A. Layton. Bonanza Books. New York, 1967.

The listings here of the world's cheeses are often sketchy, but the discussion of English cheeses is detailed. Layton's treatment of matching wine and cheese is excellent, as are his suggested tastings of both. Useful color plates of cheese.

The Cheese Book. Vivienne Marquis and Patricia Haskell. Simon and Schuster. New York, 1965.

An enthusiastic, well-written work devoted to the gastronomy of cheese. Basic groups of cheeses are discussed and described. Not organized for reference use, but well worth reading.

Cheeses of the World. André L. Simon. Faber and Faber. London, Second edition, 1960.

An excellent reference work by the late eminent gastronome and wine writer. It consists of listings and discussions of the cheeses of various countries and is particularly strong on the cheeses of England and France. Simon does not discuss the gastronomy of cheese, however.

PRINCIPAL CHEESES LISTED
BY FLAVOR FAMILIES

Note: Cheeses may be listed under more than one category.

Fresh, Uncured Cheeses
  Cream cheese, American
  Demi-Sel
  Mozzarella
  Petit-Suisse
  Queso Blanco
  Ricotta
  Scamorza

Stracchino

Bland and Mild Cheeses
  Bel Paese
  Brick
  Danbo
  Edam
  Epoisses
  Fontina
  Gouda
  Maribo
  Mimolette
  Monterey Jack
  Muenster
  Neufchâtel
  Saint-Marcellin
  Samsoe
  Sveciaost
  Taleggio
  Tybo

Crèmes
  Belletoille
  Boursault
  Boursin
  Brillat-Savarin
  Caprice des Dieux
  Crema Dania
  Excelsior
  Explorateur
  Fontainebleau
  Monsieur Fromage
  Saint-André
  see also Triple-crème

Brie and Camembert Types
  Brie
  Camembert
  Caprice des Dieux
  Carré de L'Est
  Chaource
  Coulommiers
  Saint-Benoît

Swiss and Swiss Types
Appenzeller
Beaufort
Belsano
Comté
Emmentaler
Fontina
Gruyère
Herrgårdsost
Jarlsberg
Raclette
Saanen
Sbrinz
Tête-de-Moine

Cheddar and Cheddar Types
Asiago
Caciocavallo
Caerphilly
Cantal
Cheddar
Cheddar, American
Cheddar, Canadian
Cheshire
Colby
Coon
Derby
Dunlop
Gloucester
Lancashire
Leicester
Monterey Jack
Provolone
Sage
Tillamook
Wensleydale

Grana Types
Asiago
Caciocavallo
Grana Padano
Parmigiano-Reggiano
Pecorino Romano

Provolone
Sapsago
Sbrinz

Monastery-type Cheeses
Beaumont
Chiberta
Esrom
Havarti
Maroilles
Mondseer
Morbier
Münster
Oka
Pont-L'Évêque
Port-Salut
Reblochon
Rollot
Saint-Nectaire
Saint-Paulin
Tête-de-Moine
Tilsiter
Tomme de Savoie
Vacherin

Goat Cheeses
Banon
Chabichou
Chevrotin
Crottin de Chavignol
Montrachet
Sainte-Maure
Saint-Saviol
Selles-sur-Cher
Valençay
see also Chèvres

Sheep's Milk Cheeses
Brinza
Feta
Kashkaval
Kasseri
Manchego

Pecorino Romano
Ricotta-Pecorina
Serra da Estrella

Blue Cheeses
Bleu d'Auvergne
Bleu de Bresse
Bleu de Causses
Bleu de Haut Jura
Blue Castello
Blue Cheese, Norwegian
Blue Vinny
Danablu
Fourme D'Ambert
Gammelost
Gorgonzola
Mycella
Pipo Crem
Roquefort
Stilton

Processed Cheeses
Beau Pasteur*
Crème de Gruyère*
Crème de Savoie*
Rambol*
Nec Plus Ultra*
Gourmandise*
La Vache Qui Rit*
La Grappe*
see Fromage Fondu

Spiced Cheeses
Boursin
Gaperon
Leyden
Nökkelost
Sapsago

Whey Cheeses
Flotost
Gjetost
Mysost

Strong Cheeses
   Brick
   Géromé
   Handkäse
   Liederkranz
   Limburger
   Livarot
   Maroilles
   Münster
   Romadurkäse
   Weisslackerkäse

PRINCIPAL CHEESES LISTED
BY COUNTRIES OF ORIGIN

Note: With few exceptions, versions of cheeses produced outside countries of origin not listed here.

AUSTRIA
   Butter Cheese
   Handkäse
   Mondseer

BELGIUM
   Limburger

CANADA
   Cheddar, Canadian
   Ermite
   Oka

DENMARK
   Blue Castello
   Crèma Dania
   Danablu
   Danbo

Esrom
Havarti
Maribo
Mycella
Samsoe
Tybo

EASTERN EUROPE
Brinza
Kashkaval
FRANCE
Banon
Beaufort
Beaumont
Bellétoile
Bleu d'Auvergne
Bleu de Bresse
Bleu de Causses
Bleu de Haut Jura
Boursault
Boursin
Brie
Brillat-Savarin
Camembert
Cantal
Caprice des Dieux
Carré de l'Est
Chabichou
Chaource
Chevrotin
Chiberta
Comté
Coulommiers
Crottin de Chavignol
Demi-Sel
Epoisses
Excelsior
Explorateur
Fol Amour
Fourme D'Ambert
Fromage Fondu
Fromage des Pyrénées
Gaperon

Géromé
Livarot
Maroilles
Mimolette
Monsieur-Fromage
Montrachet
Morbier
Münster
Neufchâtel
Petit-Suisse
Pipo Crem
Pont L'Évêque
Port-Salut
Reblochon
Rollot
Roquefort
Saint-André
Saint-Benoît
Sainte-Maure
Saint-Marcellin
Saint-Nectaire
Saint-Paulin
Saint-Saviol
Selles-sur-Cher
Tomme de Savoie
Vacherin
Valençay

GERMANY
Butter Cheese
Handkäse
Limburger
Romadurkäse
Tilsiter
Weisslackerkäse

GREAT BRITAIN
Caerphilly
Cheddar
Cheshire
Derby
Dunlop
Gloucester
Lancashire

Leicester
Stilton
Wensleydale

GREECE
Feta
Kasseri

HOLLAND
Edam
Gouda
Leyden

ITALY
Asiago
Bel Paese
Caciocavallo
Caciotta
Fontina
Gorgonzola
Grana Padano
Mozzarella
Parmiggiano-Reggiano
Pecorino Romano
Provolone
Ricotta
Ricotta-Pecorina
Scamorza
Stracchino
Teleggio

LATIN AMERICA
Queso Blanco

NORWAY
Blue Cheese, Norwegian
Gammelost
Gjetost
Jarlsberg
Nökkelost

PORTUGAL
Serra da Estrella

SPAIN
  Manchego

SWEDEN
  Gräddost
  Herrgårdsost
  Sveciaost

SWITZERLAND
  Appenzeller
  Belsano
  Emmentaler
  Gruyère
  Raclette
  Saanen
  Sapsago
  Sbrinz
  Tête-de-Moine
  Vacherin

UNITED STATES
  Brick
  Cheddar, American
  Colby
  Coon
  Cream cheese, American
  Liederkranz
  Monterey Jack
  Muenster
  Tillamook

Index

Index

Boldface numbers refer to main entries.

About the Author

PETER QUIMME is the author of the highly
praised THE SIGNET BOOK OF AMERICAN
WINE and THE SIGNET BOOK OF COFFEE
AND TEA. He writes frequently on gourmet
topics for leading magazines, including *New
York* and *House Beautiful*. An inveterate epi-
cure, Mr. Quimme lives in New York and
travels as much as possible.